Dear Reader:

The book you are about to read is the latest bestseller from the St. Martin's True Crime Library, the imprint the *New York Times* calls "the leader in true crime!" Each month, we offer you a fascinating account of the latest, most sensational crime that has captured the national attention. St. Martin's is the publisher of perennial bestselling true crime author Jack Olsen, whose SALT OF THE EARTH is the true story of one woman's triumph over life-shattering violence; Joseph Wambaugh called it "powerful and absorbing." Fannie Weinstein and Melinda Wilson tell the story of a beautiful honors student who was lured into the dark world of sex for hire in THE COED CALL GIRL MURDER. St. Martin's is also proud to publish two-time Edgar Award-winning author Carlton Stowers, whose TO THE LAST BREATH recounts a two-year-old girl's mysterious death, and the dogged investigation that led loved ones to the most unlikely murderer: her own father. In the book you now hold, WHILE INNOCENTS SLEPT, Adrian Havill looks at a shocking case involving money, greed, and two little children . . .

St. Martin's True Crime Library gives you the stories *behind* the headlines. Our authors take you right to the scene of the crime and into the minds of the most notorious murderers to show you what really makes them tick. St. Martin's True Crime Library paperbacks are better than the most terrifying thriller, because it's all true! The next time you want a crackling good read, make sure it's got the St. Martin's True Crime Library logo on the spine—you'll be up all night!

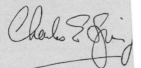

D0802915

Charles E. Spicer, Jr.
Executive Editor, St. Martin's True Crime Library

WHILE INNOCENTS SLEPT

A STORY OF
REVENGE, MURDER, AND SIDS

Adrian Havill

St. Martin's Paperbacks

WHILE INNOCENTS SLEPT

Copyright © 2001 by Adrian Havill.

Cover photographs: inset photograph © *Montgomery Journal*, background photograph by Georgiana Havill.

Library of Congress Catalog Card Number: 00-047039

ISBN: 0-312-97517-1

Printed in the United States of America

St. Martin's Press hardcover edition / January 2001
St. Martin's Paperbacks edition / July 2002

10 9 8 7 6 5 4 3 2 1

This book is for
Florence Effie Sessoms.

NOTES ON SOURCES AND ACKNOWLEDGMENTS

I interviewed Garrett Wilson, the subject of this book, nineteen times in person and at least twenty times by phone.

Both his defense team and the state's attorney's office for Montgomery County, Maryland, cooperated on an unprecedented level in giving me access to create what you are about to read. My objective in writing this account was to allow all voices to be heard.

There are more than a hundred people who helped to get this book produced or who assisted in some way. Brenda Goletz and Holly Mowery in Barry Helfand's office were always kind and helpful. The same should be said for John McLane and Pat Goodrich in the state's attorney's office. The Farley family was indispensable. In western Maryland, the entire Wampler clan welcomed me as if one of its own, as did the Jenkins family in Burkeville, Virginia.

The quotes of Mary Anastasi, Julie Stinger, Elizabeth Dodge Bahlman, and the Olivers are taken from their sworn statements, depositions, court testimony, or comments made to me. Certain police and prosecution sources cooperated with the author on a confidential basis.

My wife, Georgiana, is responsible for many of the photos that grace the center section. She was my second set of eyes and hands in the courtroom of Ann S. Harrington and at other venues throughout the writing of this book.

Registered nurses Karen Lovelace and Katie Lakin helped me understand the medical jargon. Keith Higginbotham, Bill Sessoms, Debra Dwyer, and Tom Kelly gave the manuscript a sharp read.

Countless parents have been told that their deceased childen were victims of a mysterious condition known as sudden infant death syndrome, or by its acronym, SIDS. Listen to them, and they will tell you that the deadly disorder is as old as the history of mankind. SIDS, they say, is discussed in the Bible, in the first book of Kings. Indeed, in the famous parable, King Solomon offers to cut a male infant in half for two women who both claim to be the surviving baby's mother. The story begins, "And this woman's child died in the night..."

In 1991, an international body of medical researchers attempted to create a uniform definition of SIDS. Its conclusion: Sudden infant death syndrome is "the sudden death of an infant under one year of age that remains unexplained after the performance of a complete postmortem investigation, including an autopsy, an examination at the scene of death, and a review of the case history."

The telephone operators who staff hot lines in the various American SIDS networks will quote you statistics. SIDS, they say, kills more infants each year than cancer, heart ailments, pneumonia, child abuse, AIDS, cystic fibrosis, and muscular dystrophy combined. The current number for SIDS deaths in the United States, these volunteers claim, is between six and nine thousand infants a year, or one out of every one thousand live births.

Those figures are in dispute, with others asserting both higher and lower totals. Pediatrician and author William Sears of the University of Southern California's School of Medicine, for example, cites a recent study that says SIDS occurs in one of every seven hundred babies. Whatever the actual number, the rate of deaths is presently believed to be 30 percent lower than in 1992. In that year, the American Academy of Pediatrics came forth with a landmark opinion. The organization concluded deaths from SIDS could be reduced simply by placing infants on their backs before laying them down to sleep. A productive "Back to Sleep" advertising campaign followed.

Despite the AAP's finding, SIDS is still an enigma. No medical authority has ever been able to define the cause of the lethal affliction. This hasn't stopped academicians from putting forth diverging theories on what they purport causes the syndrome. For the most part, many remain just that— theories. One can find dozens of doctors who will hypothesize on what the real reasons are for these tragic deaths.

Some physicians cite the following causes of SIDS: underweight births in young mothers who smoke near the infant, consume four or more cups of coffee per day, do not breastfeed, use an unusually soft crib mattress, or take antibiotics at the time of birth. Twins and subsequent births are said to be more susceptible. SIDS is more prevalent in the poor than in the rich. It is more frequent in African Americans than in Caucasians. SIDS also occurs in male infants 50 percent more often than in girls. The deaths nearly always take place between ten at night and ten in the morning. There are more fatalities in winter than in summer. And no less than Tipper Gore has weighed in before Congress on SIDS, testifying that she believes cold, damp weather is a strong factor. But after all this medical head scratching and political finger pointing, the cause of the condition remains yet to be firmly diagnosed.

It has been established, through examining thousands of infant death certificates, that 90 percent of SIDS cases occur between the first two and six months of a baby's life. This window of time is a critical period for "dendrite proliferation and the myelinization of neural tissue." In plain English, this means it is a key time for the development of nerve growth. The cells are still maturing and are not yet completely covered by tissue.

During this time a shift in respiratory physiology occurs. In the first few months of life, a child's breathing patterns are sent messages by the lower part of the brain. Breathing is automatic. As the baby's brain matures, the respiratory function shifts to a higher area of the brain. It is during this shift from reflex to manual control that medical experts say a baby is vulnerable to SIDS.

Many researchers have testified that before a baby dies of SIDS, it goes into a period of apnea—that is, the child experiences pauses in its breathing that become more and more pronounced in length. Eventually, the breathing stops and the baby dies. When the death is discovered, there is sometimes a pink froth that has risen from the lungs and foams around the child's mouth. It is the only external physical sign.

The physician who is responsible for the way medicine once viewed SIDS is Alfred Steinschneider, a pediatrician in Syracuse, New York. It was Steinschneider who first noticed brief apnea spells by infants during sleep. He began to conclude this might be the first warning sign of SIDS. The doctor published his findings in 1972 to great acclaim and thus gave birth to an electrical device called an apnea monitor. He endorsed the apparatus, which tracks a baby's breathing pattern and sounds an alarm if the infant's breathing stops for more than fifteen seconds. Steinschneider also maintained SIDS ran in families and that a parent who gave birth to one SIDS child had an increased risk with subsequent newborns.

One of the mothers in Dr. Steinschneider's study was named Waneta Hoyt. After the doctor sent her home with her baby and a new apnea machine, she said her daughter, Molly, stopped breathing four times and had to be given resuscitation.

Steinschneider's nurse, Polly Geer, was suspicious. "She [Hoyt] was not what I considered to be an attentive, eager-beaver mother," Geer recalled. "I just remember her not hugging Molly or holding her real close."

Three other children in Hoyt's family had already died under mysterious circumstances and were diagnosed as having SIDS. Little Molly faced the same fate. Her death was also attributed to SIDS.

Geer's suspicions were eventually confirmed. In 1995, Waneta Hoyt confessed to and was convicted of killing all five of her children by smothering them as infants, one in the first forty-eight days of life, and one as late as twenty-eight months.

"Your focus is on proving what you are proving. The denial then, comes pretty high," Geer said after Hoyt was behind bars.

Steinschneider was discredited. Not only had he done studies on a SIDS serial killer who was directly under his nose, but he had been completely unaware of her murderous actions. He had permitted Waneta Hoyt to con him into believing all five of her children had died from the syndrome, when in fact Hoyt had suffocated them one after another. She is presently serving seventy-five years to life in prison.

To this day, the good doctor asserts apnea monitors help prevent SIDS. The case of Waneta Hoyt, he says, was but a blip in his research.

Many medical authorities now believe that at least 15 percent of all SIDS deaths are infanticides—the murder of innocents who were suffocated as they slept. These forensic sleuths say that too many pathologists write off unexplained child deaths as SIDS. A diagnosis of sudden infant death syndrome is nothing but a handy wastebasket into which are dumped unexplainable cases of babies who die in the night, they opine.

Some of these deaths are thought to be a form of Munchausen syndrome by proxy, a mental disorder in which the parent, usually the mother, secretly injures or smothers her infant to get sympathy and win attention for herself. Simple rage is another motivation easily disguised by a SIDS death certificate.

A theory that multiple deaths of SIDS babies within the same family are actually serial murders is presently being pushed by prosecutors who want to make a name for themselves. A subsequent sibling who succumbs to SIDS usually creates a legal suspicion among enlightened law enforcement agencies these days. In Chicago, for example, Deborah

Gedzius gave birth to six children fathered by three different men. Each child died before its first birthday and all were diagnosed with SIDS. In 1997, Cook County prosecutors disputed the SIDS determinations and turned their evidence over to a grand jury. Gedzius denied she killed her children and at this writing has yet to be charged.

Another woman, Marie Noe of Philadelphia, admitted to murdering eight of her children by suffocation between 1949 and 1967. Those deaths were attributed to crib death, the description used for SIDS prior to 1970. Noe pleaded guilty in 1999, when she was seventy. Because of her age, she was given an unusually light sentence: five years of home detention and twenty years of probation, on the condition that she would undergo psychiatric therapy. The mental health profession says it expects the study of Mrs. Noe to shed new light on infanticide.

"It's a fair resolution," her attorney, David Rudelstein, said after the sentencing. "While facing this responsibility is emotional and troubling for her, I believe she's at peace with the decision [to plead guilty] and looking forward to taking part in her mental health treatments to try to find the causes of her past behavior."

The prosecutor, Lynne Abraham, seemed resigned to the kid-gloves treatment. Her postsentencing statement was conciliatory. "It's obvious some people would have undoubtedly wanted Mrs. Noe in prison. Given her age . . . it was the best we could hope for."

In the same year, Ron and Amy Shanabarger's seven-month-old son, Tyler, died in Franklin, Indiana. He, too, was diagnosed with SIDS. Then, just hours following Tyler's funeral, Ron told Amy he had killed their child by wrapping the baby's head in clear plastic wrap and waiting until he observed Tyler drawing a final breath. His motivation for the crime was $100,000 in insurance money and revenge on Amy. He was still angry with her, he said, when—as his fiancée—she failed to return home from an ocean cruise to comfort him when his father died. Ron admitted he married her with the murderous plan in mind. The reason that he confessed, he said, was because his child's dead face was beginning to haunt him.

"So, now we're even," he told his wife.

After Ron's revelation, Amy drove her husband to a police station where he repeated the story. In late 1999 he was still in prison, awaiting sentencing.

Yet another SIDS diagnosis found to be a baby killing is the 1980s case of Stephen Van Der Sluys, an upstate New York father who murdered his three children, Heath Jason, Heather, and Vickie Lynn. His reason was nearly the same as that of Ron Shanabarger: money from an insurance policy. Van Der Sluys received the first life sentence for infanticide done for profit to children originally diagnosed with SIDS. Convicted in 1986, Van Der Sluys embarrassed supporters of Alfred Steinschneider. During the trial he confessed he had read information from the doctor's study, which told him that secretly smothering a child might result in a SIDS determination.

The testimony of Linda Norton, M.D., a former Dallas, Texas, medical examiner, would help to convict Van Der Sluys. Her statistics on the chances or lack of chances of subsequent siblings dying from the affliction was a key to the jury's findings. Because of Dr. Norton's testimony in the Van Der Sluys case and several other court actions she soon was described as the country's "foremost expert on SIDS." Norton would launch a talk show and lecture career, further enhancing her reputation. (Dr. Norton is also a featured player in this book.)

Halbert Fillinger, the coroner in the Noe case, has an opinion on SIDS linked to homicides. He warns that any multiple deaths in the same family diagnosed as SIDS should be looked into seriously. "The first death of a child is a tragedy. The second is a medical mystery. The third is murder," Fillinger cautions.

At first glance, the case of Garrett Eldred Wilson, a former musical instrument salesman, seems to nearly replicate that of Van Der Sluys. There were two children from separate spouses. Both babies were originally diagnosed by a state medical examiner to have died from SIDS. Large insurance policies had been taken out on each child. Some eighteen years after the first child died, the SIDS determinations were changed to "undetermined" in one infant and "smothering . . . a homicide" in the other.

These changes were the culmination of a four-year investigation by a former spouse. After the autopsies were reversed, Garrett Wilson was arrested. He was charged with first degree murder in two adjoining Maryland counties, both suburbs of Washington, D.C.

But is the father of Brandi Jean Wilson and Garrett Michael Wilson "the Ted Bundy of child killers," as a former wife's brother described him? Or is he instead the victim of heavy-handed law enforcement egged on by a spurned spouse who, until he divorced her, was determined to pursue him around the country and keep their fractured marriage intact at any cost?

Garrett Wilson's case falls under the "mystery" category, as defined by Dr. Fillinger. And though he had motivation, perhaps so did his accusers. So, did he do it?

This book can be read like any other mystery thriller. The answer to the "did he do it?" question is at the end of our story.

—*Adrian Havill*
Reston, Virginia
September 2000

PART ONE

Like a city in dreams, the great white capital stretches along the placid river from Georgetown on the west to Anacostia on the east. It is a city of temporaries, a city of just arriveds and only-visitings, built on the shifting sand of politics, filled with people passing through.

—ALLEN DRURY,
ADVISE AND CONSENT

PROLOGUE

At first glance, it appeared to be some sort of parade. But it was only minutes past dawn, and on this Wednesday, May 13, 1998, there were still two weeks before Memorial Day. So, where were those fourteen speeding police cars, strung out for nearly a quarter mile, headed?

There were black-and-whites and unmarked ones, too. They were from the Maryland State Police and three of its counties—Montgomery, Allegany, and Garrett. It was an all-American auto show. Heavy, top-of-the-line Fords and Chevrolets as far as an eye could see, cruising up Interstate 68, over the Eastern Continental Divide, and onto U.S. 40, the highway historians named The National Road. The old turnpike had been a route for motorized traffic since the turn of the century and still extended from Baltimore to St. Louis.

The odd-looking police procession was led by the police chief of Frostburg, Allegany's second largest town. He had already guided the motorcade by most of the local tourist attractions in the Maryland panhandle. Here Pennsylvania, West Virginia, and Virginia converged with the far western sliver of the Old Line State. The motorcade passed a Christmas tree farm where five-year-old firs had been planted in

the shape of a crucifix. The cop cars also filed by the tallest
structure within miles, a four-story-high, rusting, iron frame
skeleton that someday was supposed to replicate Noah's
Ark. A Pentecostal preacher in the area had been trying to
get funding to complete the religious ruin for twenty-five
years.

The Noah's Ark homage and the Christmas tree farm
were two of the premier attractions for this part of Maryland. Then the National Football League's Washington Red-
skins decided to put their preseason training camp five miles
up the road at Frostburg State University. Professional football, it could be argued, was also a religion for many of the
men and women in the region.

The police drove by a local bar named the Wildwater Inn,
where you could get Buffalo wings on Thursday nights for
twenty-five cents each, past Kyle's Towing, and then back
down the hill that led to the bottom of Big Savage Mountain.
The cavalcade turned right off U.S. 40 at the junction where
the shuttered Green Lantern restaurant stood. The cops
crossed back over I-68 on a narrow bridge until they reached
Blocher Road.

The two-lane route was a three-mile ribbon of rolling
hills. Next to the road more Christmas trees were planted—
otherwise the land served as steep, forty-five-degree cow
pastures. Blocher skirted the county line. It was just inside
Garrett County with Allegany on its left as the law enforcement parade made its way down and into a hollow, the land
rising to nearly vertical walls on both sides as the vehicle
reached the end of its length. Despite being between the
base of Big Savage and nearby Meadow Mountain, the citizens of Blocher Road were some two thousand feet above
sea level.

The people who lived in this pastoral paradise had not
known they were being watched. The local lawmen had
been quiet in their surveillance of the rural neighborhood.

Near the corner of the two old roads, Ervin Wampler, a
red-billed cap pulled tightly over his head, parked his pickup
truck next to a jumbled cluster of postal boxes and plastic

newspaper cubbyholes. He had stopped to grab his morning *Cumberland Times-News* and check for mail. When the caravan turned onto his road, he figured the cops were raiding one of the trailer homes that sat away from the road in the woods. Ervin had always wondered if something funny might be going down back there. Curious, he followed the police, tagging behind in his Ford truck.

Ervin was seventy-one and in need of more repair work on some of the arteries that pumped blood into his heart. His brown brick rambler, the last home on the left at the end of Blocher Road, was his retirement house. The dwelling was small. On the main level there were two bedrooms and a single bath. There was an unfinished basement below that, a deck out back, and a TV satellite dish next to the driveway. The attached two-car garage was nearly as big as the house itself. The place was far enough away from urban civilization that it was a rare day when deer failed to graze within sight of the front picture window. A bear had once appeared unannounced on his front doorstep and had to be shouted away.

The old man's hair had faded to white. He was short, unimposing, but still sturdy, built rather like a fireplug. Ervin could be impressive while listening, fixing a gaze on you that rarely faltered. He was remembered as the kind of guy you might talk to for an hour and then tell people that "he didn't look like he had a penny, but I bet he's got millions socked away."

The theory might have been true. Most of the land running up the hills in front of and behind his home was owned by the Wampler family patriarch. His father had once controlled more than two hundred acres of land in Garrett and Allegany counties. Over the years the property was divided among members of the Wampler clan. Ervin wound up with 110 acres on which he puttered about in his December years. He had a small haying operation, selling the wire-bound bales to nearby Holstein farmers. If the deal was right, Ervin might also sell off a few acres of timber rights, keeping the land. The earth was hard clay underneath, not good for much else—it was full of rocks. The soil's chief virtue was that it held moisture well. That made it good for grass that grew high, perfect for hay.

Ervin Wampler was now the caboose for the chain of cop cars. He was surprised when they bypassed the trailers and stopped in front of his house.

Outside of it, his daughter, Vicky Wampler Wilson and her husband of four years, Garrett, sat on a shaded, raised cement slab which served as a porch. The concrete had been covered over with brown outdoor carpeting that matched the brick exterior of Ervin's house. They were dressed in T-shirts and shorts, their feet jutting out onto the Wampler lawn. In the early morning light, they appeared not to have a care in the world.

The two looked to be about forty years old. Garrett was bulky. Although the baby fat had never left his face, his muscular body was a result of a lifetime spent lifting barbells in gyms. His round countenance gave him the look of someone always ready for a practical joke or a night filled with fun. Vicky usually kept her short blond hair carefully coiffed, but at this early hour it was flat and uncombed. They had been taking turns playing fetch with her husband's golden retriever, Sassy, a recent birthday gift. Garrett had named it after a dog he'd had as a boy. Vicky had bought the animal a year ago when they were living in a lakefront community near Forth Worth, Texas.

Ervin liked his new son-in-law, despite knowing of what he believed were long-ago crimes of theft, some womanizing, and a history of free spending compounded by hiding from creditors. He thought that was over, part of the past. His church had taught him forgiveness, and Ervin now thought Garrett was one of the most wonderful individuals he had ever met.

"Garrett's heart is as big as my truck," he once told a visitor, pointing up at the dusty, rusting hulk resting diagonally on the side of the road in front of his house. He drove it only for errands—there was a new Lincoln for Sunday and wear-a-suit social affairs.

Ervin liked to tell of the time Garrett had taken some trash to the dump, then tipped the workmen at the refuse center by bringing them fruit pies from a local Amish market. Oh, he thought his son-in-law was a winner for sure.

It was Garrett Wilson who first saw the police posse pull up in front of the house, slamming car doors so loudly the sounds echoed off the mountains. The first cop ran into the woods behind the house with a K-9 Corps dog on a leash. He had a shotgun. Garrett thought there had been an escape from Western Correctional Institution, a state prison that was just over the next hill. Eager to join the chase, he began walking toward Ervin's garage. His father-in-law kept his weapons there, and Garrett envisioned grabbing a shotgun and joining the hunt for the convicts. He didn't get the opportunity. The uniforms were instead moving swiftly toward him, surrounding the house and blocking his path.

A woman in her early thirties was a part of the group. She was dressed in civilian clothing, wearing a tight-fitting shirt tucked into long pants, which gave her the shape of a Coke bottle. A brass cop's badge was fastened to her belt and a holstered Smith & Wesson nine-millimeter police special was on her hip. These two amulets announced her authority. Garrett recognized the law woman. She was Meredith Hemma Dominick, a Montgomery County detective who had shown up in Texas without warning three years ago to ask him questions about his son, Garrett Michael. His namesake had died at the age of five months, diagnosed with sudden infant death syndrome. Detective Dominick seemed to imply that he might have killed the baby.

Today she was sure.

"Garrett Eldred Wilson, you are under arrest. Put your hands on the car," a lawman next to her shouted.

Garrett tried to look puzzled, though he suspected the charge had been coming for weeks.

"What for?" he asked.

"The homicide of your child."

It gave Meredith Dominick an enormous degree of satisfaction to see the arrest being made. She went up to him and looked directly into his eyes.

"Mr. Wilson, do you remember who I am?" she asked. There was no immediate answer from her prey. This was going to be her day.

Garrett looked back at her. He was frightened.

"You do look familiar. How did you find me?"

"I'm very good at my job," she answered.

"I'm not going to miss this for anything," the female sleuth had told her friends in the homicide–sex crimes division before leaving home the day before. At the time, Dominick joked to her colleagues about needing an extra-large set of handcuffs because Garrett's wrists were so big. She had spent the night at the Wisp Hotel, normally the centerpiece of a nearby winter ski resort. She got six hours of sleep before a morning briefing at a quarter to seven. Now, her mission was nearly complete.

A uniformed lawman from Montgomery County—one of six cops she had handpicked—shackled Garrett's wrists behind his back as another drew his police special, pointing it in his direction just in case the suspect got crazy and tried to run away. At the perimeter of the property, a lanky, perpetually tanned prosecutor from Montgomery County watched the arrest. He was more than six feet tall and looked as if he could be a good basketball player, which, in fact, he had once been. His name was David Boynton. He was the assistant state's attorney and had been an important part of the Garrett Wilson investigation team since 1994. This morning he, too, was reaping the fruit from his years of labor.

The small army of lawmen served six search warrants. This allowed them to explore Ervin Wampler's house and just about anything else in the vicinity.

"Anyone else inside?" an officer asked Vicky Wilson.

"Just my mother."

One of the cops had Vicky take him to the master bedroom where her mother was still sleeping. Thelma Wampler was seventy and wouldn't have been fazed if a bomb had exploded behind her. She wore a hearing aid in each ear. Without them she was nearly deaf. Both of them were removed when she slept. Her hair was hidden inside the sateen cap she wore to preserve the hairdo she got every other week at a Frostburg beauty shop. Thelma did not hear the young officer's demand.

"You have to wake up, ma'am. You have to get dressed."

Vicky put a hand on her mother's shoulder. The old woman awoke to a strange sight. She had never seen a cop in her bedroom before. The bewildered grandmother was startled. She stuck in her hearing aids while Vicky tried to tell her what was happening to the family.

There were police in every room now. They pulled open drawers and rifled through them, opened closets and peered into boxes. They weren't being pretty or neat about it, either. Papers from Garrett's briefcase were placed on a bed and photographed. The ransacked rooms soon looked like a war zone, Vicky said later. What seemed to interest the searchers the most were photos, particularly pictures of infant children. They also seized anything that appeared to be a document or looked like old credit cards with the suspect's name on it.

The two things they missed were Ervin's safe and the barn. The old man stubbornly refused to give them the combination. Eventually an officer shrugged and the corps of cops gave up without a fight. The barn, out of sight and stuffed with hay, was passed on. One could surmise the officers simply didn't care or know of its existence.

Vicky's sister, Kathy, who lived just down the road, had been told of the commotion. Garrett and Vicky's daughter, Marysa, had slept over at Kathy's, sharing a bedroom with Kathy's daughter, Kelsey. Both children were nearly five. They arrived just in time to see Garrett taken away in handcuffs and put into the front seat of a Maryland state trooper's squad car. Marysa, a cute little girl with bangs and brown hair that fell below her shoulders, looked just like her father. The child asked her mother what was happening.

"They said your daddy did something wrong and now he's got to prove he didn't do it," Vicky told her.

"But he's in the front seat," the little girl said. "Good people sit in the front and the bad ones are put in the back."

Vicky didn't have an answer for that.

After ransacking Ervin's house, the army of police changed direction. They headed for the $700-a-month rented house Vicky and Garrett had just moved into, some twenty-five miles away. The three-bedroom home, on Lake Shore Drive near the town of McHenry, was across the street from Deep Creek Lake. The 3,900-acre man-made body of water appeared to be much larger than its size because of its multitentacled shape. The shoreline had seventy-eight miles of coves and fingers around the perimeter and was a mecca for sportsmen. Though the house was well beyond Garrett's means, the couple had laid out a $2,000 security deposit on it just a week before. The house had prestige, the kind of waterfront address that impressed people.

A rented moving van was in the driveway. This stopped the cops at first. They didn't tell Vicky whether they had a warrant for the vehicle. It wasn't necessary. When they asked her to open it, she did so without question. The van was empty. The cops had enough anyway. By the time they were finished, seventeen boxes had been collected and tagged as evidence.

On another part of the lake, in a windowless room at the Maryland State Police Barracks, Garrett Wilson was being interrogated, accused of murdering his infant son in 1987. He was told they also suspected him of killing his daughter, Brandi, in 1981. The two-month-old had also been diagnosed with SIDS. They said the death penalty would apply in each case. The questions would be fired at him nonstop for three hours.

"I'm not going to sit here and talk to you without a lawyer," Garrett pleaded.

"You don't need an attorney," a cop shot back. "Just answer the questions."

After two hours of questioning, Meredith Dominick received a letter by fax from Bill Saltysiak, a local lawyer hastily hired by the Wamplers. The message warned her that he was representing Garrett and his client was "asserting his right to remain silent." The cops ignored the attorney.

"It's the defendant who has to assert the right to remain silent, in my opinion," a detective told Saltysiak.

His interrogators showed Garrett the charges a second time. The death penalty did apply, they reminded him once again. So Garrett talked. And talked. David Boynton had thought he would. The Montgomery County prosecutor's view of Garrett Wilson was that he was one smooth, slick salesman who felt he could worm his way out of any predicament.

At four in the afternoon, their suspect was put in the back of a squad car for the 135-mile drive to the Montgomery County Detention Center. Meredith Dominick's cuffs cut so tightly into his wrists there was soon a crimson circle around them, with Garrett in danger of bleeding. The cops noticed the rawness thirty miles down the road, just after passing Cumberland, the Allegany county seat. They stopped the vehicle by the Rocky Gap State Park exit next to the interstate and recuffed their prisoner, this time allowing him to place his hands in front of his body. He was also switched from the backseat to a more comfortable position next to the driver. His captors were determined to handle him humanely.

"I guess it's been a long time since you've been to Montgomery County," Dominick said as they sped east on the hilly freeway.

Her suspect disagreed. He told her he had just been in the Washington area to show Vicky the neighborhood where he'd grown up. He had also recently driven his father-in-law to a District of Columbia hospital for surgery. Garrett chatted with the detective until he tired. Soon he nodded off and slept like a baby the rest of the way.

As the captured Garrett Wilson was being sped toward the Detention Center, his accuser, Mary "Missy" Anastasi, was summoned to the Montgomery County Judicial Center. Until 1993, the blonde, whose best feature was her large green eyes, had been Garrett's wife. After he divorced her and married Vicky, she had lobbied the police to charge her former husband with killing their son. She wondered why she had been asked to report to the courthouse once again. Missy was tired, angry and frustrated with the lack of action by the local legal authorities. A woman offered her a soft drink as she seated herself at the head of a long table.

"I know you think we haven't been working on your case, but in fact we have for years," a prosecutor at the other end told her. "Garrett Wilson was arrested this morning in Frostburg, Maryland."

Missy Anastasi began sobbing. She hugged her cousin, a Montgomery County police sergeant, who had accompanied her to the offices.

"We did it," she cried. "We finally did it."

Her cousin telephoned her mother. He said Missy was a hero.

Two weeks later a tornado descended near Blocher Road, destroying twenty-nine houses, knocking down trees, and bending steel poles. It was the first twister anyone could remember in the western Maryland highlands. For the Wilson family, the disaster felt like an omen. The life they knew had changed for the worse. With her husband in jail and charged with murder, Vicky and her family's world was filled with black clouds.

Garrett's current wife began smoking again, though she knew he hated her habit, sucking on the Salem 100s cigarettes as if each time she inhaled might be her last. In the months that followed, friends often asked Vicky about her husband's status.

"It's all in God's hands now," she told them. She believed Garrett was innocent, framed by Missy, the spurned wife who had lost him to her five years before.

ONE

A LONER IN FRIENDLY

When Ethel Mae Garrett wanted to impress people, she would tell them she was descended from the Garrett tobacco family of Virginia. The boast was only partly true. She had been born in Pamplin, North Carolina, in 1921 while her father, Kendrick Garrett, worked for the Tar Heel State, building dams and bringing electricity to thousands. His family had once been the Garretts of Garrett Snuff, a branded brown dust manufactured in Lynchburg, the beginning of the Bible Belt in Virginia. One could choose to either tuck a pinch of the powder below the lower lip, hold it inside the cheek, or inhale the mixture into and through the nostrils before spitting the residue into the dirt. All three methods forced the nicotine to seep into wet exposed tissue, providing an addictive jolt of cheap pleasure.

Ethel was one of ten. Her mother, Araminta, specialized in popping out babies as if they were sugar peas fresh from the pod. She produced one child each year throughout the 1920s. Most were girls. By that time she truly could claim to be a Garrett of Virginia. Kendrick had moved the family to Burkeville in Nottoway County after the Great Depression began. This time he built dams and bridges for one of

Franklin Roosevelt's creations—the Civilian Conservation Corps—out of a nearby army base called Camp Pickett.

Araminta and Kendrick's home was on South Agnew Street. It was a big, white, five-bedroom house with four columns in front, one of the largest homes in town. Black potbellied stoves heated it in the winter. In the summer, there were ceiling fans to move the hot, humid air.

Burkeville, population five hundred, was fifty-five miles southwest of Richmond. Outside the town, the land was justly famed for a loamy soil, which produced the highest grades of flue-cured, premium tobacco. Curing sheds, where temperatures shot up to 120 degrees Fahrenheit in the summer as workers stacked the harvested leaves inside them, dotted the rolling green fields of Nottoway County.

Araminta was an exotic moniker, but her son and daughters had plain, traditional names. The siblings were Mary, Edith, Faye, Lucie, Willard, Bobby, and Harriet. One girl, Virginia, was a victim of Down syndrome. Araminta lost another son during childbirth.

Most of the Garrett brood had reached its teens by the time the world's financial markets crashed. Living in a farming village such as Burkeville cushioned the blow. The Garretts felt the effect of the Depression far less than the unfortunates of the big cities.

By the end of the thirties, Kendrick was dead from a heart ailment and all of the younger Garretts were adults. With the exception of Virginia, they began streaming out of Burkeville. Most heeded the siren call from Washington. In the pages of *National Geographic*, they had lingered over the photos of the buildings and monuments in the great capital. Now it came to life before their eyes. On the banks of the great Potomac River, each of them sought a prize—the stability of a government job. Paychecks with a federal seal never bounced. When you reached sixty-five, you got a pension. What more could one want? Ethel Garrett, a five-foot-seven, handsome, round-faced woman who friends thought resembled Shelley Winters, had one of these coveted positions when she was eighteen. She was soon wed, and life seemed perfect.

But her modest fairy-tale beginning would have an unhappy ending. In later life, Ethel would claim that her first husband was "impotent" and that the wedding had been a sham from the start. After a decade in this near-sexless marriage that produced no children, the union was annulled.

Her closest confidante in Washington became Iris Young, who worked with Ethel at the Department of Agriculture. Iris had made her way to the nation's capital from West Virginia. The two women became so intertwined in each other's lives that when Ethel became engaged to Howard Eldred Wilson III and Iris to Carl Farley, the pair planned their weddings fourteen days apart so each could attend the other's nuptials.

Eldred—he never used his first name or the fancy Roman numerals—was considered handsome, a comer. His great-grandparents had arrived in Washington more than a century earlier from Scotland. Whether fact or fantasy, it was part of Wilson family lore that somewhere near Edinburgh was a castle in which their ancestors had once resided.

A native of the federal city, he had been a star tennis player in his youth and voted "Most Likely to Succeed" in 1926 by his class at Eastern High School. For a while he seemed to be headed for broadcast stardom. In the 1930s he was chosen to read the Sunday comics with Arthur Godfrey on a local radio station, long before the broadcaster began his CBS career.

When Eldred was a young man, his widowed mother acquired a stately home on McArthur Boulevard, a major thoroughfare in the far western corner of Washington. Eldred's sister, Eleanor, and her husband, Donald Ward, joined her in the large house. Eldred's mother would live to be ninety-eight. If genes were a factor, her son had every right to expect a long and healthy life.

Eldred had gone to a local business college named for Benjamin Franklin, which specialized in accounting and financial courses. He had parlayed this business education into a career at Lincoln National Bank, which later merged into the city's largest financial institution, Riggs Bank. In 1947, he learned that the U.S. House of Representatives wanted a professional banker to supervise its payroll inside the Sergeant at Arms office. Eldred, who was about to celebrate his fortieth birthday, jumped at the chance. He was immediately hired to the post, considered a plum position.

"I never understood why they want government desk jobs," remembered Carl Farley. The husband of Ethel's best friend managed a series of wholesale food warehouses. Farley's job allowed him to go from the inside of the building to the outside several times a day.

Ethel wed Eldred on August 11, 1951. Iris and Carl's ceremony was held on the twenty-fifth. None of their friends thought it peculiar that Eldred was forty-three, thirteen years older than his wife. Instead, they were happy that Ethel had found happiness after the disastrous first marriage. Eldred also carried personal history into the marriage. He had once fathered a child with a girlfriend and named the boy after himself. The two married for a short time, but when he divorced the woman, he failed to support her or his son. He had also married a second time, with that alliance quickly going sour. Ethel whispered these secrets to Iris, and the stories became common knowledge.

Ethel quit her nine-to-five government job. She was determined to spend the rest of her life as Eldred's wife and a mother of many children.

The newlyweds shared a love of bowling. Both became involved in recreational leagues, showing up at the local lanes until their health faltered. They also liked to play cards. There were no other joint activities.

Separately, Ethel attended meetings of the Eastern Star, the female branch of the Masonic Fraternity. Eldred's sport was baseball. As a teen, he had sold peanuts at Griffith Stadium, then the home of the American League's underachieving Washington Senators. During the long summers, so hot and humid that a foggy mist rose from the city's two rivers as morning dawned, he contented himself by listening to each Senators game on WTOP, the home team's play-by-play radio voice.

The two women were so emotionally close to one another, it seemed natural that the first homes the Wilsons and Farleys purchased were less than two blocks apart. In the early 1950s, home ownership was a tangible sign of affluence. Their small starter homes were fifteen minutes from the Capitol, across the Anacostia River, up a hill from Bolling Air Force Base, and about a mile from the Maryland state line. The Farleys' house on First Street Southwest wasn't that much different from the Wilsons' home on Second Street.

"They had a brick house with some stonework in front and a concrete retaining wall," John Farley, the eldest of Carl and Iris Farley's three children, recalled. John, born in January of 1956, would be followed by Stephen and then Linda, all in the space of five years.

Ethel and Eldred finally had a son of their own on June fourteenth, but having children had not been easy. In the first five years of marriage the Wilsons had seen three chances at parenthood go bad. The first baby was stillborn, and the other two infants died from undiagnosed illnesses during the first three months of life.

Ethel was determined to succeed. After Eldred impregnated her a fourth time, she decided to give birth alone. As soon as her labor began, she marched three blocks to a bus stop at the corner of South Capital Street in blistering summer heat, took the transit vehicle to Doctor's Hospital, and checked herself in while Eldred continued to do the work of the nation at the U.S. Capitol. She told nobody about the impending delivery.

"My mother was thirty-five at the time. She already had the first signs of glaucoma. She had gone through two heart attacks, and early arthritis was making her fingers curl like a hawk's claws. The doctors told her it would be risky to give her a lot of drugs, so I was born by cesarean. I don't think there was any anesthesia. Mom was partly propped up so she could see herself giving birth," her son explained to an interviewer.

Determined to pass on her ancestor's name, and knowing this might be her last chance to do so, Ethel named the boy Garrett Eldred. The tobacco family lineage was safely perpetuated for one more generation.

But Garrett and Ethel were close, perhaps too close. "Why, my God, she breast-fed him until he was four," confided an amazed Jackie Sandoe, who married Eldred's nephew.

Ethel teased him about it when he got older. She said she was trying to beat the record of one of Eldred's relatives who had nursed her baby until the boy was five. Her tasteless remarks in front of family friends embarrassed him as he grew older.

"You did chin-ups on my boobs forever," she would say.

After their baby was brought home from the hospital, his father purchased a female boxer dog and named it Kris. The animal was trained to protect the child from harm. It sat at the top of the stairs near the entrance of their son's nursery. When anyone other than the parents approached his crib, the canine would bark loudly.

The Wilsons and the Farleys expected Garrett and John to be friends, and they were, becoming inseparable. The green woods in front of the Wilson house was their after-school playground.

Access to power has always been the road to success in Washington. Eldred became firmly ensconced in the Sergeant at Arms office and soon began to associate with the power congressmen of the era. Framed pictures with Sam Rayburn, Carl Albert, and Thomas P. "Tip" O'Neill were displayed in his office. Ethel was equally proud of a photo of her waltzing at the White House with Harry Truman. Promotion followed promotion. This allowed Eldred and Ethel to buy a much larger house in 1967. Their new home was east of the Capitol in an unincorporated suburban Maryland town. The signs said Friendly, but the name was meaningless. There was no government, no city center, no sense of belonging to a community. And if you told someone a few miles away you were from Friendly, you would be asked, Where is that?

Prince George's County, which surrounded Friendly, was (and still is) Washington's only bordering suburb that can be called determinedly working class. In the 1960s, the county's population was 400,000. (It is nearly double that today.) Eldred wore a suit and tie to Capitol Hill, but in truth, he was resolutely blue collar and knew it. Eldred rubbed shoulders with the leaders of the nation each day, but he knew the pecking order and where he stood, which was closer to the bottom than to the top. Any resentment he had was pacified by daily doses of hard liquor, a habit that grew into an incurable dependency.

Eldred decided on the show model in a development called Caltor Manor. The Wilson family's home was the first one on Caltor Lane, a string of houses much like their own that stretched down the hilly street for nearly a mile. Eldred and Ethel's residence was a white brick split-level placed diagonally on a quarter-acre lot. The home came complete with a carport and features known as "builder's extras."

The architect for the project trimmed the front of the Wilsons' house with columns of black wrought iron, giving it a faux New Orleans feeling. Ethel, Eldred, and Garrett moved into the house in May of 1967. It was remembered as an awkward time for their son, who spent the last month of the fifth grade in an unfamiliar elementary school.

For demonstration purposes, the sales force for Caltor Manor had equipped Eldred's house with a pair of kitchens. The second one remained even after they moved in. The extra refrigerator and stove in the basement would have been costly to rip out, and the Wilsons decided to keep their little bonus. As Garrett became older, the self-contained basement became his domain. Unlike most boys, he had a virtual apartment within the family home before he was a teenager.

It was expected that the Farleys would follow the Wilsons into Maryland. They did, but moved to New Carrollton, about fifteen miles away. Their new address was closer to Carl's job. John, now in a different school district, was separated from his friend during the school week. Garrett never formed close friendships with other boys, by high school gaining a reputation as a bit of a loner, according to the neighbors who remembered the family.

As an only child, Garrett was closer to his parents than most children. Fortunately, he failed to inherit their worst habits. Though short in stature, Eldred was considered good looking by his Caltor Lane neighbors until drink began distorting his features. By the end of the 1960s he had become a barrel-chested, three-pack-per-day smoker and a confirmed double-measure scotch and water drinker, good for several shots each evening. The drinking increased as he aged. Carrying a whisky nightcap to bed became a tradition. By any standard, he was an alcoholic and a frequent drunk. Ethel was a smoker until she quit in her forties. And while she joined her husband for cocktails at five, Ethel never became bound to liquor as her husband did.

"He held court every afternoon with a happy hour when he came home from Capitol Hill," John Farley recalled. "Eldred had his bar just behind the dining room table and he'd walk back and forth to the kitchen to get the water for his drinks. He began with beer and usually switched to the scotch by nine."

John remembered a truck pulling up to the Wilsons' house twice each week. A man with a cart on wheels would deliver boxes of beer. "It was a real cheap brand called Hal's. He was usually good for two or three cases."

Eldred kept a television set in the dining room and a small radio to listen to the baseball games on during the summer. He installed a small sofa next to the table, and the room became his kingdom.

As he grew older, Garrett would join his parents in these evening drinking sessions. But he never took up smoking, rarely drank spirits, and only occasionally sipped a beer. Garrett Wilson said liquor gave him headaches and made him wake up the next day feeling sick. Nor did he ever experiment with drugs. His one vice was food—all the wrong kind. Garrett would put down glass after glass of rich whole milk while eating unlimited double slices of baloney, the brand impregnated with cheese chunks. By the time he was ten he had begun to resemble the Pillsbury Doughboy.

On Sundays, Garrett was a regular at the First Baptist Church of Friendly. He was considered a gifted baritone, able to lead the choir with his voice. Garrett's mother was usually in church by her son's side. The two didn't seem to miss Eldred. A nominal Episcopalian, Eldred wasn't much of a churchgoer. Still, he took part in Ethel's nightly Bible lessons at the dining room table, albeit with a beer and a cigarette in his hand. Eldred was more than willing to bow his head or say grace before each meal, another ritual Ethel insisted on. Despite his lack of attendance in houses of worship, Eldred could quote Scripture better than any traveling evangelist.

At ten, Garrett was able to replace the Sunday morning church pianist if needed. He had begun to play the instrument just a year before.

"When I was nine I was walking by a local piano chain, Jordan Kitt's, with my mother," Garrett recalled. "I went into their showroom, sat down at the piano, and played 'The Marine Hymn.' My mother was totally surprised. She didn't know I could play at all."

Garrett was precocious. He had taught himself the tune while staying at an aunt's house the previous week. Ethel thought she had a young Mozart on her hands and immediately hired a music tutor to give him lessons. But after a couple of sessions, Garrett quit.

"My teacher, Mrs. Galloway, wanted me to play one type of music, and I wanted to play another. Except for a few lessons on the organ when I was fourteen, those were the only ones I ever had," Garrett said.

Most people would say Garrett was spoiled. His indulgent parents refused to command a classic musical discipline for him and never found a mentor who might have made his talent bloom to the fullest. They had problems of their own. Ethel's health was growing more precarious. Eldred's lifelong dependency on nicotine and booze was beginning to take its toll. He was often short of breath, experiencing the first signs of what would be diagnosed as emphysema.

Garrett certainly had enough talent to make others take notice. He could listen to any melody on the radio and usually duplicate the tune within an hour. He played Chopin without difficulty, but instead chose to learn the pop melodies of the day—bland soft rock offerings by the likes of John Denver or Neil Diamond. Garrett's interpretations were more than passable, yet after reaching this middle plateau, he seemed to be satisfied. He made no effort to take his considerable skills to higher levels.

At times Eldred could be a disciplinarian. Until he was eleven Garrett was beaten with his dad's belt whenever he got out of line. His father's other method of punishment was to creep into the bathroom when his son was showering and whack him on the back with the flat of the hand. The pain was magnified by the contact with the wet skin.

"He would have the belt out as soon as he walked through the door from work. It was usually because I had argued with my mother. The beatings never lasted long. He was always in a hurry to open up the liquor cabinet and have his first drink," Garrett said.

By high school, Garrett was grossly overweight. He had grown to his final height, five foot ten, and his weight was above 250 pounds. In his early teens, he had tried to toughen up by working a summer construction job, but the baby fat that filled his cheeks would never leave. He tried out for, and made, Friendly High School's varsity wrestling squad, but he was just average. His mediocre record inspired him to begin lifting free weights in an attempt to become more successful at the sport.

The rotund teen was more successful in his high school choir. As a senior he was an "All County" selection. And though he had few male buddies save for his steady friend, John Farley, he more than made up for it with the girls. Garrett Wilson's greatest success was as a teen Romeo, given to smooth compliments and extravagant romantic gestures. His gifts would wow scores of impressionable young women.

"He could talk the fleas off a dog," remembered John Farley.

A typical Garrett romance was Jane Edmunds, a girl who lived next door, the daughter of the minister of the Baptist Church he and his mother attended. In her sophomore yearbook he would write,

You're a crazy girl (sometimes). But you can be as sweet as sugar. I love the privaledge [sic] of living next to you for several years???? Ha! Ha! Well Sis, Good luck in the future with the boys.

Love, Garrett.

The next year, at the age of seventeen, he proposed.

"He asked me to marry him in the eleventh grade," the preacher's daughter recalled. "He once sent me several dozen roses, and when he popped the question he had a diamond ring with him. We hadn't gone out *that* much, but I have to say, he certainly was a ladies' man. I suppose that was surprising, considering what he had to work with."

He didn't have a fancy car. Though Garrett bought a clunker at age sixteen, he continued to catch the school bus to and from Friendly High, sometimes walking the one-mile distance by taking a shortcut through the woods. His dates were simple. They usually consisted of inviting a girl to his family's home and into the basement, where he would serenade her with music, sometimes singing along to a hit tune of the day. Eldred Wilson's 1970 Chevy Monte Carlo was available, but it wasn't Garrett's first line of romantic offense when it came to comely young girls and affairs of the heart.

He was a talker, as smooth as silk. His personality was enough to get Virginia Fort, a blonde in the drama club described as "the prettiest girl at Friendly High," to go to the senior prom with him. Though it was a coup and cause for envy, he remembered it as a platonic night out. The two were buddies only. Eldred had just purchased a new 1974 Chevy Impala, and let Garrett borrow it for the event, held at Washington's Mayflower Hotel.

The other high point of his high school years came when his Spanish class made an Easter week journey to Mexico City. Garrett was a fifteen-year-old sophomore when the trip was announced, and both parents balked at letting him loose in what Eldred called a "Third World country."

"On Christmas day they put a camera and some pesos in my stocking. At the bottom, near the toe, was a card that read ONE TRIP TO MEXICO CITY, with a copy of the two-hundred-fifty-dollar check they had written as a down payment for the plane fare," Garrett said.

The Mexican adventure was not without mishaps. Garrett went out alone and promptly became lost, his Spanish not quite good enough to assure his quick return. He was also seduced by an older senior girl who then conned him into lending her his last seventy dollars. When he came home, he told his parents about the money. Eldred became so incensed he went to the girl's house and made her father pay the money back. Later, Eldred gave Garrett some fatherly advice about women that his son took to heart.

"There are lots of them. And sometimes, if they don't want you, they don't want you."

The Wilson family made two out-of-town journeys each year. The first was a regular Thanksgiving pilgrimage to Burkeville. Araminta, who lived into her nineties, would preside over the holiday feast. Garrett's Uncle Willard would always drive over from Lynchburg, and some of Ethel's sisters would make an appearance. The holiday get-togethers were as close as the Wilsons ever came to sibling reunions.

The other holiday was a weeklong summer vacation trip to Piney Point, on Route 5 in southern Maryland. The three Wilsons would rent a waterfront cottage near the mouth of the Potomac River, just before it joined the Chesapeake Bay. There they would play long card games—canasta and pinochle—or their favorite board game, Scrabble.

"The Potomac is five miles wide at that point and we'd go fishing. But I would have to catch him early, before he got drunk," Eldred's son explained.

His father was a formal, pretentious man. He wore a different suit each day and wouldn't take it off until his bedtime. At one time he owned nearly fifty such costumes, filling several closets. Dinners were a ritual. Eldred expected three-course meals, and the one in the evening was expected to be the likes of a pot roast, or a whole stuffed chicken. Ethel spoiled him as she did her son, giving him just what he wanted.

After his graduation from Friendly High School, on June 30, 1974, Garrett drifted. Surprisingly, his parents, who always said their son would be a doctor when he reached adulthood, had given him no education plan or real push in any scholarly direction insofar as what he should become. Eldred and Ethel never drove him to visit a university campus. Grades, remembered as mostly A and B marks, and SAT scores between 1200 and 1300 were good enough to get him admitted to most colleges. His parents never even encouraged him to apply. Eventually, Garrett took a couple of business courses at a local community college and that became the extent of his higher education. Instead he became good at golf, played piano on weekends at Lyle's (a steak restaurant near his house), and, with Eldred's help, got some short-term menial jobs in the government. They were usually at the U.S. Capitol, where he toiled as a $3.15-per-hour carpenter's helper, and later, as an elevator operator for five dollars an hour.

Garrett's father also found him his first steady employment. In November of 1975, he pushed his son into taking a position in the computer division of Riggs Bank at the corner of 9th and F Streets in Washington, one block from FBI headquarters. The salary was $240 a week. Since Eldred had jump-started his own career at Riggs, it was assumed Garrett would surely want to follow in Eldred's footsteps. The job was far from glamorous. The bank started him out on the midnight-to-dawn shift in an interior room.

A year out of high school, Garrett had become, at best, a weekend piano player and a graveyard-shift banking clerk. Did he want more? If he had higher dreams and ambitions, they were not evident to those who knew him well.

His parents seemed happy to drift. Eldred was forced to retire from his job at the U.S. House of Representatives within days of Garrett's high school graduation. After twenty-eight years of government service, his health had been poisoned from a lifetime of too much liquor and far too many cigarettes.

"I remember my mother appearing at the end of Friendly High School's stadium in the fall of 1973," Garrett remembered. "I was running track after a wrestling practice. She was petrified with fear. My father had collapsed at the Capitol and we had to go to pick him up. It was an emphysema attack. He couldn't function anymore."

Eldred received 80 percent of his salary, and was guaranteed yearly cost-of-living increases after he ended his career. He appeared to be financially set for the rest of his life.

It was doomed to be a short and unhappy retirement. His health was failing badly. By now he needed to clamp an oxygen mask over his face several times each day. Ethel's condition was worse. Her clogged heart was severely damaged. The arteries that provided blood to the life-giving organ had been partially blocked for years.

In 1970, Ethel walked outside the house to saw down some tree limbs in the backyard. After the chore, she felt a burning inside her breast. Ethel thought she had torn a chest muscle. A few days later, when she went to her doctor, he told her that besides the injury, she had also suffered a third coronary. Her heart had been damaged further because of her stoic refusal to seek medical attention for the pain.

Whatever status Eldred had once enjoyed on Capitol Hill quickly evaporated. When he tried to return to the hallowed U.S. House of Representatives, he was embarrassed.

"I went with Dad when he attempted to go back to the Sergeant at Arms office for a visit after he retired," Garrett recalled. "He was wearing a loud Hawaiian shirt, some funny-colored slacks, and moccasins. The clothing was totally out of character for him. When he tried to get on the elevator he had been whisked up in every day he worked there, the operator didn't recognize him. He argued with my father about whether he should let him get on. Dad never went back."

Neither Ethel nor Eldred had any wants left. Experiencing the joys of world travel or attempting something new during their senior years was not part of their personalities. They were content enough just to drink, smoke, and occasionally indulge themselves with a night out at a booze-and-beef chain restaurant until the end of their days. With no urgency in their lives, they felt no need to take risks or take on challenges. Their health was now in steep decline and became their primary concern. These frequent medical traumas, combined with Eldred's ever-increasing expenditures on liquor and cigarettes, also prevented them from partaking of luxuries.

"Yeah, I did have good grades—a 3.2 high school average," Garrett recalled. "The reason I never made a commitment to go further in school is because there was always a crisis of some kind at home. Every time I tried to focus on a career, something would happen to their health. I think I always had the idea in my mind of becoming some sort of performer, but that never worked out."

By the end of 1975, his father's alcoholism had progressed to a point where on most nights he would drink himself into a liquor-induced coma. Eldred often fell down or stumbled badly as he made his way up to his bedroom. On one occasion, a drunken fall fractured a bone in the lower part of his spine, immobilizing him for months. The cigarettes and the scotch had exacted a severe price. He was diagnosed with tuberculosis in 1970. A year later, a diseased kidney was removed, followed by the gall bladder, with the final signs of emphysema beginning to painfully immobilize his body. He had to take medicine to keep his pancreas functioning.

Eldred's once handsome face now appeared unhealthy, a beet-red mass of inflamed broken blood vessels. He began to gasp with each step, unable to walk more than a few feet at a time. Garrett became both the family bookkeeper and the parental caretaker while barely out of his teens. None of these medical nightmares put any damper on his father's drinking and smoking, though. Stubborn to the end, Eldred did make the concession of switching to low tar and nicotine cigarettes, but immediately neutralized any benefit by upping the number he smoked by a pack a day.

"My mother would come down after he was asleep and talk with me about ways we could get him to cut back. But my dad would never consider any of this for a moment."

Garrett Wilson said he knew both of his parents were slowly dying before his eyes. He always thought his dad would go first.

Garrett's reign as the Casanova of Caltor Manor eventually got him into trouble. In the mid-1970s, he met an eighteen-year-old brunette named Shelly at a Baptist Church in nearby Camp Springs, Maryland. Shelly had been a year behind Garrett in school and was a senior at Friendly's sports nemesis, Crossland High.

Both must have slept through the normal fire-and-brimstone Baptist Church sermons. They quickly became intimate, and within months Shelly was with child in the most Biblical sense of the phrase. Garrett promised to marry her so the child wouldn't be labeled a bastard, and he did that, on March 17, 1976, at a courthouse ceremony in Upper Marlboro, the Prince George's county seat. Shelly was seven months pregnant at the time the ceremony was performed. Both of them were still in their teens. Still, Garrett lived up to his rakish reputation by secretly dating one of Shelly's rivals, a blonde looker named Kim, before and after the short-lived wedding. The day after the ceremony, Shelly announced they were separated. The news was given in writing to the courts by her just-hired divorce lawyer, Gary Alexander.

A boy, whom Shelly named Billy Alan, was born on May 16, 1976. Garrett would never take part in the infant's care, and after Shelly fulfilled the state's requirement of a year's separation, she filed for divorce on the first day of April in 1977.

After the divorce complaint was filed, Garrett denied he was the father of the boy in an attempt to avoid paying child support. When he filed a financial statement showing he had a negative net worth, Shelly's demand for child support was tabled by the divorce court judge. Her plea for financial aid was not presented again.

Eldred managed to keep the squalid affair so quiet even Ethel didn't find out. Few of their neighbors ever knew Garrett had married, fathered a boy, separated, and gotten divorced, all in the space of less than two years. Shelly moved to California and remarried. She tried to forget the youthful error.

"Shelly? I never knew about that one," said Garrett's best friend, John Farley, when asked about the relationship.

TWO

ROBBERY ON THE HILL

Garrett Wilson was talking to me about what he said was one of the saddest days of his life. The voice dropped to a near whisper.

"It was on July 4, 1976, the Bicentennial. I had plans for the holiday but got stood up. My friends were supposed to come for me that morning at nine, and they didn't. I was moping around with nothing to do, sitting on the front steps, feeling sorry for myself.

"My mother found out I'd been left behind. She felt a little sorry for me and said, 'Come on, let's go down to Washington and spend the day on the Mall.' We did, and parked the car about eight blocks from the Washington Monument. Mom wasn't all that well, but she was determined to do it. We took our time. We'd stop every couple of blocks and buy a snow cone from a vendor or get something to drink. It was a hot day. We got a good spot and by two there must have been three hundred thousand people around us. There was a long free musical concert that day—the Beach Boys headlined. After dark there was the most spectacular fireworks I've ever seen, followed by a laser light show."

Garrett remembered this long-ago event as if it were yesterday.

"We waited two hours for the laser light show, but it got screwed up and didn't come off right. By the time we got home it was past midnight. We were hungry so we drove to the all-night IHOP in Marlow Heights for an early morning pancake-and-eggs breakfast."

But shouldn't that have been a happy day?

"Yeah, but because of what happened a month later, it was one of the saddest."

His eyes were filled with tears. Was the sorrow sincere, or was Garrett Wilson just a good actor?

On an August Saturday in 1976, Garrett got up at eight o'clock to finish mowing the front lawn before it got hot. He had started the night before and was able to complete the task by nine. Then he walked into the house and made breakfast for his mother. He put coffee and toast on a tray, and walked up the stairs and into his parents' bedroom.

He couldn't make Ethel stir, even after shaking her. She was dead at fifty-five, the victim of a final massive coronary eruption which had taken place hours before. Partial rigor mortis was already present. Eldred, in one of his scotch-induced comas, snored beside her. Instead of telephoning an ambulance, Garrett called Iris Farley to ask for advice on what he should do next.

Ethel's funeral had an open coffin. Everyone agreed she looked wonderful in repose. She was buried at Cedar Hill Cemetery, just inside the District of Columbia line, where Eldred had purchased a plot for three. Following her death, Garrett, witnesses say, appeared as if in a trance. Eldred was worse, sitting at the dining room table in his pajamas until just before the funeral, an ever-present drink in his hand. The arrangements with the mortuary were made by his son.

"He never cried. In fact, I don't think I've ever seen him cry," John Farley said. "After his mom died, we would drive around in his car and sometimes he'd park and then stare through the windshield for more than an hour without ever saying a word. He would say out loud, 'I need to be strong,' over and over again."

"A lot has been made of me being always under control," Garrett responded when asked about John's comments. "I had to be. I had to take care of things."

He ran his father's checking account, paying the bills and taking his mother's role in running the household. He began telling people he could feel her presence whenever he went into the master bedroom. Garrett said the room gave him a chill when he entered it. He attributed the eerie shivers the space imparted to the spirit of his mother being nearby.

"A week after my mother died, my dad walked into the house and said, 'Come on, we're going to the beach.' We went down to Piney Point. For a week he was a real dad. He went there without his oxygen tank, and I spent the week amazed. We'd wake up early, go to a little store for eggs and bread, then take out a boat and fish.

"The last day he lost his shine. He realized my mom was gone forever. We came home and he reverted back to his usual habits."

Garrett's voice trailed off. His eyes were filled with tears again.

"I was caught between a rock and a hard place. I had to make dinner for him and do all the things my mother had done. But by then, drinking was his only priority."

With Ethel gone, Eldred deteriorated fast. The emphysema slowly strangled him. He needed to wear the oxygen mask in the house for much of the day. With flammable tanks around, his doctors banned any smoking. Eldred, however, defied them. Again, he actually increased his habit by taking to True, a cigarette brand that claimed to offer the lowest tar and nicotine available. With a True in his mouth, he believed he was even doing himself good. But he needed the addictive poison so often that after pulling hard on the miserly white cylinders for months his cheeks became hollow and sunken just from the effort. He consumed them in record numbers—one hundred a day.

Eldred simply no longer cared. He took his chances on the house exploding and often roared dangerously down the roads of the county in the family car. He drove alone, the oxygen mask on, a portable steel tank on the front seat beside him. Motorists who saw this masked man hurtling toward them would veer away in terror. Eldred deemed immediate death preferable to the slow painful one he was experiencing. And he didn't care who he took with him.

A practical nurse was hired, but she didn't work out. So Eldred was removed, protesting, to a nursing home in September of 1978. After he was installed at the institution, Garrett found thirty cartons of the blue-and-white True packs stashed in cubbyholes and drawers in the rooms that had once represented his family's dream of a better life. Eldred spent the last year of his life in a grim second-rate asylum, alternately gasping or begging for a cigarette, bribing the attendants to bring him scotch, and cursing anyone who dared to prevent him from practicing his vices. This included his son.

"I'd go to the nursing home to visit and would drag a piano down the hall to his room to play for him. Often, he would shoo me away. I never let it bother me. I just played for the others instead," Garrett said.

Eldred died on August 12, 1979, three years after Ethel, almost to the day. He was rushed from the nursing home to a hospital during his final hours. His son was with him when he passed away. Eldred's remains were cremated, the ashes placed on top of Ethel's body at Cedar Hill Cemetery.

Eldred didn't leave his son much of an estate. The house and bank accounts had already been put into joint accounts with Garrett, who had controlled most of the assets for years. There was a small life insurance policy. The only other person remembered in the will was his first son, Howard Eldred, who was awarded a single dollar. The buck bequest was a legality to prevent Howard from contesting the legacy. A lawyer had told Eldred he needed to show he was aware of the other son's existence.

His father lived long enough to see Garrett take a second step on the career path he had chosen for him. In 1977, Eldred used some remaining chits to get his son a solid position on Capitol Hill, the kind he had once gloried in. His son's new job was identical to his own bootstrap position in 1947. Garrett became a clerk in the House Finance Division, working in room 263A of the Cannon House Office Building, at the foot of Capitol Hill. The finance section of Congress was responsible for doling out twelve thousand employee payroll checks a month. Garrett would be virtually retracing his father's life in spades. He had already duplicated Eldred's youthful indiscretion of fathering a child out of wedlock. Only his rejection of Eldred's addiction to hard drink and tobacco prevented him from being a true clone.

Garrett began at thirteen thousand dollars a year. While the amount wasn't a king's ransom, he could look forward to a regular workday, security, promotions, raises, and a fat federal pension in thirty years, just like his late father.

With Eldred dead and all the remaining family assets deeded to him, Garrett, by all accounts, went on a wild spending spree. He installed the beginnings of a recording studio in the basement of the Caltor Lane house, placing black acoustical tiles on the ceilings and walls. In another part of the cellar he added a weight room and a pool table. He purchased two dogs, a German shepherd he named Sassafras, and a Norwegian elkhound. The second canine soon ran away and was killed by a passing car. Garrett then had a chain-link fence installed around the perimeter of the backyard to confine the German shepherd. Besides spending money on a dog, Garrett indulged in that most expensive of luxuries, a horse. The Appaloosa gelding was boarded nearby at the rate of $60 a month and quickly ran up a $2,500 vet bill because of a saddle sore that was passed on by the previous caretaker.

"The owner was in the military and he wanted a thousand

dollars," Garrett recalled. "Then he came down to five hundred. On the day he was due to be shipped out to Alaska he gave him to me. So, since the horse came to me out of the blue, I named him Blue."

There was one inexpensive enthusiasm. Garrett mixed some cement and built a concrete patio at the rear of the house. This soon became a summertime muscle beach for his weight-lifting regimen, his only discipline. The drummer from a musical group he would put together, Bobby Henley, became a bodybuilding partner.

Other expenditures seemed even more lavish, though much of the money he spent seemed designed as an attempt to win the love and admiration of others, including large checks written to the Baptist Church. When John Farley's sister, Linda, graduated from high school, Garrett insisted on giving her a one-hundred-dollar bill. Then he took the teenager and other members of the Farley family to a private club for Republicans on Capitol Hill. He had once proudly played piano there for President Gerald Ford. To celebrate the milestone, Garrett hired a limousine to whisk the Farleys into Washington. He lent John $5,200 to buy a car and didn't seem eager to get it back, exclaiming to him that, "It's from the Bank of Garrett!" He bought a car for himself as well.

In spite of coming into a small inheritance, Garrett seemed unable to pay his creditors, no matter how big or small the invoice. A tiny $4.31 charge from the Register of Wills in Prince George's County went ignored for three years, even though the government sent dunning notices every quarter. The county clerks eventually gave up on collecting the amount and took the bill off their books.

His father hadn't left him *that* kind of cash. The costs of the emphysema care and his nursing home stay had reduced Eldred's net worth. Garrett, an immature twenty-three-year-old, went through what was left as if trying to meet a midnight deadline, determined to spend it all before the clock struck twelve. It didn't occur to him to plunk money down on a four-year college education. Advanced academics had never been stressed by his parents, despite Ethel's fantasy of her son becoming a surgeon—like the ones she had seen on television doctor shows. Love had been measured by the Wilsons with awards of material possessions. Garrett got a set of golf clubs for his fourteenth birthday. This kind of giving offered instant gratification and made no long-term demands on the intellect.

Garrett daydreamed of stardom in the pop music world. He put together two- and three-piece bands, sometimes naming his soft rock group Cirrus. He had a short career playing in clubs in Waldorf, a former southern Maryland hot spot on U.S. Highway 301. The town had once housed slot machine casinos, but in the mid-sixties the state changed its gambling laws. The former one-armed-bandit gambling destination was now a strip of seedy second-rate night clubs, attached to single-story motels that rarely filled up.

John Farley would sometimes show up at one of the places where Garrett played. Whenever his pal appeared, Garrett would launch into the theme from *The Banana Splits*, a popular children's television show of the day that they both liked. It was their private joke.

No Hollywood talent scout ever came calling in this lost area of Maryland. Garrett quickly came to realize that all he had was another job, a sometimes pleasurable and glamorous one, but one with a low salary and without much of a future.

By 1980, the cash left by Eldred was gone, there was a second mortgage on the Caltor Lane house, and Garrett was in hock up to (and maybe above) his neck. He then made a stupid but conscious mistake. Garrett stole money, a lot of money, from his employer, the U.S. House of Representatives. In later years, he would refer to this event as "the fiasco."

The theft of funds from the U.S. Congress is a bizarre story. Just before midnight on March 6, 1980, Garrett suddenly appeared before Officer G. F. Landers of the U.S. Capitol Police, the law enforcement branch of Congress. Appearing bruised, cut, and shaken, he had an amazing tale to tell the law enforcement officer.

The twenty-three-year-old clerk said that just three hours

before, he had gone into his office after noticing the door was unlocked. Garrett said "a white male" was already inside and had put a pistol to his head, telling him, "Come in, you work here. Open the safe."

"No, I don't work here," Garrett claimed he answered. An accomplice of the gunman then punched him in the right side of his face.

With a revolver to his head, Garrett supposedly opened the safe, and, while the man with the weapon continued to point it at him, the other stuffed the cash and checks into the pockets of his overcoat. After getting the money, the gunman pistol-whipped him with three more blows to the face, this time with the butt end of the weapon, he said. Then a strange capsule was crushed under his nose, rendering him unconscious for more than an hour. He awoke, he claimed, because the phone in the office was ringing. After getting his bearings, he contacted the Capitol Police in the person of Officer Landers. The cop wrote out a report, classifying the event as a "robbery, holdup, gun" and noting that the method used was "fear."

District of Columbia police detectives were called in when Landers realized a security guard had been stationed less than fifty feet from Garrett's office. The night watchman said he hadn't seen anyone enter or leave the room.

"How two men could creep by the officer without being seen or heard in the empty hallways was a puzzle," the Capitol Hill policeman said later. He also noted that the wounds on Garrett's face from being punched and pistol-whipped appeared to be superficial.

The D.C. detectives, Henry Daley and Ronald Carpenter, began grilling him at the District of Columbia's police headquarters interrogation room, making Garrett retell his account over and over. After he spun his tale a few times, Daley looked him in the eye and said, "I don't believe you." There was a dead silence. The suspect quickly caved in.

"What will happen to me if the robbery didn't occur the way I said it did?" Garrett asked.

The cops didn't answer the question immediately. Instead the investigators told him what *they* needed.

"We want the money back," Carpenter said. They told him if he returned the cash, both would try to put in a good word for him with the prosecutors.

"Okay," said Garrett. He told them he had stolen the money from the safe and taken it to his Caltor Lane home that afternoon. He also admitted returning that night to fake the robbery.

"Then let's go get it," said Henry Daley, and the three drove to the house at two in the morning. Their suspect led them down the hallway and into a bedroom. There was money in a briefcase, and even more money in a chest of drawers. In all, it totaled $41,044.12 in cash and $704.49 in checks. The three returned to Washington police headquarters, and Garrett wrote out a four-page confession. His motivation for the crime, their suspect claimed, was desperation. He had just been physically threatened by a loan shark for repayment, and he didn't have the money.

Surprisingly, the police did not lock Garrett up that night or even charge him with any crime. They simply told him he was a suspect in a robbery, read him his Miranda rights, and sent him home. It was nearly five in the morning.

John Lawler, Garrett's boss and the director of the House Finance Office since 1975, later seemed more concerned that Garrett had been up all night answering questions. Police records show that he gave his employee the day off after the arduous night.

"This is the first time this has ever happened," Lawler told a reporter, appearing shocked. He explained that Garrett's story at first seemed plausible because although his people signed out at 5:30 P.M., they often came back to work late, leaving as late as ten at night.

In his statement admitting the crime, Garrett wrote that he took the money from the safe and then made a false report to the police. The case appeared to be solved with his willingness to accept the consequences. The police issued a warrant on the Saturday following his arrest, and three days later their suspect surrendered at police headquarters, where he was again released on his own recognizance.

When the story appeared on the front page of the local news section of *The Washington Post* the next day, Garrett began getting dozens of calls from people he hadn't seen or talked to since high school. Iris Farley was one of those who read the newspaper account. She wept. Her tears and the embarrassing calls from his former classmates appeared to bother Garrett more than any possible penalty.

At first, Garrett's release by the detectives in what was obviously an open-and-shut case seemed to be the end of the episode until his sentencing. Garrett found another job, selling pianos at Jordan Kitt's, the local musical instrument chain where he had first demonstrated his musical talent. At the same time, he retained Richard T. Colaresi, a Maryland criminal attorney. Colaresi, who twenty years later remembered Garrett as "a genteel, well-spoken young man," tried to wriggle out from the charge. He filed a motion to suppress the evidence from the D.C. police already admitted to by his client.

"The confession was not voluntary," argued Colaresi, writing that Garrett's case was similar to one where a defendant had been "weakened by shock and isolated from his family, friends, and legal counsel."

Wrote Colaresi:

> ... the defendant's will was overborne at the time he confessed. The Supreme Court has on numerous occasions taken many facts into account. The relevant ones in this case are that the defendant was not assisted by counsel; there was a prolonged interrogation by numerous officers, including a car trip to the defendant's home; the defendant had no sleep during the entire night of his investigation. The interrogation was designed to elicit a signed statement of the police's view of the proof; and the defendant had no food. He had already been advised by a doctor to go to a hospital, and was in contact with no one else. In addition, the defendant had never been in trouble with the law before and as such was not acquainted with his rights.

Colaresi summarized:

> In this case, defendant would answer all of the questions
> prepared by the court in a different way ... defendant would
> contend that there were promises and subtle forms of coer-
> cion, that the defendant was in the police station, that he was
> a newcomer to the law, and he was not given his Miranda
> rights. For these reasons and for other arguments to be made
> at the hearing, the defendant would move for the suppres-
> sion of statements made by the defendant and any evidence
> obtained through a search of the defendant's premises.

Colaresi's arguments on behalf of Garrett quickly fell on
deaf ears after U.S. District Court Judge Harold Greene read
the brief. Garrett pleaded guilty to the charge of embezzlement in June.

At the sentencing on July 29, 1980, he got lenient treatment based on a new federal statute for first-time offenders
who were still under the age of twenty-five. Under the law,
known as the Federal Youth Corrections Act, he was given a
suspended sentence of three years, providing he pay a fine of
$5,000 within sixty days. (Of note is that his prosecutor the
day of the sentencing was Charles F. C. Ruff, who then had
the title of Attorney of the United States. Ruff would reach
national fame eighteen years later as an eloquent defender of
President William Jefferson Clinton in his impeachment battle before the U.S. Congress.)

Everyone deserves a second chance at love and happiness.
Garrett certainly had several. The next such opportunity was
with Deborah Lynn Oliver, a girl he met in 1976 and began
dating in 1977 between the deaths of Ethel and Eldred. She
was twelve and he was twenty when they became friends.
They met in church, virtually under the nose of a Baptist
minister.

"I had conducted the chorus in high school, and the pastor of the Fort Foote Baptist Church asked me to conduct his
chorus when their choir leader went on vacation. Debbie

was sitting with her older sister Melissa after practice, and I thought she was the oldest. I was going out for pizza after the rehearsal, and I decided I wasn't going to go alone that night. So I asked her to go with me," Garrett recalled.

It didn't occur to him when they started dating that some people might roll their eyes at the sight of a nearly twenty-two-year-old man taking out a thirteen-year-old girl. It also wasn't forbidden by Kyle and Jean Oliver, Debbie's God-fearing parents. Kyle was a government auditor and Jean was a secretary at a Baptist church in nearby Temple Hills. While their occupations might have been bland, their residence was not. The Olivers lived in a unique white stucco house that looked like it would have been at home on the Riviera. The glitzy two-story villa was trimmed with bright blue awnings and matching clay roof tiles and stood out from the conservative colonial houses that were the standard in Prince George's County.

The Olivers were willing at first to let Garrett take their daughter to dinner and to shows like *Oklahoma!* and *The Nutcracker Suite* at the Kennedy Center, though later they said they thought the relationship was only a friendship. They seemed impressed with the trips into Washington, calling it, "going to the opera."

Garrett remembers that the prim-appearing Mrs. Oliver was upset when she discovered the two were romantically involved. In Garrett's mind, at least, it wasn't only for the reason one might suppose.

"I'm more of a woman than she'll ever be," he alleges she said to him. At Christmas time, she gave her future son-in-law a three-pack tube of bikini underpants. After that, Garrett believed his future mother-in-law had the hots for him.

"Jean Oliver was a pistol," remembered Linda Farley.

Garrett proposed in the fall of 1980 with his usual lavish style. He asked his near–child-bride-to-be to marry him during a lavish dinner at Hugo's, an expensive restaurant inside the Hyatt Hotel at the foot of Capitol Hill. His style was dated, right out of a dime-store romance novel. It would have made the genre's current cover boy, Fabio, proud.

"I had the waiter bring a dozen red roses with a single white one in the middle to the table. Then I dropped an engagement ring into her glass of champagne," he remembered. Garrett said the waiter didn't card the sixteen-year-old, instead turning his head and looking the other way.

On October 12, Garrett and Deborah Oliver walked down the aisle of the Fort Washington Baptist Church with seventy-five people present. The place of worship was three miles from Garrett's house. Debbie was a grown-up-looking teen. She was pretty, bosomy, a five-foot-four blonde who knew how to turn heads and who could also throw a baseball better than most boys her age. She had given up her chance at high school for an adult who was eight years older and who had just missed a Federal prison term by inches only months before.

Were the Olivers aware of his criminal record? Records show that Kyle Oliver himself volunteered to be a character witness for Garrett before Judge Harold Greene at his probation sentencing. The Olivers also knew of the eight-year age difference between their daughter and her new husband.

Debbie Oliver was five months pregnant at the ceremony. Her condition was discreetly overlooked by those present. The newlyweds celebrated with a Saturday night honeymoon at the Key Bridge Marriott, in a room overlooking the Potomac River.

Garrett appeared to be in great spirits on the day of his second marriage. There was good reason. A few days before, on October seventh, he had gotten an extension on the $5,000 fine he had been ordered to pay by Judge Greene. He had managed to pay the U.S. District Court $2,800 of the penalty—of which $1,000 was a loan from his uncle, Donald Ward. Stealing nearly $42,000 from the safe on Capitol Hill had only cost him cash and an indelible criminal record. It was money he didn't have. His probation officer, P. J. Watkins, wrote to the court: "His plan now is to sell the home and as soon as the proceeds are available, pay off the balance of the fine."

The probation officer also praised Garrett's "regular contact and lawful conduct," in her plea for more time. She appeared to believe that Garrett's previous bad behavior had been an aberration.

"In view of Mr. Garrett's otherwise compliant behavior and good attitude at this point, we would respectfully recommend that the Court grant him an additional ninety days to make payment in full," she wrote.

Garrett was given the extra time to make amends. He was married again, had a job, with many years left to make something of his life. He made a fresh start by spending less time in his basement domain and began sleeping in his deceased parents' master bedroom, a new wife beside him and a baby on the way.

THREE

BABY BRANDI IS DEAD

Anxious to pay off the rest of his fine to avoid imprisonment, Garrett made a hurried deal to sell the family home on Caltor Lane where he had lived for almost fourteen years. A local real estate agent, Leo B. Iserman, agreed to buy the house for $55,000 in cash.

The contract Iserman drew up on November 7, 1980, put $15,000 in Garrett's pocket after the first and second mortgages were paid off. The realtor was frank in telling his financially strapped seller he intended to resell the property for $79,000, its appraised worth. But that would have to wait six months. As part of the deal, Garrett and Debbie were allowed to rent the house back at $600 a month, providing Garrett repainted the house's white brick exterior. The property, Iserman said, would be shown to prospective buyers beginning in April. They would have to be out by June.

"We thought we'd pay off the debts and get an apartment. We didn't need a big house," Garrett recalled.

A teenage Debbie Wilson wasn't always the ideal mother-to-be. She often drank during the nine months of her pregnancy and got roaring drunk at a party just a month before the baby was born.

On February 26, 1981, Debbie gave birth to a seven-pound, two-ounce girl at Fairfax Hospital, on the Virginia side of the Potomac River. Garrett was allowed into the delivery room for the forceps procedure. Except for a high bilirubin count, a condition caused by too much iron in the blood resulting from an immature liver, the infant appeared completely healthy. They named her Brandi Jean. Garrett said Brandi got the trendy name not from the hit song of the day, but because each liked the way it sounded. Jean was for Debbie's mother. Garrett, who had purchased cigars weeks before the birth in both pink and blue because he didn't know the baby's sex, passed the pink ones out to strangers in the hospital lobby.

"She was a beautiful baby," John Farley's sister, Linda, recalled. "Lots of dark hair and violet eyes. I remember visiting them and Garrett showing me the baby pictures. He seemed so proud. He was thrilled to be a father."

Linda remembered Garrett purchasing an album for the photos. On the first page, he smeared a small amount of Brandi's first bowel movement. He claimed saving infant excrement was a Wilson family tradition.

Some eighteen years later, Debbie would remember Garrett's involvement with his daughter differently. She said her husband didn't have a relationship or any involvement with his daughter and that he seemed to be detached from her emotionally.

A month after Brandi's birth, Garrett bought two different insurance policies on his daughter's life. The first, from Lafayette Life, was worth $30,000 if Brandi were to die. The second was from a weight-lifting buddy, Eddie Aragona. It was the first policy Aragona had ever sold. Eddie worked for American National Life, and Garrett purchased a $10,000 Universal Life plan. Garrett never told Debbie about his purchase of the insurance.

Years later, George Smith, the salesman at Lafayette Life, recalled he thought the insurance purchases were a bit high for someone of Garrett's income. Garrett was then just a salesman at Jordan Kitt's making about $10,000 a year.

"I mean, thirty thousand dollars. I was surprised," he

said. On the other hand, Garrett claimed Eldred had always purchased a lot of insurance for the family. His father had believed in it and he had been conditioned to buying lots of insurance by both of his parents, partly due to his mom having had three babies die before his birth. Shortly after buying the policies on his daughter, he also bought $25,000 worth of joint life insurance for himself and Debbie.

Eddie Aragona, for whom he sometimes spotted free-weights at a gym, and a person he occasionally hung out with, was someone he was just trying to help get started in the insurance business, Garrett said.

Toward the end of April, Debbie came down with the flu. Her mother helped with the baby while Garrett worked. On the last day of the month Garrett gave his wife some pills he said were vitamin C capsules. After taking them she fell into a deep sleep.

Sometime during the night, Brandi stopped breathing. Garrett said he discovered his daughter at six in the morning, her face visibly discolored and distorted. Debbie was still asleep. He repeated the action he took when his mother died by not calling the police. Instead, Garrett telephoned his mother-in-law, Jean, with the news.

"Baby Brandi is dead," Garrett told her. Jean said later she thought his voice sounded unusually calm.

"Have you called 911?" she asked.

"No, I haven't."

"Then for God's sake, call them," she shouted.

The Olivers, a squad car from the Prince George's police department, and the Allentown Road volunteer fire department unit all raced to the scene. Brandi was immediately pronounced dead by a paramedic. Debbie, in a comatose state, slept through the commotion until she was shaken awake by her mother. When she learned of her child's death, she became hysterical and had to be restrained by the police. Only Mark Cashman, a volunteer fireman, thought there was something suspicious about Brandi's death.

"There's more here than meets the eye," he told a policeman after viewing Brandi's mottled face. The cop thought otherwise. He did not question Garrett or Debbie on the events preceding Brandi's death.

There are two distinctly different memories of the tragedy that unfolded. The Oliver family remembers Garrett as being unemotional, cold, and aloof from the grieving process. But Joseph Edmunds, pastor of the Friendly Baptist Church and the father of Jane Edmunds, his high school sweetheart, had a different recollection.

"I went over to the house. Garrett was in the basement and we prayed together. He was tearful and appeared to be in a state of total shock."

John Farley, who also came to the house that day, echoed Edmunds. "Garrett was crying and catatonic," he recalled.

The Oliver family remembered Garrett staying in the basement most of the time Debbie was grieving, blithely playing eight-ball on his pool table. Garrett said he had sold the pool table a year before to make room for more weight equipment, a statement echoed by John Farley. After the firemen and paramedics left, the Olivers recalled their son-in-law going flying with his pal, Bobby Henley. Garrett denied that it ever happened. But if he appeared callous to some observers that day, Linda Farley wasn't surprised.

"I expect he might have reacted that way. Garrett had lost so many people in his life, he expected everyone close to him to die," she said.

Before their baby was allowed to be delivered to the funeral home, her body was autopsied by two pathologists from Maryland's Medical Examiner's office, Matthias Okoye and Ann Dixon, as well as a neuropathologist, John Martin, who focused on the infant's brain. They found no irregularities.

"The body is that of a thirteen-and-a-half-pound, two-month old female child measuring twenty-two inches from crown to heel," the autopsy began.

The clothing on the body consists of a white tee-shirt, a soiled white diaper, a baby jumpsuit with yellow floral design, pink bedspread and a yellow-white bedspread. Rigor mortis is moderate in the cold body and livor mortis [a pooling of blood after death] is dorsal except over pressure points. The scalp is covered with fluffy brown hair. The jaws are edentulous [toothless]. The external auditory canals and oral cavity are free of abnormal secretions or discharges. The external genitalia are those of a female child. The posterior torso and anus are unremarkable. There is no evidence of penetrating or blunt force injury. There is no evidence of recent medical intervention.

After the external examination of Brandi's body, the pathologists dissected the torso with scalpels, examining the cardiovascular system, the trachea, and the respiratory system. The neuropathologist removed and examined the brain.

"There is no evidence of soft tissue injury," the report read, under the neck subcategory. "The lumen of the larynx and trachea are free of foreign material and abnormal secretions."

The report showed that the lungs were expanded and had "acute congestion and edema [swelling]." There was also "acute congestion and mild cloudy swelling in the liver" and "acute congestion" in the spleen. Within the respiratory system, the medical team discovered that the parenchyma [lung support system] was "moderately congested and edematous [swollen]" but without lesions. There was also a "fine petechiae [a pattern of small black and blue blood spots]" on the lungs.

The tongue, kidneys, musculoskeletal system, bladder, and pancreas were all normal. Dr. Martin, the neuropathologist, found no abnormalities in the brain, but did note it was immature.

Summarized the two pathologists in their report: "The death of this two-month-old white female, Brandi J. Wilson, is attributed to Sudden Infant Death Syndrome (crib death). The manner of death is natural."

Garrett said he knew a little about SIDS.

"I had heard about it from relatives. They believed there was a possibility some of my mother's babies died from it."

Brandi's body was sewn back together and returned to the funeral home. Her service took place the next day. She lay in a tiny white coffin, opened so everyone could see her. Garrett read a long poem that he said was a favorite of his mother's. Debbie wept throughout the service. Their daughter was buried next to Eldred and Ethel at Cedar Hill Cemetery. Neither parent ever paid the last one hundred dollars of the funeral bill. The grave would stay unmarked for more than a dozen years.

On the same day Brandi died, Garrett telephoned George Smith of Lafayette Insurance to announce her death. It was mere hours after she was pronounced dead, but he wanted to know when he could collect.

The insurance agent thought the call was, at the very least, poorly timed. Garrett told the salesman he didn't know what else to do or who else to call. He would later admit not telling his wife about the insurance. His reasoning was that because his wife was only sixteen, he wasn't sure if she understood the concept of insurance or would have approved of the purchase. Garrett repeated again and again that buying insurance was a concept his father had drilled into him when he was in his teens.

Five weeks after Brandi died, and with a $40,000 windfall about to land in his lap, Garrett got permission from a probation officer, Jud Watkins, to take an extended vacation in Florida. The probation officer referred to Brandi's death in his court report as a miscarriage, and it is not clear if he knew what had actually happened. A judge granted the request so that "Mr. and Mrs. Wilson can vacation in Florida and recover from the trauma of losing their baby."

"I quit my job at Jordan Kitt's. I had been working sixty-hour weeks, and it had been getting to me," Garrett remembered. He said he had been assigned to stay in the store until its nine-thirty closing and then had to add up the receipts and make the night bank deposit. He usually arrived home after eleven.

Debbie wasn't working at all, which enabled the two to go on their free-spending, whirlwind holiday in the Sun-

shine State, staying at first-class hotels like the Daytona
Hilton and visiting two Oliver family friends, Joe and Jan
Church.

"It was two and a half weeks," Garrett said. "We went up
and down both coasts—Tampa, Clearwater, Daytona Beach,
Orlando, Miami, Fort Lauderdale . . ."

His voice delighted in reliving the June 1981 trip that had
been financed by his daughter's death.

When they returned, the real estate agent, who knew
about the tragedy but hadn't as yet been able to sell the
house, let Garrett and Debbie continue to live at the Caltor
Lane residence. Garrett wrote Iserman a check for $4,230.
The amount was for overdue rent plus several months in advance. Iserman was wary of his tenant by now.

The insurance money disappeared in a hurry. Garrett
bought a new car, a black Pontiac TransAm, for $13,178.20.
He paid an overdue $358.99 hospital bill for Brandi's deliv-
ery. He wrote a check for $400 for a new vacuum cleaner
and paid more than $800 for a stereo system. By the last
days of summer, Garrett was broke again, and the two immature newlyweds were at each other's throats. The ill-fated
marriage appeared to be unraveling even before they observed their first anniversary.

Garrett came back from Florida unemployed. In mid-Au-
gust he found a position with United Bank and Trust, a small
financial institution two miles from the Caltor Lane house.
Debbie began working, too, at a local mom-and-pop construction company. Garrett failed to tell his new employer
that he had been convicted of embezzlement at the U.S.
House of Representatives finance office just a year before.
Dismissal, of course, would have been immediate. Instead,
he told his probation officer about the job, which alarmed
the court-appointed official.

Garrett's watcher waffled. He neither forbade Garrett's
employment at the bank, nor did he notify the financial institution's executives about his client's past. As Garrett's probation supervisor would later report to the U.S. District
Court, an error certainly had been made.

On Tuesday, August 26, 1981, the probation officer wrote to Mr. Wilson fully explaining the disclosure requirement, the probationer's obligation to make the previous embezzlement offense known to his employer, or seek work elsewhere. This same correspondence, a part of our official record, explained to Mr. Wilson the probation officer's willingness to meet with bank officials and make representations if necessary pertaining to Mr. Wilson's exemplary conduct while on probation.

On September 2, 1981, the probation officer met with Mr. Wilson for an appointment at the probationer's request. Mr. Wilson pleaded first, that any disclosure of his record would mean an instant termination and permanent loss of livelihood. Second, Mr. Wilson stated emphatically that his present job description posed no risk in that he handled no funds, performed only low-level clerical duties, and even repaired small business machines at the bank. The probation officer granted Mr. Wilson an extension, with the condition that the probationer provide documentation regarding the nature of his present employment and show that his duties could not permit a reoccurrence of previous offense behavior.

On November 18, 1981, the probation officer reminded Mr. Wilson by correspondence (copy in file) of the need to provide documentation, or the probation officer would intervene and make notification to bank officials. The same letter restated the disclosure requirement fully, and set a November 30, 1981, deadline for resolving the matter by providing conclusive documentation of no risk, or proceeding promptly to notify bank officials of the instant offense.

On December 1, 1981, the probation officer received a letter from Mr. Wilson and a written job description outlining duties such as stockroom inventory control, records maintenance, small business machine repair, and preparation of certain reports. The written information in this job description matched identically the verbal description Mr. Wilson had presented earlier, and the title "Accounting Clerk" matched the job title on Mr. Wilson's written monthly reports for the period September, October, November, and December 1981. Mr. Wilson's letter accompanying this material expressed once more the probationer's plea to continue his job without disclosure, saying that he had found immense satisfaction in succeeding at his work and "...as is your [the probation officer's] concern, doing it honestly and earning it."

The case worker decided to overlook the matter and let his charge continue on. Neither did the officer think it necessary to inform Garrett's supervisors of his criminal record.

Garrett Wilson was a well-liked figure at the little bank and its five branches. He endeared himself to the staff by volunteering to play Santa Claus at the firm's 1981 Christmas party. He also began an intimate relationship with one of the bank's female employees. The marriage to Debbie Oliver was already disintegrating.

Garrett began the adulterous affair at United Bank and Trust with a young woman who had the same first name as his wife. The new Debbie in his life was a Debra who worked in the bank's customer service department. She was his age. His wife continued to live in the Caltor Lane house, but for all intents and purposes, they were separated. Debbie, Garrett claimed, had met a man by the name of Steve Fennell at the construction company where she worked. The husky, handsome Fennell would eventually marry her and become Debbie's second husband. But first, there was a dramatic altercation on a fall evening in 1981, which Garrett remembers vividly.

"I was in the house with Debra, and Debbie came home. She tried to get at Debra, but I came between them. Debbie ran out of the house, and I followed her in my car because I was worried about her mental state. She drove to her parents' house, speeding all the way. I stayed right behind. The Olivers lived off Allentown Road down a long twisting street that ended in a dirt dead end. Debbie had to drive past some recreational vehicles. She was going so fast, she crashed into one of them and broke her finger."

The marriage had now unofficially ended in less than a year in a most ugly way. Fourteen months later, Deborah Lynn Oliver would file for divorce, charging Garrett with extreme cruelty. She also accused Garrett of committing adultery with the other Debra in the documents, her attorney noting he had exhibited "vicious conduct towards her, including the breaking of her finger... although the conduct of the plaintiff has been that of a faithful, kind, and chaste wife who has always been kind, affectionate, and above reproach."

In early 1982, after the fight with Debbie, his probation officer reported that Garrett was becoming difficult to reach. Four calls by the court failed to reach him. When he was contacted in mid-February, Garrett convinced the probation officer that he was about to terminate his position at the bank. He promised he would make a decision soon on a new career direction and would resign within the week. But when the time limit elapsed, Garrett became hard to find. After the probation officer located him, he discovered his client had done a complete turnabout. The news gave the court a start when it got the latest report.

By way of explanation, Mr. Wilson stated that his wife had left him after a bitter dispute, and that there was no hope for a reconciliation. Mr. Wilson followed that with a statement of his intent to stay with the bank, and seek more responsibility, applying for a branch manager's position.

Garrett's decision to move from a low-level bank employee to an attempt at managing a financial institution with all attendant responsibilities and temptations was the last straw. On March 8, the probation officer telephoned his client, at the same time sending him a registered letter. Both communications ordered him to resign within thirty days, "terminating all affiliation with the United Bank and Trust."

With a quit-or-else edict before him, Garrett went out with a bang. Literally. On March 30, 1982, in a near-duplication of the Cannon Office Building theft, he stole $10,338 from the bank at seven in the morning, after letting himself in with a key. Again he faked a robbery, claiming he was held up by two gunmen. This time, instead of saying he had been pistol-whipped, he shot himself on the side of his stomach, the bullet grazing the surface of his skin. But when he left the bank, he panicked, thinking he had been seen by a fellow employee arriving at work. He wound up tossing the stolen cash into a green metal Dumpster at the rear of a McDonald's restaurant near his home. The money, buried under a mess of greasy fast food wrappers, was never recovered.

"He called me at Temple Hills Baptist Church where I worked," Jean Oliver recalled. "He told me he had been shot at the bank. I asked him how badly he was injured, and he said it was just a flesh wound."

The police and FBI agents showed up at the Caltor Lane house. Garrett was given a polygraph test, which he failed. There was another confession. The police report to the court noted the similarities:

> The facts of this new offense parallel almost exactly those of the first offense which resulted in Mr. Wilson being placed on probation in July 1980 in this district. That is, there was a theft of bank funds, a reported robbery, an attempted cover-up, and then a full admission of guilt. In this offense, however, FBI agents have been unsuccessful in attempting to recover the stolen money. Although the indictment in this matter was handed down on April 13, 1982, it was not until April 27, 1982 that the probation officer was able to get Mr. Wilson to respond to numerous calls, letters, and directives, some of which were related in person by FBI agents. Mr. Wilson told us that he removed the money, not for personal gain, but to attract the attention of his estranged wife, or to somehow elicit her sympathy by way of this self destructive act. Mr. Wilson also revealed at this interview that his job description at the bank had allowed him access to bank funds throughout his period of employment, and that he had misrepresented the nature of his responsibilities to his probation officer.

The court recommended a hearing on the violation. The dry, understated report failed to mention this fact: Garrett was now certain to be confined to a federal prison. Considering the severity of the two offenses, the sentence of the court could be viewed as a light rebuke.

The sentence committed Garrett to a federal prison for a period of not less than six months or no more than eighteen months. It ordered him to report to the prison on July 9, 1982.

A Baltimore judge duplicated the sentence for the United Bank and Trust offense. The court then made the two terms consecutive.

Judge Harold Greene strongly suggested that Garrett be committed to an institution where he could receive psychiatric treatment. The federal facility the jurist had in mind was in Lexington, Kentucky.

FOUR

HARD-BODIED LADIES' MAN

The day before he was to report to prison, Garrett telephoned his last remaining friend, John Farley. Both John and Garrett were now twenty-six, but life had taken them in different directions. John had graduated from the University of Maryland, was working as a certified public accountant, and if one excluded his raffish mustache, looked much like the stereotype one would expect to see in the occupation. John was, if anything, loyal. He thought his pal's mood was upbeat, almost nonchalant, considering the predicament he was facing, which was several years behind bars.

"Hey, John, what are you doing tomorrow?" he asked over the phone. His voice sounded as if he were about to suggest going to a ball game.

"I don't know. What did you have in mind?"

"I made a deal with the government to turn myself in at the prison. Would you help me drive there?"

Garrett told John he estimated it would take twelve hours to drive from the Washington, D.C., area to Lexington, Kentucky. Would five-thirty in the morning be too soon?

"I'll be ready," John promised.

The next morning Garrett put the keys to the Caltor Lane house in the Oliver family's mailbox. With them was a message to Debbie. It said she could have anything in the house and asked her to give the rest away. The Oliver family wasn't impressed with this show of generosity. Everything of value was already gone, the Olivers would say, when they arrived later in the day. They also claimed they had to clean the house or face the ire of the owner, Leo Iserman.

. Garrett showed up at John's in a spanking new American car. He said he had rented it through a dealer. Uh-oh, John remembered thinking, this car could be stolen. He asked Garrett to see the rental contract. His friend reached in the glove compartment and produced the ownership papers, which showed it belonged to a local dealership. He again said he had leased it. His friend let the matter slide.

"He didn't show any concern during the trip," John recalled. "And he was going away for years."

Was Garrett a brave man or a sociopath? One could only wonder. On the way, he answered John's question about how he had reached this low point in his life.

"He said, 'I tried something stupid and I shouldn't have done it,' " is John's recollection.

On Interstate 64, near the Kentucky–West Virginia border, the two pals stopped for a last meal together at a cafeteria-style Ponderosa steakhouse. Garrett ate a particularly big dinner, believing it would be his last real feast for a long time.

As the sun began to set, John drove Garrett through the Leestown Pike gates of the U.S. Federal Correctional Facility that borders the outskirts of Lexington. Garrett then issued John some final words of instruction.

"When you return the car," he told him, "put it back on the lot either before it opens or after it's closed."

Uh-oh, John thought a second time.

It would be nearly two years before he saw his friend again.

In 1982, the minimum security correctional institute in Lexington more than lived up to its reputation as a country club prison. It had some 1,500 prisoners and was co-ed. Men and women were allowed to wander freely at times, even holding hands if they liked. Kissing or committing more intimate acts though, resulted in a month of solitary confinement. The penalty rarely stopped anyone from doing that and more.

"They had a swimming pool when I arrived," Garrett remembered. "But they paved over the pool and put in tennis courts instead. Too many of the women were getting pregnant in it."

The Lexington facility has had its share of important prisoners. Female disciples of the mass-murdering gang leader, Charlie Manson, have resided here. More recently, the colorful Whitewater figure, James McDougal, entered its gates. He would die two months later from heart disease.

The new arrival met his first celebrity within days. The big shot was former Congressman Frank Thompson of New Jersey. The politician had been one of four members of the U.S. House of Representatives convicted of soliciting bribes in an early 1980s FBI sting called ABSCAM. The AB in ABSCAM was for Abdul. The U.S. government had its agents impersonate rich Arab oil sheiks who pretended they were willing to pay off elected officials for legislative favors. When Thompson was caught in the government dragnet, he tried to win in court on an entrapment technicality, but lost.

"He knew my father," Garrett remembered. "But we didn't hang out together. He had a cushy wing all to himself."

Garrett's prison days seem to have been almost enjoyable. Besides tennis, there was a plethora of recreational opportunities at Lexington, including a golf course. Inside, there was a big screen movie theater suitable for necking in the dark. Still, it was a sort of prison, so one might expect Garrett to try to talk his way outside the grounds as soon as possible. And he did.

He accomplished this feat by using his natural talents as a pianist and organist. This quickly earned him a prominent place within the prison's Christian ministry program. Garrett's "good Christian" attitude led to a tour on the road with former Watergate felon Charles Colson's Prison Fellowship Ministry. Colson's organization took the former Caltor Manor Casanova and a group of other prisoners to Memphis, Tennessee, where they spent their days repairing old houses for the poor or aged. The nights however, were a different matter.

"I got calls from women after they left the prison, looking for Garrett," John Farley recalled. "They had met him on the inside."

After twenty months of this gentle incarceration, he was paroled and allowed to leave Lexington. During his time there, Garrett never once had a visitor. He returned to Washington in March of 1984, assigned to a halfway house in the Anacostia section of the federal city. The residence was less than a mile from where he had once lived as a small child.

In the years that followed, he would sometimes try to laugh off his time inside. Whenever asked, he called the prison term "a sabbatical."

Before heading off to Kentucky, Garrett had stored his good furniture at Carl and Iris Farley's house. Iris cried a second time when she heard Ethel's only child would have to serve a prison sentence. She considered Garrett to be another son and felt a responsibility to her deceased friend. When Iris wanted to visit Garrett at the halfway house in Anacostia, Carl told her that it was in a rough part of town. He wouldn't allow her to go there alone and instead, reluctantly drove her and his daughter, Linda, to the building.

"Iris was one of those people who always wanted to give everyone a second and a third chance," Carl recalled. "But I was still surprised at Garrett's attitude when we visited him. He blamed his probation officer for letting him work at the bank. He was upset because there had been embezzlers in prison like him who had actually stolen millions instead of a few thousand dollars. They'd been sentenced to less time, and that seemed to bother him. When we left the halfway house, I said to Iris, 'He just blames the system. He has absolutely no remorse.'"

Linda was more charitable. She felt Garrett was pleased that at least a few friends had not forsaken him.

Iris Farley died within weeks after her visit to the halfway house. The funeral service was held on the Virginia side of the Potomac River at the First Christian Church in Alexandria. Garrett showed up late. He stood quietly in the back of the balcony and left immediately after the ceremony without talking to anyone. The Farleys did not think that unusual. He had seen so much death in his short life he had become numb to it, was their belief.

Garrett was a natural salesman. In the spring of 1984, he was able to find a situation that suited those talents. Crystal City, a northern Virginia community of high-rise apartments and offices next to one of Washington's airports, was loaded with professional young men and women who were both on the rise and on the make. When a sales job peddling memberships for Fun and Fitness—a health club chain with a spa adjoining a small ice skating rink on the ground floor of an office building—opened, he grabbed the opportunity.

"He instinctively knew how to sign them up," said Dennis Awe, who became a friend in the 1980s. "His standard technique was to put a five-pound barbell into each hand of a chunky rich guy at the beginning of the spa tour and ask him to hold them. After walking around the club he'd steer him into his office. By then the prospect was usually huffing and puffing from carrying the weights and Garrett would say, 'That's only ten pounds. You weigh thirty pounds more than you should. You're carrying that extra weight right on your body. This is what your heart has to deal with every day.' They'd usually sign up after that pitch."

Garrett discovered that a smooth, well-muscled talker could also meet a virtually unlimited number of women at a health club. Some 70 percent of the club's business came from slightly neurotic, chubby women. They generally suffered from low self-esteem, a result of the doubts they had about the desirability of their bodies.

The newly minted health club salesman stopped taking the bus from the halfway house and began living in the home of a woman, Ronnie Malamud, near his workplace. He began borrowing money from her and by the end of 1984, owed the woman thousands of dollars. When he didn't pay, she sued, got a judgment, and began garnishing his paycheck. Ronnie was justly vindictive. She pursued him from job to job for several years until every dollar was repaid.

There was another problem, too, indicating he was still pushing his luck. Garrett wrote a bad check for a Toyota Supra and was arrested. The incident wasn't prosecuted when he returned the car.

A more important female than Ronnie Malamud came into Garrett's life in April of 1984, just after he began selling the memberships at Fun and Fitness. Her name was Elizabeth Gardner Dodge. Garrett met Liz when she came into the club in an attempt to lose a little weight. It was her father, Bill, a U.S. Central Intelligence Agency employee, who brought his twenty-one-year-old daughter to the health club and introduced her to Garrett. They had worked out together and he thought the spa salesman might be a catch. Signing Bill Dodge's daughter up for a membership became one of the easiest contracts Garrett would ever close. Strongly attracted to each other, the two began dating.

At first, it was the usual pattern. There would be dinner followed by a movie—the only twist on their dating dance was the joint gym workouts before going out on the town. The relationship soon deepened, and they became intimate.

Liz Dodge was full-figured and lovely. Some seven years younger than Garrett, she had a habit of brushing back her honey blond hair away from her face. Her age may have made her more than a little gullible, because she came to be serious about her muscular older lover. After Garrett started to talk of marriage, the couple began living together at her apartment in Alexandria.

"He would buy me a lot of gifts. Jewelry, flowers, clothing," she remembered. "But he didn't always have the money to pay for them, so he would charge the presents on my credit card."

Garrett spent some $3,500 of Liz Dodge's money this way. He promised to pay her back when his ship came in.

They began to have "an understanding." The agreement was that they would marry each other within the year.

By 1985, Garrett's adventures with the opposite sex began to get a bit complicated. The six Fun and Fitness locations had never done as well as their then-rival, the undisputed king of Washington-area health clubs, Holiday Health Spas. Holiday was a national chain with hundreds of clubs. It spent a fortune on television advertising compared with Fun and Fitness's puny ad budget. So when Garrett was offered a chance to train to be a manager there, earning more money and the opportunity to eventually run things his way, he accepted the competitor's offer.

The Holiday Spa they wanted him to manage was back across the Potomac in Maryland, on Rockville Pike in Montgomery County, reputed to be the least pretty, but most profitable, commercial strip in the Washington area. The Pike, as it was known, was an unfastened six-mile clunky charm bracelet hung with gas stations, strip centers, fast food emporiums, and car dealers. Holiday Spa, in the middle of this miniature America, was thirty miles of heavy traffic from Liz Dodge's apartment in Alexandria.

And Montgomery County? It was everything Prince George's County wasn't, with 800,000 people, arguably the richest county in America. Montgomery was flush with castlelike mansions that housed sports celebrities—Sugar Ray Leonard was one—and fading television stars like Lynda "Wonder Woman" Carter. Garrett felt he was moving up again and that his troubled past was behind him.

In December of 1984, Liz gave up her apartment in Alexandria and moved back in with her mother, some ten miles away. Garrett's new job had him working long days, and the couple began to share an apartment in Maryland near the Holiday Spa. The pair's plans included saving for the large, formal marriage she favored. Though they might have seen each other less frequently, there was the promise of a wedding day that both of them would remember forever.

Except Garrett met another woman in January of 1985, soon after moving from Liz Dodge's apartment. Her name was Mary Anastasi, but she told everyone she met to call her Missy.

There are two versions of their first meeting. The first is Missy's:

> A teacher I knew wanted me to join Holiday with her. Garrett began to show me around, but I said, "Don't bother, I'm going to join anyway." He told me right away he was divorced and had lost a baby to what he called crib death. He said his daughter's name, but I misunderstood him. I thought he called her Randi. My name was McCune when we met, but I told him I was about to be divorced and was changing my name back to Anastasi.

Garrett's version is more graphic. He believed that Missy, a pale, sad-faced blonde, three years older than he and very overweight at the time, seemed to know exactly what she was doing. His impression was that here was a no-nonsense woman who was very much in control of herself. Her personality intrigued him. She had been taught by nuns in a series of strict Catholic schools, but despite the religious upbringing had developed a salty tongue.

"She said, 'Let's cut the crap. I just got a divorce and I'm going to St. Thomas. I need to lose fifteen pounds, so sign me up.'"

Garrett believed his potential member was behaving a little bitchy and he let her know it. "It sounds like you need to go down there and get laid," he said.

The relationship didn't blossom immediately. Liz Dodge may have been dreaming of a formal white wedding, but Missy wasn't earning an A for attendance at the Rockville Holiday Spa. Thus, a dual romance developed, with Garrett dividing his time between Liz and Missy. Each believed he was devoted to her alone.

"I didn't go to Holiday right away," Missy recalled. "But

he called me and said he'd lose his commission if I didn't attend. So I went. He was a good conversationalist, and we'd usually meet and talk near the Coke machine. We started to do things. We'd go out for rides, to dinner, to the beach. I showed him my favorite spot, the National Seashore near Bethany Beach in Delaware. It's always quiet and deserted. And he escorted me to a friend's wedding in Ocean City, Maryland."

Missy thought Garrett had a muscular body. He was good looking, but if anything, maybe he was too big, she thought. Unlike her own controlled, step-by-step approach to life, she liked her new beau's seemingly impetuous style, his way of wanting to do things on the spur of the moment.

According to all three in this developing love triangle, there was an incident at the Maryland–Delaware beaches on the final August weekend of 1985 when the simultaneous but separate wooings of Liz Dodge and Missy Anastasi were discovered, with dire results. What follows is Garrett's version.

I was at the beach with Liz. We were sitting on the sand near Missy's secret spot. Missy had followed me in her car to the beach. She was walking along the waterline barefoot towards us, carrying her sandals. I think she was stalking me. She came right up to Liz and me and then she hit me with the shoes. Liz and I left in a hurry, but she followed us. I remember driving down the ocean highway and Missy pulling alongside of us and shouting. She continued to cry and yell and Liz said, "She's crazy," but Missy read her lips because she has a degree in special education as an oral interpreter for the deaf. And what Liz said just made her madder.

Liz went back to the hotel room while Garrett stopped the car and attempted to tell Missy she had no hold on him. Garrett left the beach without being intimate with either woman that weekend.

Missy would refer to the incident as "having a falling out." Garrett managed to somehow explain the altercation away to a believing Liz Dodge, who agreed to go away on a vacation with him. Liz had just won a trip to the Caribbean, and so off they went, the pair enjoying a weeklong romantic tropical island holiday in October 1985.

"We went to Jamaica," Liz remembered. "It was apparently some sort of time-share scam, and we wound up buying one. Of course, it was me who ended up making the payments. The gentleman showing us the apartment tried to talk us into tying the knot. He said, 'We have a wonderful colored marriage certificate, so why don't you just go ahead and get married?' We thought about it and chickened out."

"We flew to Montego Bay," Garrett added. "Then we were driven to Ocho Rios in a van. I remember waking up the first day, and there were all these naked German tourists on the beach. It was wild!"

When they came back, Garrett switched jobs. Again, he began selling pianos and organs for Jordan Kitt's, this time at a new store inside the Lake Forest Mall, which was also in Montgomery County, ten miles west of the Holiday Spa. On November 12, Missy came into the store and walked up to him as if the traumatic incident at the beach had never happened.

"It's my birthday tomorrow. Why don't you take me out for a drink?" she said. The next night, after Missy had several Manhattan cocktails, he drove her home and kissed her good night.

"She was pursuing me," he claimed.

Pursuit or no pursuit, Garrett proposed marriage to Missy Anastasi during the Thanksgiving weekend of 1985 while they were parked in front of the high school where she had graduated.

"Well, I guess we should get married," is Garrett's memory of how he asked the question. He said it was a response to a teasing taunt Missy had just made to him.

A few weeks later, during the Christmas holidays, he put the same question to Elizabeth Dodge at her mother's house. That promise was sealed with an engagement ring. The wedding was scheduled to take place in her mother's Blue Ridge mountain hometown of Bedford, Virginia, on June 7, 1986.

Amanda and Michaelangelo Anastasi, Missy's mom and dad, seemed to take to Garrett as much as Liz Dodge's parents had. So did her brother Frank, his wife, Susan, and her sister, Melissa. That was important to Missy. Garrett thought Missy's balding father was a little like Eldred.

"I got along with Mike the best. He worked for the Montgomery County school system, purchasing supplies. Sometimes he would work part-time at Sears. He drank and smoked a lot like my dad, except he was a vodka and gin man. I liked to hang out with him," Garrett said.

He introduced Missy to his old friends. Linda Farley recalled his first description of his new fiancée.

"You're not going to like her, but you need to give her a chance," he told Linda. She agreed with Garrett's prediction, remembering a "bleached blonde with big hair and lots of makeup."

Missy set a wedding date which, unbeknownst to her, beat Liz Dodge to the altar. Missy and Garrett walked down the aisle at Christ Episcopal Church in Rockville on March 1, 1986, and then flew to the Bahamas for a honeymoon. Friends and family of both were in attendance. Garrett's best man was his uncle, Donald Ward, who hadn't yet been paid the thousand dollars his nephew had borrowed from him in 1980 to avoid imprisonment.

"On Valentine's Day, he showed up at eleven o'clock at night and gave me an engagement ring," Missy remembered. "We began looking at rental properties, but didn't like what we saw, so on February twenty-eighth, we signed the purchase papers on a town house in Germantown—that's in Montgomery County—the day before we got married."

The couple paid $15,000 down. The money came right out of Missy's checking account. (When Garrett had given Missy her ring, he used the same romantic trick he had pulled on the night he proposed to Debbie Oliver. She went into the bathroom and he dropped a one-carat, pear-shaped stone into her glass of champagne.)

Did Missy know about Garrett's time in prison? One of Missy's friends said she did.

"He told her about what had happened and how he got in trouble. But he didn't tell her everything. His version was that he had been working for a [bank,] and said a manager had okayed a scheme where he would take some money and quickly put it back. But, he said, after he did it, the manager wouldn't back him up, so he got arrested. Missy said, 'You would never do that again, would you?' And Garrett's answer was, 'I'll never go to jail again.'

"He also talked a little about Debbie and Brandi. He conned Missy by saying Debbie couldn't get over the baby dying, so he took her to Florida with some insurance money from Brandi's death. He blamed Debbie for getting him into debt. She wrecked his cars, cheated on him, and indulged in all sorts of sexual shenanigans, Garrett told her."

Both began to talk about children. Garrett said he wanted a family. Missy, who had just turned thirty-two and had never been a mother, said she felt her biological clock ticking. The closest thing she had to children were her two part-Siamese cats, Floyd and Felix. The felines were aging twelve-year-olds, not long for this world. Missy became an expectant mother five months after her wedding day. Garrett seemed thrilled.

"The doctor confirmed the pregnancy in July. I was very excited. Garrett made me breakfast in bed when I got morning sickness. He would shop for the groceries and cook for me," Missy said.

After learning she was pregnant, Missy had an amniocentesis procedure performed. There had been a Down syndrome child in each family, and she was concerned. Besides getting a clean bill of health, the fluid drawn from her abdomen revealed they were going to have a boy. The name was decided upon early, Garrett Michael. The middle name was in honor of Missy's father. Garrett celebrated by purchasing an eighteen-karat gold ring for Missy. But what about Liz Dodge? The pesky problem of Garrett's betrothal had been cleared up in May.

Elizabeth Dodge had been preparing for her marriage following all the classic rules of etiquette. Just after Garrett had married Missy, Liz's mother mailed out engraved wedding invitations. The formal card read:

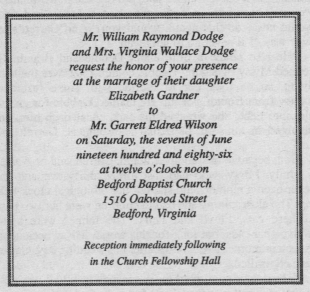

Mr. William Raymond Dodge
and Mrs. Virginia Wallace Dodge
request the honor of your presence
at the marriage of their daughter
Elizabeth Gardner
to
Mr. Garrett Eldred Wilson
on Saturday, the seventh of June
nineteen hundred and eighty-six
at twelve o'clock noon
Bedford Baptist Church
1516 Oakwood Street
Bedford, Virginia

Reception immediately following
in the Church Fellowship Hall

Even after marrying Missy, Garrett found time to visit Bedford a couple of times with Liz Dodge to map out details of the wedding. On his way there, he mentioned that his Uncle Willard lived nearby, in Lynchburg. The two became so busy in Bedford, they never found time to visit his relative.

On the morning of May 6, a month before the scheduled ceremony with Elizabeth Dodge, and just nine weeks after marrying Missy Anastasi, Garrett entered a Fairfax County, Virginia, courthouse with Liz. They took out a marriage license together. The engaged couple immediately celebrated the occasion with daytime sex.

"We returned to my mother's house and made love. Garrett left, saying he had to return to work. He left his wallet behind, and I opened it up. I began to feel a little funny. There were lots of credit cards inside with the name Mary Anastasi Wilson on them. My fingers were trembling, but I thought at first it might be a cousin," Liz recalled.

She tried to telephone Missy at home several times. Each call was met with silence and then the connection was cut off. She then called Jordan Kitt's. Liz talked to a male coworker who she thought was supposed to be an usher at their wedding. Instead, he told her Garrett had been married for several months to Missy.

His fiancée got a sick feeling in the pit of her stomach. She called him and arranged a meeting. Garrett was sheepish about the betrayal.

"We went for a drive. I basically asked why. He said he didn't know how to break it off," Liz said.

"I asked him if he was going to stand me up at the altar. I had already begun receiving gifts. He told me he had been trying to think of a proper way to tell me."

"I thought it was going to work itself out," Garrett said. "Missy was talking as if she was going back to her last husband, Dennis McCune. When that didn't happen, I didn't know how to get out of it."

Bill and Virginia Dodge mailed out a second announcement to the same people they had invited to the wedding just a few weeks before. They also took out an ad in a newspaper. The card and the ad read:

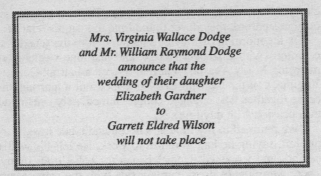

*Mrs. Virginia Wallace Dodge
and Mr. William Raymond Dodge
announce that the
wedding of their daughter
Elizabeth Gardner
to
Garrett Eldred Wilson
will not take place*

There was one unfinished piece of business—the $3,500 worth of charges Garrett had made on her credit cards. Liz wanted to be repaid. Her mother had taken the engagement ring to a jewelry store and tried to sell it to recoup the loss. The jeweler said the stone was worthless and made of cut glass, and not even cubic zirconia. (Note: The ring Garrett gave to Missy *was* cubic zirconia, purchased from a Madam Wellington, a Washington jeweler who in the 1980s advertised herself as "the queen of fakes.")

"I would like to get that money back from you," she told him.

"No problem," Garrett answered. He promised to pay her back at the rate of between one hundred and two hundred dollars a month.

Missy's pregnancy became difficult. She developed gestational diabetes, a form of the disease that usually leaves after a baby is born, as long as one stays away from sugar. Her blood pressure began rising to such levels that in late February of 1987, two weeks before the baby was due, she was hospitalized by her doctors as a precaution. Garrett, she thought, behaved perfectly through the difficult time.

"He made me feel cherished," she recalled.

Missy liked to cuddle with Garrett during those winter nights. Her only criticism was that he insisted on sleeping in ragged T-shirts and boxer shorts. She always wore elegant nightgowns. Her husband refused to wear pajamas.

On March 12, Missy went into labor. Garrett was scheduled to assist in the delivery room, but at the last minute their baby was found to be turned. It was a breech birth. A cesarean procedure was performed, and her husband was chased away from the operating arena. Because of her many difficulties, Missy spent the next ten days in a room at Shady Grove Adventist Hospital. When she came home, Garrett painted a corner bedroom they decided would be the nursery. He had the baby stay in the master bedroom while the paint was drying.

By now, Garrett was working as many hours as he could find in the day. There were lots of bills to pay and lots of women who wanted to be paid. Missy, a fastidious woman, also liked her house to be spotless, something he failed to accomplish. She was not happy about her homecoming from the hospital.

"The day he brought me home he said the house was clean, but it wasn't. Garrett showed up at the hospital with someone from his job and then he just dropped me off, saying he had to go back to work. He said he'd taken so much time off visiting me in the hospital, he had no choice. I had to stay home to take care of our son."

Missy always claimed it was she who became the primary caretaker for Garrett Michael. She said her husband never volunteered to change a diaper or feed the baby. He was rarely there. She said she thought his absence was because he was working long hours. Her husband's only responsibility was to buy diapers on the way home and to mix the baby formula.

"Garrett Michael would eat every two and a half hours. He was healthy and smart. He had regular checkups. It was exhausting. I never got enough rest," Missy recalled.

Garrett may also have been exhausted. He was involved with yet another woman. Her name was Julie Stinger.

FIVE

A CLASSIC SIDS CASE

Six weeks after he was born, Garrett Michael Wilson received holy baptism inside Washington's National Cathedral children's chapel. Missy chose three godparents: her sister, Melissa, her brother, Frank, and his wife, Susan. Garrett seemed pleased that the tobacco family name had been passed on to yet another generation.

"He let it be known the baby was going to be named Garrett. And I didn't have a single problem with that," Missy recalled.

An ultraorganized Missy kept a calendar of Garrett Michael's progress and highlights. She noted that on April 1, he had "kissed Daddy" for the first time, and on April 2, had eaten "Gerber rice." A week later, a memo read that he had "recognized Daddy." There was a notation for nearly every one of these miniature milestones into August when Missy wrote on the fourteenth of the month that their son had "smiled and laughed when I saw Daddy at work." Garrett wrote his observations on the calendar, too, but not nearly as often as his wife.

Like many married couples, they made baby videos. Garrett played director and held the camera while Missy positioned the baby. On one, Missy's voice can be heard cooing in disjointed phrases as she played with their baby: "I can't believe it, Garrett....Look at this....Where's Garrett Michael? Mommy's coming to get your picture....Where's the baby?...Daddy doesn't know what you do in the morning, does he?" Missy thought the video would help explain the infant's personality to his frequently absent father.

"He slept better during the day and not as well at night. I think he had his days and nights reversed," she remembered. The birth of their child had made Missy into an ecstatic mother who cared first for the welfare of their son. Garrett played the role of the hardworking but loving father.

A month after Garrett Michael was born, his father strolled over to an Allstate Insurance booth at the Sears store in the Lake Forest Mall, within walking distance from Jordan Kitt's. He purchased a $50,000 policy on the life of his son, naming himself as the policy's owner with he and his wife listed as the beneficiaries. A few weeks later, on March 27, the sales agent, Lee Smith, was asked to change the beneficiary to read Garrett E. Wilson as the primary beneficiary and Mary Anastasi Wilson as a contingent recipient. Thus, for Missy to collect, both her husband and son would have to predecease her. Garrett paid the year's premium of $207.96 in advance.

On April 16, a few days after buying the Allstate policy, Garrett went to the offices of Metropolitan Life Insurance, a couple of blocks from Jordan Kitt's. He found a twenty-six-year-old salesman, Daniel Sullivan, who had worked for MetLife for just five months. The young agent sold Garrett a $100,000 policy on his infant son. In one space on the application there was a question: "Are there any other life insurance policies in effect or now pending?" Garrett checked the "no" box. He again named himself as the primary beneficiary and Missy as the contingent. The young salesman would remember the encounter as "the easiest sale I ever made."

Why a policy on an infant and not himself? Garrett would claim he already had that kind of insurance through his employer. It was term life, he said, and had he died, would have paid off at the rate of four times his annual salary. He also said Missy had a similar policy with the Montgomery County school system.

Garrett came home and handed the MetLife policy to Missy. His wife couldn't be bothered with reading the insurance papers and tossed them in the bottom of a closet, which served as a repository for their personal records.

Julie Stinger's first meeting with Garrett was in April of 1986, a month after he married Missy and just before he applied for the wedding license with Liz Dodge. Julie loved kids. Despite being single, the thirty-two-year-old earth mother, who was even bigger and heavier than Missy, had adopted or provided foster care for five small children. She also ran a crafts store in Gaithersburg called Julie's Quilt Shop. Julie had played piano in her youth. She was looking to rekindle the avocation when she wandered into the Jordan Kitt's store inside Lake Forest Mall.

"I wanted an oak piano, and they had one for five thousand dollars. I got the information from Garrett to give to my father. He said he was willing to pay for it. My dad owned a Pepsi franchise in Indiana, and was about to sell the plant. Garrett seemed to be real interested in that," she recalled.

"So, I bought it. And a few weeks later he showed up at my shop. He was dressed real casual, in shorts and a T-shirt. He wanted me to buy an organ that cost thirty thousand dollars. I said no, no, no—I don't want that big a thing in the house, but he was persistent. He would call me nearly every day to ask about my dad or my financial resources, and yes, I bought the organ, too."

Julie said she was surprised when Garrett came to her house just before Christmas of 1986 and asked to meet her father. She was even more surprised when he gave her a gold bracelet.

"He talked with my dad a long time. After that, he called me constantly. Money was always on his mind. My dad had bought a retirement house on Hilton Head Island in South Carolina and I guess I lived in a large house for a single person."

Julie began to believe Garrett might have a gambling problem. She would meet him for breakfast and he would buy scratch-off lottery tickets, spending as much as seventy-five dollars while she would play five dollars. And, according to her, he would spend even more money on the Saturday night Lotto drawing.

She also thought that Garrett was beginning to show a romantic interest in her. She remembered him promising to take her on a cruise where the two were to share a cabin.

"He was constantly buying me gifts. It bothered me. My family is extremely wealthy, but we never flaunt it. He was getting personal, but I didn't even know his phone number or where he lived. I told him he was a con artist and he had to come clean with me."

Julie may have already been conned. She remembered Garrett as bringing pianos and organs to her house to store for weeks. Julie said she learned later that this was her admirer's way of getting an advance commission on a piano sale he hadn't as yet made.

The single mother claimed Garrett eventually gave her a thumbnail history of his life, altering a few facts along the way. He told her there had been a wife and they had a baby who died. Garrett also said he was living with a woman, but they weren't having sex. The reason they were staying together was because he didn't know a polite way of telling her to leave. When she asked for his address, he gave Julie the name of a street a few blocks from where he was really living.

A week after that meeting Garrett telephoned Julie. He said he was calling from a hospital. The woman he had been living with had been taken there because her blood pressure was extremely high, he told her. The statement made a lot of points with Julie. She thought Garrett was showing his humanitarian side. A few days later he showed up at her house again. This time he told her he was married and his wife had just given birth to a baby boy.

"I just came unglued. I'm thinking—the way I'm brought up—and he's married and has a baby. I said, 'You've got to go.' He started to walk away, but came back and hugged me. He asked me not to give up on him. I told him, 'Garrett, please go.'"

But her admirer continued to call, and she continued to receive him. Julie claimed he also upped the ante by offering to run away with her.

"He said, 'She means nothing to me. I didn't want to marry her. She came after me.' I told him, 'You've got to look after the baby. The baby should come first,' and he would say, 'We could bring up the baby. We could pay off Missy and raise the baby together.' In my heart, I began to think this child was going to be mine."

After that, Garrett asked to borrow $1,300 from her. When she asked him why, he said he needed the cash to pay off the birthing fees at the hospital. "Why don't you have any insurance?" she asked him. He said he did, but it had gotten tangled in red tape at the hospital. Julie lent him the money and after she did, he asked to borrow more.

"I told him, 'You've got this musical talent. You should use it.' And so then he wanted forty-four hundred dollars to buy instruments. Garrett said he was going to make a recording. I gave him the money by taking an advance from my credit cards. But I made him sign a blank, post-dated check I could use if he didn't pay me back. That way, if I went to cash it, he'd be charged with writing a bad check. He was supposed to pay the minimum amount on my credit cards each month. But getting it out of him was like pulling teeth. He never paid me more than the minimum."

In July of 1987, Garrett brought his four-month-old son to her quilt shop. It was the first time she had ever seen the child. When he told her he was taking his wife and baby to the beach, she asked him about the loan.

"I kept pushing him and he said the money was coming. 'I'm getting the money,' he told me. 'It's coming soon,' he said. 'I swear it's coming.'"

* * *

Missy and Garrett took two beach vacations with their infant son in the summer of 1987. The first, in July, was to Nag's Head, the resort town on the Outer Banks of North Carolina. The second was in August, at Bethany Beach, Delaware. Missy remembers walking down the boardwalk with her husband and Garrett Michael on August 12. Because Garrett had told her Brandi had died from SIDS, she had studied the syndrome and believed the day was an auspicious one.

"Do you know what today is? It's our baby's fifth-month birthday. We're out of the woods," Missy said. Garrett didn't respond. Instead he ran into a nearby shop and bought Garrett Michael a toy bear.

Missy had read that after the fifth month of life a child was immune to SIDS. Nevertheless, she still kept a monitor at her bedside, connected to the nursery. It was turned on at all times, just in case. One could never be too sure, she thought. Their baby seemed healthy and, thankfully, was beginning to fall asleep just before ten at night, lessening her stress. An early morning feeding was still necessary, but it was now taking place closer to dawn. Everything seemed well. Missy felt comfortable enough to go back to work with the Montgomery County school system. Her first day was to be August 24.

On August 22, ten days after Garrett bought his son the teddy bear, Missy awakened to the baby crying. It was just before five in the morning. Her husband awakened as well.

"Garrett said, 'I'll feed the baby.' I was shocked," she would remember. "But he said, 'I'll do it. I have to take the baby to day care. You're going back to work.' I knew he had to learn, so I was excited he was willing."

Garrett got up out of bed. There had been a bottle warmer installed in the hallway, but Missy couldn't remember if she heard him use it. Then she heard him going into the baby's room. She didn't know exactly what he was doing, but she could hear him pick up the baby and take him to the rocking chair. She remembers hearing footsteps, a sound of the rocking chair, and a patting noise. And she heard what sounded like a sigh or a breath. She would say later it appeared to be her son exhaling.

Then Missy said something that didn't seem to make sense. She expressed concern but didn't go directly to her child. "I had never heard that sound before. My hair stood up on end. I got up out of bed and went down to feed the cats. They had been climbing up on me in bed, bothering me. I came back up the stairs and went into the nursery. The baby didn't feel right. He was limp."

Later, she could never tell this part of her story without sobbing: "I ran out of the nursery and into the bedroom screaming, '*Garrett, what did you do to him?*'"

Garrett opened a bathroom door and came out. Missy thought he looked pale. She dialed 911 and told the police their baby wasn't breathing. They told her to do CPR by holding his nose and blowing into his mouth.

The police dispatcher said help was on the way. Were the outside lights on? Missy handed off the baby to Garrett and raced downstairs to make sure.

A county paramedic team was there in six minutes, the time of arrival logged in at 5:56 A.M. They examined Garrett Michael. He was not breathing, and there was no pulse. Medical protocol required them to defibrillate the baby first. So, there in the driveway, they placed electric paddles on the five-month-old chest of the child and tried to jolt him back to life. The heart appeared to start and then was measured as a flat line. They tried it again with the same results. Then the medics started the ambulance and began racing to nearby Shady Grove Adventist Hospital. On the way they attempted to put in an IV but, as one of them, Tony Lombardi, would recall, "You can't do this when you're bouncing down the road."

The baby's parents followed the ambulance to the hospital. But before they left, Garrett did something that appeared to be inexplicable. He took the baby seat out of Missy's Saab and tossed it into his Mazda RX-7. Then he drove Missy to the hospital. They sat together and waited for the doctors.

"He never said a word. The doctors came out and said they couldn't do anything. Garrett and I went to my parents' house. I needed to talk to someone alone."

Missy huddled with Susan Anastasi, her sister-in-law. The first words out of her mouth shocked Susie.

"Garrett did this for the insurance money."

Susan Anastasi didn't say anything. Her sister-in-law was in an aggravated emotional state, and Susan tried to ignore the charge. Then Missy made a similar statement to her mother, Amanda. She remembered Garrett staying in the basement of her parents' house most of the day. This time there was no pool-playing accusation. Instead, he would be remembered as "watching videos." Garrett would confirm this, with what sounded like a reasonable explanation.

"Nobody seemed to want to have anything to do with me. We had made duplicates of the baby videos for Missy's parents. And so I went down to the basement and watched them again."

Garrett would also say he attempted to assist in reviving his son. He claimed that when the paramedics arrived, he was down on his knees pressing up and down on Garrett Michael's chest on their bed, following instructions from the dispatcher who was on the phone.

Missy sat on the front steps of her mother's house, alone and inconsolable. A friend with whom she had worked in the Montgomery County school system, Mary Ann Finnegan, arrived. She had heard of Missy's suspicions.

"Where's Garrett?" she asked.

"He's in the basement," Missy answered.

"Do you think he did it?"

"Yes."

Garrett commandeered her brother Frank and had him go over to their town house with him. The two stripped the bed of the sheets and threw them away. They placed the rest of the bedding in black trash bags. The bags were put in the basement on the theory that the less Missy had to see of where and how Garrett Michael had died, the better. Then Garrett ironed some shirts.

Missy spent the night at her mother's house. She did not want to go home. And, despite everything she had said about him, it was hard for her to believe the unthinkable—that her husband had killed his namesake.

The Office of the Chief Medical Examiner for the State of Maryland at 111 Penn Street in Baltimore has a factory in its basement. It is an important part of its departmental function. The workshop is for solving death's mysteries, a labyrinth where bodies are wheeled in and wheeled out on stainless-steel gurneys. Inside this underground cavern of the dead, cadavers are sliced apart, examined, and stitched back together again. There are usually at least a dozen procedures in various states of progress at all times of the day. If a corpse has a gunshot wound, it is the duty of a pathologist to determine whether the deceased died from the wound or another as yet undiscovered reason.

Finding the cause of death in an otherwise healthy baby who has stopped breathing is difficult, maybe as difficult as the process becomes. Often, in these examinations, there is what is known as a negative autopsy, defined as an analysis that does not disclose any significant findings. The doctor is left without an explanation for the infant's passing. Distraught parents of such a child will, understandably, not accept an answer that is inconclusive. Thus, a pathologist will often state that a baby succumbed to sudden infant death syndrome whether or not the infant had any characteristics of the condition. The doctor does so because the term offers closure.

At 10:30 A.M. on the day following his death, Garrett Michael Wilson's tiny body was wheeled into these chambers. Because he had been declared dead at the hospital and not at home, there was no police report or investigation. Julia Goodin, an associate pathologist for the medical examiner's office, did the autopsy, while Charles Kokes, her boss and an assistant medical examiner for the state, supervised. Other than evidence of the IV hookup and the emergency measures that had been taken, the body appeared to be externally normal.

> The partially clad body is of a nineteen pound, twenty-five inch white male reported to be five months of age. Rigor mortis is fully developed in the cool body and livor [the pooling and settling of blood] is present dorsally [the back surface of the body] except over pressure points. The scalp hair is relatively sparse, fine, blonded and has a maximum length of one inch. The anterior fontanella [soft spot on top of skull] is patent and neither bulging or depressed. The irises are blue, the cornea clear and the sclerae and conjunctivae are unremarkable. There is a nasogastric tube present in the right nostril. The natural facial orifices are free of foreign material and abnormal secretions. The lips are without evidence of injury. The gums are without note. The teeth have not erupted. The nasal skeleton is palpably intact. There are fresh needle puncture wounds in the right and left antecubital fossa. The abdomen is moderately protuberant. The extremities are symmetrical. The external genitalia are that of a circumcised immature male with bilaterally descended testes. There is a large testicular hydrocele of the left testis. The posterior torso is without note. There are no antemortem injuries or congenital abnormalities evident. There is a femoral cutdown in the left upper thigh. Clothing with the body consists of a yellow print hospital gown and a baby blanket.

The doctors found "20cc of water and curdled milk" in Garrett Michael's stomach, evidence he had been fed just before dying. They also found the same pattern of fine black-and-blue blood spots on the lungs that the other doctors had found in Brandi. There was congestion in the kidneys.

One remarkable difference between the autopsies of Brandi Jean and Garrett Michael stood out. Pathologist Juan C. Troncoso, who examined Garrett Michael's brain, noticed some swelling. He thought the protuberance significant:

On coronal sections, there is evidence of marked postmortem artifact. Diffuse edema of the cerebral hemispheres
is noted. No focal abnormality is present in the gray or
white matter. The basal ganglia are normal. The ventricular
system is collapsed. The cerebellum and brainstem are normal. SUMMARY: Infant brain with diffuse swelling and
absence of focal or congenital abnormality. Microscopic
sections are pending.

The sections from the cerebral cortex, the hippocampal
formation, and the brain stem were normal. The cause of
Garrett Michael's death was determined to be sudden infant
death syndrome, said the state of Maryland.

Representatives from the medical examiner's office contacted Missy's family. They said Garrett Michael's autopsy
had come back clean.

"It's a classic case of SIDS," they told her mother,
Amanda.

Because of that news, Missy decided to go to a nearby
conference in Bethesda, Maryland, on sudden infant death
syndrome. A SIDS support person at the University of
Maryland confirmed the medical examiner's findings, saying flatly, "There is no foul play."

So, Missy changed her mind. It had been inconceivable to
believe that her own husband would murder the son he had
named after himself, she thought. Still, she vowed never to
give birth to another baby. She also punished Garrett by re-
fusing to have sex with him for one year following the
baby's death. She also told her friends she couldn't understand his attitude. It was unlike her reactions.

"Why does Garrett play music? He doesn't seem to be
grieving," she would ask her family.

Her husband remembered this period differently. While
admitting they weren't having sex for a year after Garrett
Michael's death, he said it was because his wife had become
so obese she was no longer desirable, and it was he who rejected her. He also claimed Missy discouraged him from
playing music in the house because, in her words, "The day

Garrett Michael died is the day the music died." On the other hand, he said, Missy continued to play her Bruce Springsteen CDs. Missy, he recalled, was such a devoted fan of the New Jersey rock icon, she once drove two hundred miles through a driving snowstorm to see him perform.

Then, if all this was going on, why stay together? he was asked. He didn't have an answer to the question.

"I don't know. I just don't know."

Garrett went with Missy's father and brother to make the funeral arrangements. Missy wouldn't go with them, telling them, "I don't want anything to do with it."

The service was held at the same Christ Episcopal Church in Rockville where his marriage to Missy had taken place a year and a half before. A weeping Missy was walked down the aisle by a stoic Garrett, the two arm in arm. Garrett's uncle, Donald Ward, who had been his best man at the wedding, was also at the somber event. He had attended Brandi's funeral seven years earlier. He remembered his nephew making a peculiar remark afterward that stayed in his memory for years.

"It's most unusual to have two SIDS deaths in one family," Garrett told him.

Garrett Michael was buried at Gate of Heaven, a Roman Catholic cemetery, in the Maryland suburb of Silver Spring. His final resting place was an unmarked grave in the children's section officially called The Holy Innocents. Most visitors simply referred to it as "Babyland." The grave was still unmarked as a new century began.

Missy's husband began to put his house in order. Again, there were many bills to pay and women who wanted to be paid.

"Garrett called me in August," Elizabeth Dodge later recalled. "He told me he had a baby and it had died of SIDS. He said to get a copy of the newspaper that day because there was an obituary in it. He said, 'I'll be getting insurance money, and when I do, I'll pay you a thousand dollars.' A few weeks later we met and had lunch and he gave me a check."

Garrett also gave Liz the phone number of the bank and told her to wait a week and then call to make sure it was good. He didn't want it to bounce.

And Julie Stinger? She happened to call Jordan Kitt's on the Saturday Garrett's son died, looking for her money. She was told by a salesman in the store about his family's tragedy.

"I was shocked. I was going to be the child's stepmother." Garrett showed up on Julie's doorstep the next day.

"He said the money would be there soon because he'd taken out insurance policies on the baby," Julie recalled. "I said, 'Who takes out insurance policies on babies?' He said it was for his education and 'just in case.' "

Julie attended Garrett Michael's funeral services, but not the wake that took place the night before. Garrett asked her not to be present at the smaller gathering.

"Then he showed up at my store in October with a check for all the money he owed me. He said, 'The insurance money came through, see!' He showed me a receipt for more than a hundred thousand dollars. I guess it was the insurance money. I didn't care. The baby was dead. The child who was going to have been mine was dead."

SIX

A DIVORCE IN FLORIDA

After their baby was buried, Garrett was promoted to manager at a new Jordan Kitt's store in Landover Mall, a shopping center some forty miles from the townhouse in Germantown. Missy was surprised when her husband suddenly seemed rich.

"One night Garrett came home and threw money on the bed. It was ten thousand dollars in cash. He said it was some of the insurance money he got for the baby's death. I wanted to do some good with it. My father wanted me to have another child and then he suggested we adopt. So I thought we could use the money for that. At first Garrett seemed interested, but he wouldn't go to the adoption classes."

Missy instead deposited the money into their joint checking account.

Garrett's memory is different. He recalled a meeting with an attorney in a shabby neighborhood in Washington to discuss the adoption process.

"The lawyer wanted fifteen hundred dollars down and fifteen thousand total to adopt a child. I said, 'This is buying babies for bucks.' I didn't like it."

Garrett said the only reason he considered it was because

Mike Anastasi, Missy's dad, was pressing them for another grandchild.

"If you can't make one, adopt one," was Mike's edict.

Garrett collected a substantial settlement. There was $150,000 plus interest—$100,788.30 from MetLife, $50,328.77 from Allstate—in insurance proceeds from Garrett Michael's death. The cash was gone within months. Even though there was plenty left after paying off Julie Stinger and Liz Dodge—money that ensured they would not expose him—he spent it the way he always had: trying to buy love and respect. This time his target was Missy. There was a new Saab for her, and then a $212,000 just-built house for the both of them. Garrett wrote a $36,000 check for the down payment and closing costs. The two then added $5,000 worth of upgraded carpeting to the price and bought a cherry dining room suite for $2,000.

The home was isolated, next to a cornfield at the end of a cul de sac in Damascus, the most western, least populated outpost in all of Montgomery County. Missy's parents told them they could get a lot for their money that far out, and they were right. The brick two-story estate came with a double-size garage and lots of green lawn. The street wasn't saddled with a meaningless name like Caltor Lane. Garrett finally had an address that fit the image he was seeking—Kings Valley Court!

With the rest of the money, Garrett purchased jewelry for Missy. It wasn't cheap costume stuff, either. There was a diamond tennis bracelet. (Garrett used his now hackneyed "dropping it in the champagne" ritual when he gave it to her.) There were gold earrings and gold necklaces. Each piece cost thousands of dollars. Missy began to buy clothes from Lord & Taylor, and Garfinckel's—the haute couture address for Washington fashion. While the money lasted, Garrett played the role of big spender with Missy along for the ride. There were fancy three-course meals for the self-indulgent pair at restaurants like Windows inside the *USA To-*

day building in Arlington, Virginia. Windows offered a breathtaking view of the capital city's monuments. The couple sometimes ran up three-figure dinner tabs. Garrett explained the frequent dining out in this way: "We never got into fights when we went out to dinner," he said. "When we were home we were always bickering."

Any suspicion that Missy once had that her husband had killed their child was forgotten. The autopsy had come back as SIDS. The SIDS organization had confirmed the diagnosis, calling Garrett Michael's case a classic one. And Garrett had told her that his first child had died in the same way. Maybe it did run in families, just like he said. Missy didn't link the insurance money with motive. Garrett had told her that his father was heavily insured and he was just following that example. Missy said she didn't see all that money slipping away until it was too late.

"Garrett ordered a lot of credit cards," she recalled. "But he wasn't paying our bills. I was the one who thought a larger house would make it easier to adopt. He told me he was making lots of money. I didn't know what we owed—he handled the bills. Then we started getting phone calls from creditors. I honestly didn't know what was going on."

In response, her husband said he felt his wife didn't support his career at Jordan Kitt's no matter how hard he worked. He remembered that on Christmas Eve of 1988, he wanted Missy to go with him to several customers' homes. He was responsible for delivering and setting up three pianos and one organ in individual residences, just hours before the holiday began. There were big commissions involved. Missy, not exactly a piano buff, dragged her feet.

"In the end she went, but she acted like it was a big chore," he complained.

By the time 1990 began, Missy and Garrett were flat broke. They filed for bankruptcy. The big house purchased just two years before already had several liens against it totaling more than $50,000. It was about to be taken away. The location had been a mistake. When Garrett had been made a manager of the Jordan Kitt's store in Landover Mall in Prince George's County, it forced him to fight his way through more than a hundred miles of traffic each day.

"In January, my next-door neighbor said someone had knocked on our door and looked at the house to see if they liked it," Missy recalled. "They were going to foreclose the next day. I called up my father and he helped me scrape up some money. We saved the house."

The rescue proved to be only temporary. It would belong to someone else a year later.

Garrett's reaction to the house crisis was to pledge to Missy to work longer hours. He lamented that his wife had not taken a higher salaried position in the school system when it was offered.

"If she had just taken that job we would have been all right," he claimed.

After Missy's father, Mike Anastasi, helped to stall the house foreclosure, the old man had a heart attack and then a stroke. He died in 1990 at the age of sixty-five. After Mike died, Garrett claimed he would have left her earlier, but had pledged to her father to stay by her side. With Missy's dad dead and their financial reputations shattered, it was time to look for a fresh start somewhere far away from Montgomery County. Garrett told her he knew of an opportunity in Houston, Texas.

"I got recruited by Holcombe Music," Garrett said. "People who sell instruments usually know each other. Holcombe only had one store, but it was huge, as big as a warehouse. So we drove to Texas with what we had left. The trip meter said 1,514 miles when we got there."

In addition to the financial reasons behind the relocation, there were also personal ones. There certainly hadn't been fidelity in the marriage on Garrett's part during the final year in Maryland. He had begun a sexual affair with a nineteen-year-old lifeguard at a private swimming pool where they were members. Missy had volunteered to work at the snack bar during the summer, and while she did, Garrett advanced the relationship virtually in the presence of his wife. John Farley was the contact point.

"After they left town, she came to my office wanting to know where he was," his friend recalled.

Garrett and Missy lived in a small Houston apartment for five months. But Garrett decided he didn't like the job or Houston from the day they arrived. He was upset when the store wouldn't pay the expenses of their trip to Texas. He was also unhappy when Missy wouldn't try to find a job at the Galleria, one of the largest malls in the country, right across the street from their apartment. When he found out Holcombe Music had taken out a "Going Out of Business" license, he began to believe he had been duped, hired only to help the owners shut down the store.

"The day they ran the first 'Going Out of Business Sale' ad in the paper is the day I quit," he said.

Missy wanted to head to Florida and, for a change, her husband agreed. Garrett was a womanizer and may have been missing other virtues, but he could sell pianos for his employers. Lots of them. His impromptu piano performances to gullible females were loaded with charm. With that going for him, any musical instrument emporium in America was willing to consider hiring him, even if his criminal record was discovered. Corporate store spies who dropped in at Jordan Kitt's to check out the competition had often tried to hire him away. So Missy and Garrett left Texas and drove to the Sunshine State, this time with their expenses paid. Garrett had been recruited to sell pianos in the Tampa–St. Petersburg area for Fletcher Music, a chain similar to Jordan Kitt's. They rented a garden apartment in Largo, a small town just south of Clearwater in Pinellas County.

"He was so good at what he did," said an admiring Dennis Awe. "When someone walked into his store, Garrett could look at them and read their age. Then he'd sit down at the keyboard and begin to play something that fit their era. If it was a couple in their sixties, he'd do a Frank Sinatra standard. If it was a young man in his twenties, he's do something by Billy Joel."

His friend remembered Garrett as a man who was willing to sacrifice his own comfort for others. Every gesture Garrett ever made always seemed to be for the benefit of someone else, Awe believed.

"Once it was raining cats and dogs outside. But Garrett insisted on walking this old woman out to her car. There was nothing in it for him. She had already bought the piano. But he held the umbrella over her, opened the car door, put her cane and umbrella inside, and then ran back to the store. He was soaking wet when he got back, but it didn't bother him."

And despite having just a high school education Garrett had a keen sense for mathematics, remembered John Farley. "He could figure out the commission from any sale in his head instantly," he recalled. "He had a good head for business."

The sales job with Fletcher Music didn't pan out, either. Garrett liked Florida, but not Fletcher. Missy, who did not work in 1991 except for a six-week stint at a Hickory Farms store during its Christmas rush, spent most of her days sitting on the beach. Each thought the other was becoming depressed. Missy remembered coming home in January of 1992 to find her husband sitting in their apartment in the dark. When she turned on the lights, Garrett was in tears. He said, "I've been thinking about our son." Missy said he had been reading a magazine article about a child who had slowly drowned.

Garrett found what he thought was a better opportunity, the kind of position that was not only prestigious, but offered more money and allowed him to travel. After being hired at his third job in a year, the new employer, Casio Electronics, hired him to demonstrate and sell electronic pianos, its eighty-eight-key traditional models, and karaoke machines. Casio, a Japanese corporation, was trying to find a foothold for its music division in America. The territory found him traveling through eight states—from Florida to North Carolina and then all the way west to Arkansas and on into Texas. It was during one of these journeys, on May 7, 1992, that he met Vicky Frihse in Cumming, Georgia. Vicky was separated and in the midst of a divorce from a second husband. And Garrett was fed up with Missy.

He began spending a lot of time in Georgia, encouraging Missy to go back to Maryland to visit a pregnant relative. In retrospect, he pushed her out the door. He began to call Vicky, "the love of my life."

On October 9, 1992, Garrett filed dissolution of marriage documents in Pinellas County. The papers requesting the simple divorce were filled out without the help of an attorney; Garrett instead used an independent paralegal. Point four of the fifteen-point legal brief emphasized: "This marriage is IRRETRIEVABLY BROKEN." And point five falsely stated: "There are no minor or dependent children born of the parties and my wife is not pregnant." He also requested that no financial maintenance be awarded to either party. Missy would later claim the divorce was done in a stealthy manner and that there had been no prior discussion of any separation or divorce.

In order to file in Florida, one has to be a resident for at least six months. Garrett was, but Missy had to be formally notified of the action. Garrett first tried to send Missy notice through a sheriff's deputy at a Cocoa Beach address where he thought she was visiting a friend. When he was unable to serve Missy there, the divorce court in Pinellas County threatened to dismiss the case "for failure to obtain service." Eager to move the case along, Garrett went to a storefront law clinic to keep the divorce process in play.

The lawyers suggested mailing the summons to Missy using what they called an "alias summons." He did so, on March 3, 1993. However, the court would still not recognize Missy as being served, and on April 28, 1993, dismissed the divorce again. He was forced to start over.

By now, Garrett was no longer living in Florida. But he knew a woman who had lived in his apartment complex when he lived in Largo. She certified that he had resided in the state of Florida for at least six months. In August of 1993 he tried to serve Missy at two addresses. The first was at a friend's residence in Cocoa Beach and the second was at her mother's home in Rockville. Finally, a Montgomery County deputy sheriff served Missy with the divorce action on October 4, 1993.

Garrett was now in a hurry. The love affair with Vicky had become passionate and had borne fruit. The two already had a daughter, delivered by Vicky in July of 1993, long before Missy had even been served. He was impatient to marry her. Yet, in spite of an infant child and his professed love for Vicky, he had found time for sexual flings with Missy both in August of 1993 and May of 1994. At the time, Missy didn't know of his adultery or the child.

"Garrett called near the date of our wedding anniversary in 1993 and told me he had filed for a divorce in Florida," Missy would recall. "He said he did it because he had been depressed. So I said, 'Can't you stop it?' Garrett told me not to worry. He said, 'We'll go on a cruise and get remarried.'

"Then I met him in May of 1994 for a weekend in New Orleans, and we had a good time. We rode in a carriage and ate on top of a hotel in the French Quarter. At the end of the weekend I told him I was going to Florida. He was back in Texas, so I said, 'Call me on my voice mail and tell me where you are.'"

Before deceiving Missy a final time—Garrett had never revealed his relationship with Vicky, told her they had a child, or even talked to her about the divorce—Garrett went back to Texas and Vicky.

In Florida, the legal wheels inside the Pinellas County Courthouse continued to churn. On October 9, the order for a final divorce hearing was served on Missy at her mother's address in Rockville. The hearing was set to be heard on November 15 in a Pinellas County Circuit Court. In the application, the civil court noted again that "there have been no children born of this marriage or adopted and the wife is not now pregnant." The notice from the judge sent Missy into a frenzied last-ditch effort to try and save the marriage. On October 12 she wrote this letter to the Circuit Court, attempting to invalidate Garrett's action.

> To: Circuit Court for Pinellas Co. Fl.
> Case # 92-008614-FD-023
> Please be advised that neither Mr. Wilson or myself have resided in the state of Florida since October 15, 1992.
> It is my best understanding that Mr. Wilson was under extreme distress due to a job layoff at the time he initiated this action. He does not desire the same course of action at this time. We have worked out our difficulties. Should any further court be involved it will be in the state in which WE reside.
> Mary Anastasi Wilson

The court ignored the letter and went forward. On November 18, Missy sent a final missive. Her argument was forceful and candid.

> Re Case # 92-008614-FD-023
> I object to the action being taken in this order. Re statement #17 [the court had written that "both parties have waived the ten-day objection period" and then recommended that "the court enter said final judgment if no written objections to the report are filed within ten-days of service upon the parties."] I did make written objection to this—I have not had legal advice or time to respond due to the fact that I am living in Maryland and am unable to afford legal counsel or travel to Florida at this time.
> My husband and I were reunited in Texas in August of 1993 and had decided to work out our marriage. We had sexual relations at that time. He was under the impression that he did not have to do anything further and this case would be dismissed.
> I absolutely do not just intend to be "dissolved of a marriage."
> Dismiss this case.
> Mary Anastasi Wilson

The Florida court ignored Missy's pleas again, and on November 30, 1993, wrote "that the bonds of marriage between GARRETT E. WILSON, the petitioner, and Mary F. Anastasi-Wilson, the respondent, are hereby dissolved because the marriage is irretrievably broken. The wife shall have her former name restored and shall hereafter be known as: MARY F. ANASTASI."

Missy would later say she never knew the divorce had been finalized. She continued to talk and meet with Garrett, believing they were still married. Garrett certainly didn't tell her. As with Liz Dodge, Debbie Oliver, or the other romantic relationships in his life, he was unable to completely let go. Like the others, a dramatic incident was needed. Missy began making plans to move to Texas to be with him. She thought he was encouraging the move, so she made a date to interview with Pulte Homes, the national residential building firm, on the day she arrived.

On Mother's Day of 1994, Garrett called her at home. He said he was sad. He told her he had been thinking about Garrett Michael a lot lately.

Garrett's next question was peculiar, Missy thought. "Did we get him a Social Security number?" he asked.

"No, he didn't really need one yet," she answered.

"Too bad. He would have seemed more real."

A dramatic incident wasn't long in coming. Garrett had given Missy a voice mail number in Texas so she could call to let him know of her whereabouts. From time to time she did just that. Near the end of May 1994, she called in to his answering service to let him know she was in Pensacola, Florida, visiting friends. A few hours later, while watching the action movie *Backdraft* on television, she got a telephone call.

"Hello, Missy, don't hang up until I tell you who I am," said a woman Missy would later learn was Vicky. Missy hung up on the caller. Missy drove back to Maryland upset and in a foul mood because of the call. On the way home, she had an epiphany.

It suddenly dawned on her Garrett might be married to someone else. More importantly, Missy also made this mental hurdle: She began to feel once again that he had killed their child. Soon after she arrived at her mother's house, Garrett was on the telephone. Missy wanted to know what was going on.

"A woman called me and said don't hang up, but I did. Since you're the only one who had the number, Garrett, I'll ask you—are you married or are you seeing somebody else?"

Missy claims Garrett denied it by saying, "No, that was probably someone from work."

A week later, Garrett called again. This time Missy could hear a baby crying in the background. She was more accusatory.

"Garrett, you are married and have a baby, don't you?"

"Yes, I do, Missy," he answered. Missy screamed her next line.

"Garrett, you son of a bitch! Now that I see what you're capable of, I know you killed my baby!" she shouted into the phone.

Garrett immediately hung up on her. He was shaken. Missy then called John Farley at his office. She asked him when the last time was he had spoken with Garrett.

"Not too long ago."

"Did you know he has divorced me and has a new wife and a baby?"

John said he didn't. He seemed to believe Garrett needed psychiatric counseling. "Missy, Garrett needs help. He can't deal with money, and he's needed help for a long time. You can't believe how many women have been in here crying over him," he said.

"You mean, while he's been married to me?" she asked. She was incredulous at the revelation.

"Yes. At least three."

Missy begged John for an office phone number for Garrett. He gave her one. She collected herself and punched the digits into the telephone. Her former husband answered.

"How could you do this?" she began. Missy recalled Garrett's next statement as frightening.

"You'd be dead if you were here," he said.

"What do you mean by that?" Missy asked.

"You said I killed our baby. I always thought *you* did it, but those SIDS people said there was no foul play."

Missy hung up on him this time. Later in the day Garrett called Missy and asked her not to put messages on his answering machine anymore. Missy remembers this conversation taking place:

"Garrett, you have killed me. I'll be okay though."

"I guess you don't think I have any feelings," Garrett said.

"Well, you're right. I do think you have no feelings," Missy told him.

Then she hung up on Garrett again.

Garrett's recollection is different. "She told me, 'I am going to destroy you,'" he said.

Three days later, Missy said she got a call from Vicky Wilson. Missy wanted final confirmation that Garrett had married Vicky behind her back.

"Do you have a child?" Missy answered.

"Yes, a ten-month-old. Her name is Marysa."

"Then you better get that baby out of there," Missy warned her, telling the tale of two dead infants and the insurance Garrett had purchased on Garrett Michael.

Vicky said Garrett told her he was divorced when they met. She didn't find out he was still officially married until she was already pregnant, and it was too late. But she seemed optimistic about her situation.

Did Marysa have insurance? No. Vicky said she wanted to buy a policy on their newborn, but it was Garrett who refused, because, "What if something happens to her?" Vicky thought about taking out insurance secretly and not telling him, but she had insurance on Marysa through her job. It wasn't much, but it was enough.

Garrett had a completely different story, an incredible

one. He said Missy had asked him to snatch Marysa and run away with her, that they would raise the child together.

Missy recalled Vicky as being completely comfortable with the father of her baby. She told her they were going to marriage counseling.

"Even Charlie Manson can be rehabilitated," Missy remembers Vicky telling her.

Vicky also claimed Garrett had taken a psychological test that showed he wasn't a sociopath and thus couldn't have killed anyone.

Frustrated, Missy began to sob. Vicky heard her tears through the phone. "I know how you feel," she sympathized.

"Just get that baby out of there," Missy repeated. The two women would never speak to each other again.

PART TWO

Reserving judgments is a matter of infinite hope. I am still a little afraid of missing something if I forget that, as my father snobbishly suggested, and I snob-bishly repeat, a sense of the fundamental decencies is parceled out inequally at birth.

—F. SCOTT FITZGERALD,
THE GREAT GATSBY

SEVEN

THE PROUD
PANHANDLE PEOPLE

Allegany is derived from a Native American phrase that means "land of endless mountains." It certainly looks that way entering the world of the Wampler family, whose land has straddled the Eastern Continental Divide for centuries.

The gaps and valleys here are surrounded by giant green hills that turn white in winter. The names of these mountains are not always politically correct. Besides the earlier mentioned Big Savage Mountain, there are appellations like Dan's Mountain, named for a local character by the name of Dan Cresap. Then there are the ones named for ethnicities like Polish Mountain and Negro Mountain. The federal government makes noises about changing the name of the latter peak every few years, but always fails.

Garrett County adjoins Allegany County, and except for Deep Creek Lake, which attracts well-heeled visitors, the two feel much the same. Named for another Garrett, the former president of the Baltimore and Ohio Railroad, it is the westernmost county in the state of Maryland, some three hundred miles from the state's ocean beaches. Amish people settled here early and still influence local politics to such an extent that beer and liquor sales are banned on Sunday. This is a sore subject in the lakeside bars and restaurants that cater to the tourists.

Naturalists make pilgrimages to Garrett County to find the source of the Potomac River. The origin is a spring that gushes forth on the side of Backbone Mountain before meandering 343 miles where it empties into Chesapeake Bay, and eventually the Atlantic Ocean.

The region has long been an area of benign neglect by the bureaucrats in Annapolis, the state capital. While America enjoyed prosperity in the last decade of the twentieth century, Allegany and Garrett counties were depressed. Their unemployment rate hovered at 9 percent, more than twice the national average. The citizens of the area seemed not to care. Those who were employed would have willingly deserted an employer at a moment's notice if it came to choosing between the job and ten days of deer hunting during the fall season.

Allegany and Garrett counties, truth be told, are in the very heart of Appalachia. They have much more in common with, and are closer to, the gritty white ethnic ghettos of Pittsburgh than the shiny, slick suburbs of Washington and Baltimore, where most of Maryland's population live.

Vicky Wilson's father, William Ervin Wampler, was descended from a long line of German immigrants who settled first in Garrett County. He was also proud of the Native American blood that is part of his heritage. Ervin's grandmother, Molly, had copper skin and hair that fell to her waist. She looked every inch of what she really was—a princess whose Cherokee name was Meadowlark. Though Ervin was Baptist, his father had been a part-time preacher for the Church of the Brethren. The Wamplers were a well-known force in the region. They had a family plot spanning three generations just off old U.S. 40. Ervin was the fourth in the Wampler line, which dated back to the middle of the nineteenth century.

His daddy had once been a coal miner. Ervin was as proud of that as he was of the preaching. He liked to show off an old hat his father had worn down in the mines. Made long before electric batteries were invented, the now ragged old cap had a carbide-burning blowtorch installed above its brim to illuminate the man-made caves.

In the nineteenth and the early part of the twentieth century, coal mining had been the mainstay in nearby Frostburg. The mountain town had five coal companies working the region, as well as smaller, family-owned mines. Children once crawled in darkness through the veins that ran beneath the streets to snatch enough lumps for their mothers' stoves. In those long forgotten days, the black gold would be loaded into wagons and then pulled by mules to the freight yards where steam-driven trains hauled the mineral to the cities of the Eastern seaboard.

Frostburg, whose population never quite reached ten thousand, was named after Meschach Frost, a nineteenth-century hotelier and owner of one of these coal mines. Newcomers to the community thought otherwise. The three feet of snow it averaged each year and the dangerous icy roads made them believe the village was named for its winters.

Ervin graduated from high school in 1944 and for a short while tried welding at the Big Savage brick company. A few months later, on his eighteenth birthday, he enlisted in the Merchant Marines. When World War II ended and he came home, he tried coal mining himself.

In the postwar years, the Wampler elder met and married Thelma, the daughter of a family that operated the only roller rink in the region. It was thoughts of Thelma that made him decide to stay above ground. Ervin signed on at the nearby Allegany Ballistics plant, helping to create the Polaris Missile. Former Nazi and guided-rocket pioneer Wernher von Braun was the company's consultant, probably the most famous visitor to the area during the postwar years.

Ervin soon left the missile manufacturer and spent the rest of his working years bringing home a paycheck from the Kelly-Springfield factory. Kelly made car and truck tires in Cumberland, the region's only city, some twenty-five thousand people strong. Kelly was the largest employer in Allegany County, with fifteen hundred workers on its payroll. In its heyday, its unionized employees got fat regular paychecks.

Ervin started off unloading boxcars where Kelly-Springfield's freight train spur stopped. It was tough, physical work, but he stuck it out. In a few years he became a supervisor. That was easier and paid more, too, though he never got used to walking through the union pickets when strikes interrupted the assembly line. The friends he had grown up with would snarl at him, spitting on the ground when he passed by.

Kelly-Springfield finally got weary of these hassles and the union's unrelenting demands. Cheaper foreign tires were killing its bottom line anyway. In 1987, the production plant closed down completely, the jobs sent south to low-cost, right-to-work states. By then, Ervin no longer cared. His career at Kelly had ended in 1984 with retirement and a pension. He was back to what had always been first and foremost in his life, the steep green hills of his beloved mountain land.

Ervin and Thelma were unable to have children, and in the late 1950s began adopting. The couple signed contracts with single, pregnant women prior to their delivery. The sex of the child was never known in advance. The first was a girl. They called her Kathy. Two years later, there was another opportunity. They named her Vicky Lynn. Both were picked up three days after the mothers gave birth in a hospital. Vicky was born in Richmond, Virginia.

Is that short for Victoria and Katherine?

"No, just Vicky and Kathy. My parents are plain people. It would never occur to them to put names like that on a birth certificate," Vicky Wampler Wilson said.

Growing up together, Vicky and Kathy were as close as two young girls can be. Few knew they weren't natural sisters. They even seemed to look alike. But their personalities were as different as mud is from chocolate. Vicky was outgoing, confident, and talented. She flourished at the piano, beginning her lessons at the age of six. Kathy was so shy, she ran from strangers. And Kathy was a Goody-Two-Shoes while Vicky could be rebellious.

Ervin tried to keep a tight rein on his adopted daughters. When they reached their teens he allowed them to date, but established a ten o'clock curfew.

"I was always home before ten. That was usually the time when Vicky was sneaking out," Kathy recalled. "Vicky sometimes came home early and then went out again through a bedroom window."

One evening when Vicky was fifteen, she stole away late at night and went drinking. She came back in through the front door well after midnight and fell over Ervin. Her father knew she had broken the rules and sneaked out. He was sleeping lengthwise on the floor just inside the house so he could literally trip his daughter up. Ervin chased after Vicky and let her have it.

"It was the only time he hit me, before or after," she said. "I deserved it, and I never did anything like that again."

While it may have been Vicky who had the wild ways, it was Kathy who married first. She wed her boyfriend, Smitty, in Frostburg's Welsh Memorial Baptist Church when she was seventeen. Kathy quickly had two boys, Jimmy and Jason. Both infants arrived before she was twenty-two. Twenty years later, she found herself pregnant for the third time. Kelsey, her only girl, was born a month before Garrett and Vicky's daughter, Marysa.

Vicky wanted a different future. She believed her mezzo soprano voice was good enough to sing on the stage in New York. The piano lessons she had taken all her life had given her professional status in the community. Vicky enrolled at Frostburg State University, majoring in music education. She thought her future was set.

"I was going to be a music teacher. I decided to become one in the eleventh grade. Then, when I tried it, I hated the experience. I did some substitute teaching at a middle school, and I remember the kids throwing chairs and spitting on each other. I became disillusioned fast. Even though it was all arranged that I would be replacing a teacher who had lupus and was retiring, when I graduated from college, I just couldn't go through with it."

While in college, Vicky married her teen sweetheart, Alan. The wedding took place a few months before her twentieth birthday. Alan was a budding Frostburg fireman. Again, another Wampler was walking down the aisle of the venerable Welsh Memorial Baptist Church, named for settlers from Wales who had founded it in 1868. Ervin, who had high hopes for his college-attending daughter, was frank about not having much optimism for the union's success.

"You're not in love, you're infatuated," he told her when she apprised him of her intentions.

And on her wedding day in 1979, even as he offered his arm, he uttered this prophetic warning: "This won't be the last time you walk down this aisle."

Vicky's marriage to Alan lasted six years. It was during this time that a single violent incident changed the direction of her life forever.

In 1983, four years after she married Alan and just after Vicky got her degree from Frostburg State, her husband's aunt died from cancer. The widower, Alan's uncle, William Eichorn, was a local insurance adjuster. He wasn't sure what to do next. While one son was grown, the forty-seven-year-old widower had two other boys who were not yet in their teens. He consulted his family. They told him to employ a housekeeper.

Bill Eichorn hired a pretty thirty-four-year-old woman, Lois Faye Crowe, to take charge of the children. It wasn't long before her duties included taking intimate care of him as well, in addition to her child-rearing responsibilities.

Lois's husband, Dennis, a rangy six-foot-three mountain man, caught wind of the affair. On October 23, 1983, just before midnight, an armed and angry Dennis Crowe entered Bill Eichorn's house. He discovered the two of them together. Alan's uncle was dispatched first, with a .45-caliber handgun that sent bullets through his head at close range. He then fired at his wife as she ran, critically wounding her with two more shots. The first shot was through her head and the second was aimed at her genital area, but went into the lower abdomen. As his shots were being fired, the young children cowered in the house. Dennis Crowe escaped in a red pickup truck, and Lois Crowe was rushed to Allegany Memorial Hospital. When the cops arrived, they found the children outside, in shock, covered in blankets to ward off the cold rain.

Lois Crowe never recovered. Three days later, she succumbed to the gunshot wounds, which made it the first double murder case anyone could remember in Frostburg. Alan organized a manhunt using men from both the Allegany and Garrett County fire departments as his posse. Dennis Crowe, it was rumored, was hiding in a swamp outside of the village of Finzel, near Ervin Wampler's house.

Four days after the murders, Dennis Crowe called the police and gave himself up. He was held without bond, charged with two counts of first degree murder and two counts of committing a felony with a handgun.

"They moved the trial downstate," Vicky Wilson recalled during a Sunday night pizza dinner at Smiley's, a Deep Creek Lake restaurant. "He got seven years. We wound up taking care of the two boys for a couple of years. A court mandated they have psychiatric counseling, and I took them to their sessions. That was what inspired me to go back to school and get a second degree so I could do social work."

By then her marriage was falling apart. Alan had decided he didn't like being a fireman, particularly after he had made a mistake by driving the town's new fire truck into a wall during a practice session. The two parted as friends, with Alan's family and Vicky's family retaining their adjoining pews at Welsh Memorial Baptist, where Alan's people still sit just in front of the Wampler clan to this day.

Vicky enrolled at West Virginia University in Morgantown for the 1984 fall term, prepared to put in two more years so she could become a state-licensed social worker. It wasn't long before she married again. Her new husband, Paul, was very different from Alan. He was eighteen years older, balding, and filthy rich. He specialized in brokering purchases of jumbo jet airliners, acting as the middleman between the manufacturer and the purchaser. To make these deals he headed up a specially created department in a large money center bank. An affluent new life opened to Vicky for the first time in her life. Paul's world was light-years away from Frostburg and its proud but plain panhandle people.

"He was one of their top executives," Vicky said. "He owned three houses. A lot of his money was made through investments."

Paul reimbursed Ervin for some of Vicky's college loans. The two moved to Pittsburgh—the Iron City was the same distance to Morgantown as Frostburg. Vicky began using her new degree at the Veteran's Administration in western Pennsylvania. She became, for the only time in her life, a woman of real means.

Vicky stopped working. There was no need for her to bring home a paycheck. Instead, she blossomed culturally. Vicky joined the city's famed Mendelssohn Choir, her mezzo soprano voice at times accompanying the Pittsburgh Symphony in choral performances of Handel's *Messiah* or the final movement of Beethoven's Ninth Symphony at Heinz Hall. On another level, she was chosen to sing "The Star-Spangled Banner" before an Atlanta Braves game.

Paul seemed to travel for business reasons constantly, and Vicky would often go with him on these trips. She remembered averaging eighteen of these road journeys a year, at first thinking it was impossible ever to get tired of ordering from room service or raiding the mini-bars in the sophisticated, big city hotels.

But life with Paul was turbulent. Her husband was demanding. There was the age difference, and the patina of sophistication Paul had acquired over the years began to wear thin with her even as his wealth continued to grow. He was a divorced man with children and all the baggage that came from a long previous marriage.

The union lasted exactly as many years as her wedding to Alan. Toward the end, it got ugly. Paul threatened to send a video of them in compromising positions to Ervin and Thelma.

By early 1992, they were separated. Vicky moved out of one of Paul's homes, where she had been living alone. The house sat on Lake Lanier in Forsyth County, Georgia, north of Atlanta. Divorced for the second time, she rented a small lakefront efficiency apartment and began supporting herself by giving voice and piano lessons to children.

Vicky met Garrett in May of 1992 when he was demonstrating keyboards for Casio Electronics. Vicky remembers seeing him for the first time as she walked into Take Note, the Cumming, Georgia, music store near Atlanta. When Garrett saw her, he launched into a medley from the Broadway musical, *Phantom of the Opera*, beginning with its romantic anthem, "All I Ask of You." Both seemed smitten immediately, though it was Vicky who admits to making the first move.

"When do you get off?" she asked him when he took a break. The two had lunch together the same day. The next night there was dinner and wine at an Atlanta Marriott Hotel.

Vicky and Garrett appeared to have been made for each other. Both played the piano and organ, both sang exceedingly well, and both had strong ties to the Baptist church. Each was willing to say grace not only at the dinner table at home, but at a restaurant in public. Anyone would have predicted they would probably be lovers within months. Actually, it was weeks.

Ervin and Thelma met Vicky's new boyfriend soon after they met. Her parents thought he was wonderful, the salt of the earth. Garrett remembered the first meeting as taking place under sad circumstances.

"I had gone over to her apartment for the weekend. I couldn't wait. She had thrown her back out, so I was wondering how I was going to get this beautiful woman upstairs to the bedroom and what I was going to do when I got there. But she got a phone call from Maryland and began crying. Her grandmother had died. Vicky didn't know how she was going to get home. I still had this company van from Casio, so I lifted her into a backseat and put Vicky on her back with her knees up. I drove fourteen hours, straight through to her parents' house in time for the funeral."

Vicky said Garrett told her of his wives, his two dead babies, and his criminal past within weeks after meeting her. Some women might have fled on hearing such news, but apparently in Vicky's case, love overcame all.

Garrett soon began finding excuses not to get back to Florida where he still shared an apartment in Largo with Missy. He failed to return in time for the July 4, 1992, Independence Day holiday after telling her he was going on a road trip to the Carolinas. Missy remembers Garrett calling just before midnight to let her know that even though he had been taking the caffeine pill NoDoz, he said he had fallen asleep at a rest stop. Garrett didn't get back to Florida until the fifth of the month.

Juggling at least two or more women wasn't new to Garrett, but it took its toll. Casio terminated his employment that month, which sent him into a dark depression. Missy rushed back to Florida to be by his side, but since Garrett always seemed to be either traveling or looking for a job, he wasn't home long. So Missy left the Tampa Bay area and went to visit her friend Carol in Cocoa Beach.

In August of 1992, Garrett had Missy ride with him from Florida to Maryland, supposedly to celebrate a birthday in her family. The plan was that Garrett would go on to Pittsburgh, where he had a job interview. In truth, he was going to visit Vicky, who was trying to sell the townhouse she got as part of her divorce settlement from Paul. A day later, Garrett called Missy and talked her into renting a car, driving it to the Pittsburgh Airport, and dropping the vehicle off. He said he would meet her there and then they would drive together to Florida because it was a straight shot down the interstate. Vicky was put on a plane to Atlanta, so that Garrett could drive Missy to Largo.

Missy thought Garrett was in a black mood on the long drive south. Her husband told her they were broke again and he was jobless with no prospects in sight. A few days after arriving in Florida, Garrett gathered up some of Missy's good jewelry, a television set, and their stereo speakers and took everything to a pawnshop. The money he received was a last-ditch attempt to buy time.

By September, Garrett's luck changed. He found a new position managing a warehouse-style piano store for Westbrook Music in Columbia, South Carolina. Garrett had known Sam Westbrook for years because Sam also imported pianos made in China. He sold the inexpensive models to stores like Jordan Kitt's under the Brentwood label. Missy, who again was visiting in Cocoa Beach, was told to come home and pack their bags. The new job was $40,000 a year plus a bonus plan. Garrett said he would go ahead to South Carolina and familiarize himself with the area, returning a few days later.

Missy recalled that her husband hated leaving Florida, and blamed his misfortune on her. Garrett's wife, who hadn't worked in years, save for her Hickory Farms stint, was berated by him for her sloth.

"This is all your fault," Garrett yelled. "If you had a job we would still be in Florida." Arriving in Columbia during the first week of October, the two lived in a Ramada Inn for three days. Sam Westbrook, a crusty, seventy-six-year-old music mogul, liked Garrett. He thought he had found a winner who could not only run the store but build its reputation. His new manager quickly found a nice two-bedroom residence at a garden apartment complex in Columbia called Paces Brook.

Missy remembers unpacking the boxes, and then Garrett coming home on a Thursday night to announce he had to fly to Pittsburgh to repossess some pianos, telling her he would be back that Sunday. Missy was suspicious of this surprise event until Garrett had roses delivered to her as he flew out of town. He came back late Sunday night, saying he had missed his first flight from Pittsburgh.

On October 28, a duplicitous Garrett said he was depressed again and shipped Missy off to Boston, this time to visit a girlfriend. He did so by presenting her with a ticket on a train that passed through Columbia at four in the morning. There was an argument before they left, with Garrett knocking down the shelves in a bedroom closet as she packed. In an attempt at placating her, he promised to meet Missy at her mother's house in Rockville for the Thanksgiving holidays. When she left, he telephoned Vicky.

"She's gone," Garrett said.

"Then I'm on my way," Vicky promised.

Vicky was by now deeply in love with Garrett. When she arrived, he hired her to be Westbrook Music's Director of Music Education. The two began working blissfully together. It was to be idyllic for a few short months. Vicky remembers seeing a side of him that was almost saintly.

"Sam Westbrook had a black man named Eddie Wilson who worked for him," Vicky recalled, citing one such example. "Sam underpaid him. Poor Eddie only made five-fifteen an hour, even though he had been there for years. Garrett's the kind of person who would give someone the shirt off his back, and that December he went out and bought each of Eddie's five children a pair of shoes as a Christmas present."

But Vicky's career at Westbrook was soon cut short by her inability to get along with the owner. "She wanted to attend a convention in California. Sam wouldn't let her go, so she quit," is how Garrett remembers the termination.

Unable to totally let go, but eager to be with Vicky, Garrett telephoned Missy two weeks before the beginning of the Christmas holidays in 1992 to let her know he wouldn't be home for the holidays. He was still too depressed, he claimed. Missy was incensed.

"Then forget it," she yelled into the phone. She packed her bags and took another train to Raleigh, this time to stay with her younger sister, Melissa, and her sister's stockbroker husband, Chris Shoffner. Missy spent only a few days with Melissa and Chris. While she was in the North Carolina capital, her girlfriend in Cocoa Beach called and implored her to come to Florida for the New Year's holiday, and then stay to try and get a job there after the first of the year. Stop thinking about Garrett for a while, she counseled. Missy borrowed her sister's car for the short drive to Columbia, South Carolina, to collect some clothing and her cat—the other elderly feline had died—for what she thought would be a few months' stay in Cocoa Beach.

But when Missy went to the apartment, her key wouldn't work. Garrett had changed the locks. She went to Westbrook Music and confronted him.

"He had Vicky working there as his Director of Music Education, and now here's Missy coming in one door and Vicky going out the other," a former employee of the store said. "Garrett gave her a hundred dollars, but he wouldn't give Missy her clothes. He didn't want her in the apartment. Garrett became so angry during the confrontation he kicked at her sister's car."

Missy drove her sister's car back to Raleigh and then went on to Cocoa Beach. Inexplicably, Garrett soon called her there, saying he was depressed, but that he still loved her. He would make it all up to her by coming to Cocoa Beach for Christmas, he promised. A few days later Missy got a Federal Express overnight letter saying that even though he loved her he wouldn't be coming to Florida for Christmas after all.

Missy soon got a chance to give tit for tat.

Garrett and Vicky showed up in Maryland the day after Christmas and wanted to get into a mini-storage room he had rented with Missy to keep their possessions. But Missy had changed the locks because she was afraid he would sell everything in it if he got the chance. Garrett became angry at being locked out, but was unable to get her to budge.

Missy's girlfriend in Cocoa Beach began urging her to get her cat and the clothes in South Carolina before Garrett disposed of them as a kind of revenge. Two days after Christmas, Missy, who tried to avoid planes at all costs, arrived by train in Columbia well after midnight, took a cab to the apartment, and knocked at the door.

"It's Missy, it's Missy," she said. There was no answer. She went around and knocked on the sliding glass doors, repeating the refrain again. When there was no answer, she decided there was no one home. What happened next is her version of the altercation.

"I saw our car wasn't in the lot, and so I picked up a log to break a window. A flashlight and a gun appeared, and the next thing I knew a policeman has thrown me to the ground and he's threatening to arrest me for burglary. Garrett came out and told the police that we had been separated for months. He was lying. I asked for my cat and he said it was at the vet's. The police wouldn't help me and offered to take me to Red Roof motel, saying it was a domestic dispute between us."

One of the reasons Garrett wouldn't let her in the apartment was because Vicky was inside with him. And Vicky, who later admitted being there, thought the altercation was "one of the most bizarre situations I've ever faced."

Missy got on the next train to Florida, but Garrett, still unable to ever shed a woman willingly, showed up in Cocoa Beach with her cat and some other possessions a few days later. Missy remembered that he claimed he was miserable at Westbrook Music and wanted to be back in Florida with her. Garrett said he was depressed about the way his career was going. He apologized for everything he had done to her, adding that he thought about their son a lot and saying how much he missed him.

A month later, midway through the last week of January 1993, Garrett got another chance in the wholesale music business, this time working for the Technics division of Panasonic Electronics. Sam Westbrook seemed happy to have him go. His boss said Garrett left owing him a lot of money.

"I told Garrett I would pay for his move and he wanted four thousand dollars cash. I told him fifteen hundred would be enough," Westbrook remembered in 1997. "He asked me to wire him the money and then he said the brakes on his car were bad and wanted another eight hundred. The next thing I knew he called me on a Tuesday from the Ramada Inn and said, 'We're here.' A few days later he said, 'I know the nicest person. She used to be the director of a church choir in Pittsburgh.' Then I came in one Monday morning, and there was this lady, and Garrett said, 'Here's your new employee. She'll work for nothing. If she sells something, she'll get a commission.' "

Female employees at Westbrook who worked with her said Vicky appeared concerned about her future. She told them she was pregnant and didn't know what to do next.

The women wanted to know the father's name. "He's a friend," Vicky answered.

Sam Westbrook later accused Garrett of stealing five pianos worth about $8,000. His cash advances were never paid back.

"He got me for about fourteen thousand dollars in all," he recalled. Garrett and Vicky disputed Westbrook's claims, adding that the store owner had lowballed Garrett's salary in order to recoup his cash advance, which Garrett admitted was indeed $4,000.

EIGHT

LIKE A LAST BREATH?

Marysa Delores Wilson was conceived on Halloween night, October 31, 1992, in Columbia. Garrett and Vicky had just seen the fish-out-of-water comedy film, *My Cousin Vinny*, and Garrett wanted to name a girl after the movie's female star, Marisa Tomei. When Tomei won the Academy Award for supporting actress the following spring, the choice was assured. Marysa weighed more than seven pounds when she was born on July 18, 1993, in Dallas.

Vicky was more practical. She also wanted to honor her dad Ervin, by giving the child his mother's name, Mary. They both agreed that Marysa would be a great compromise. The middle name, Delores, was Thelma's mother's name. This made for two very happy grandparents despite Vicky's being unwed and as yet legally unable to marry Garrett. The divorce from Missy was still months away. Always unable to restrain himself from the big romantic gesture, no matter how thin his bankroll, Garrett brought a hundred red roses to Vicky's hospital bedside.

Both claimed that Marysa was planned in spite of their being unmarried. They were soul mates, Vicky said. For that reason, they wanted to go ahead and have a child as soon as possible.

Garrett appeared concerned whenever something went awry with their new child. Marysa began to have spells of apnea, with sporadic pauses in her breathing. They placed apnea monitor straps on her chest, using a gel to make the contact points, but it would often malfunction, sending off a screeching alarm. Once, Marysa did stop breathing and began turning blue. Vicky punched her in the chest until she began gasping for air. Garrett became worried he had passed something along to his daughter that was genetic. He talked about testing her at Johns Hopkins Hospital in Maryland.

"I don't know what I'd do if I lost another baby," he told Vicky.

"One night, when she was about eighteen months old, Marysa scooted herself up and into a corner of the crib," Vicky recalled. "She wedged herself in a corner, and I heard a strange noise. Garrett went in. He discovered the trouble. He got her out and handed her to me, but it really shook him up. He cried all night."

Vicky and Garrett made Texas their new home. In January of 1994, a month after the divorce from Missy became final, the two stole away and were wed at the Baylor University Medical Center's chapel. A local piano dealer and his wife were witnesses. At that time, Vicky was employed by Baylor's home health care program.

"I was doing hospice visits and physicals for them. They would pay me fifty dollars for a three-hour visit and then bill me out at one hundred twenty-seven," Vicky recalled. Her second degree was proving to be valuable.

With Missy gone from Garrett's life legally and with all contact between them severed, his next three years would be remembered as golden ones. Vicky said she knew Garrett had cheated during the first six months of their union and admits she did the same. Vicky, though, was determined to make the marriage work, if only for the sake of their daughter. She pressed Garrett into group therapy and he took to it, attending meetings with her every Friday night.

The other reason for these good years is that both were

bringing home substantial salaries. They could finally pay most of their bills. With Garrett selling for Technics and Vicky working for Baylor's health plan, their combined annual income was well over $100,000. The two lived in a number of large houses, each better than the last. They hired a Chinese nanny to take care of Marysa.

The final dwelling was a handsome four-bedroom, three-bath brown-and-beige brick home, rented for $1,300 a month. The house was on Pelican Court, in an upper-middle-class neighborhood a block from Lake Arlington, and midway between Dallas and Fort Worth. It was a lovely residence, perhaps the nicest Garrett had ever lived in, nicer by far than the tract mansion that had forced him into bankruptcy in Damascus, Maryland. There were more than 2,500 square feet, with a soaring thirty-foot-high ceiling in the living room. Three extra-wide French doors in the rear of the house led to a deck and an outdoor whirlpool. Despite the luxuries, Vicky remembered the first months of the marriage as being far from peaches and cream.

"We sure did have some fights," she admitted. "Once I got so angry I spit in his face. Garrett didn't strike back. He's never been violent with me, and for that matter, I've never seen him behave violently with anyone. I don't think he can behave that way."

At Panasonic's Technics division, Garrett was considered one of their star salesmen. He was given several nicknames. One such moniker was the Tin Man, after the Danny DeVito/Richard Dreyfuss film, *Tin Men*, a 1987 Barry Levinson comedy-drama about fast-talking aluminum-siding confidence men. Traveling five days a week, Garrett had most of the larger southern states as his domain—Arkansas, Louisiana, Mississippi, Oklahoma, and Texas. Part of his job found him arranging trade shows for piano dealers in hotel ballrooms, where the retailers were hosted and Technics keyboards were demonstrated.

His pal Dennis Awe, who once toured with Liberace and often wore two of the flamboyant showman's old rings on his fingers, was one of the performers at these exhibitions. Liza Minnelli's former music arranger, Dom Chiccetti, was another. Garrett's beefy strength was called upon several times. He helped to install musical equipment in Elton John's Atlanta home and became a Technics sales hero by arranging to trade a $60,000 organ to the management of the baseball stadium that housed the American League's Texas Rangers. In return, the firm got three years' worth of season tickets with which to entertain piano dealers, and advertising promotions.

"He was a natural," Awe raved. "Once we gave an organ demonstration in Hot Springs, Arkansas, where we hired dancers to do a scene from *Carmen*. It was the one where the man and the woman exchange a rose they're holding between their teeth from one mouth to another. Garrett rushed out at the last minute to buy a hundred and seventy-five roses. He passed one to each of the women in the audience. It went over big, real big. After that we started calling him our pied piper of warmth."

His boss at Technics, Tim Storrs, said that no matter what the company would ask of him, Garrett tried to be the ideal employee.

"I remember a trade show in Dallas. We were setting up in a hotel. We had to do it mostly ourselves, and Garrett was called upon to move these desks from one side of the room to the other. He lifted them up as if they were feathers. Then someone decided we would do it another way, and so Garrett had to lift them up again and put them back where they came from. He laughed about it afterward. 'You just wanted to see if I could do it,' he told me."

Garrett was considered a model citizen by his employer, convincing Technics to adopt East Handley Elementary School in Fort Worth, where the company donated free instruments to the music department and gave money so that the indigent students could have music lessons. Garrett would sometimes show up there, performing concerts for the children in the school cafeteria.

But after three years, Panasonic revamped its Technics

division, cut back on territories, and Garrett was out of a job again. His short period of making more than $60,000 a year in the wholesale music business was over.

Mary Floyd "Missy" Anastasi was a woman obsessed with vengeance. She believed, with justification, that her former husband was a philanderer and a con man. It was more than that, though—much more. She saw him as the murderer of his own flesh and blood, a man who was pure evil. Missy was determined to get justice for Garrett Michael.

Missy contacted her cousin, Joe Anastasi, a sergeant in the Montgomery County Police Department. He was more than willing to serve as an unofficial listening post for her. She also knew a lawyer, Patricia Schrein, a friend whom she had met while working a part-time job. Missy knew her well enough to call her Patty, a nickname only friends used. Schrein had been a public defender in the Seattle area courts before moving to Maryland, and though some of Missy's friends warned her against working with a bleeding heart, she encouraged the attorney to work for her as a volunteer. It was Schrein who had voiced the magic words she most wanted to hear.

"I believe you, Missy," she said.

On June 14, 1994, Missy visited Patty Schrein. The lawyer had already gotten things moving by contacting Lee Smith at Allstate Insurance to find out the amount of Garrett's policy. Missy had never been told the exact figure. She didn't as yet know the $100,000 MetLife policy existed.

Schrein told Missy they needed to hire a private investigator, and Missy went along with the suggestion. Missy also made an appointment to visit Peter Banks at the National Center for Missing and Exploited Children across the Potomac in Alexandria. After Missy told her story, it was Banks, a former Washington, D.C., cop, who contacted the police for her.

Several days later, Missy and Schrein met with Larry Robinson, a stocky private investigator who headed Chesapeake Investigations. At 7:30 on the evening of June 20, they had a meeting with the Montgomery County cops. It was there she met Detective Meredith Dominick for the first time.

Missy and Schrein began telling their story to Dominick. The lawyer was about to be married and still used her maiden name of Hemma.

Patty Schrein had put together a crude timeline on Garrett for the meeting. She had some of the details of his criminal background already. The biggest piece of evidence was in learning a day before the appointment with Dominick that the Allstate policy had been for $50,000. The evidence was not enough to bring even the thought of an indictment by those in Montgomery County's police department. Why would someone come forward seven years after her baby's death? The woman could be a neurotic or worse.

Dominick was a husky woman with broad shoulders honed by her teen years as a female jock. She had once been a competitive swimmer—the butterfly stroke was her specialty. She had also been on her high school field hockey team and had wanted to be a nurse until she learned she couldn't stand the sight of blood. Dominick was a rare commodity—a female homicide detective with a degree from a major university. Becoming a cop who dealt with rape and murder was never in her mind as a youth.

She looked at the timeline politely. There wasn't nearly enough evidence to prosecute a former husband for murder, Dominick thought. Missy might be imagining mayhem where none existed.

The report from Larry Robinson came back in September. It showed that Garrett had sometimes reversed his name and gone under the name of Wilson E. Garrett. It also validated Missy's suspicions that he was far behind on his credit card payments. Details surrounding his criminal convictions were handed over. And Robinson had the court records of his previous marriages and divorces.

Larry Robinson soon located Debbie Oliver, now Debbie Fennell, but about to begin divorce proceedings from her second husband. Debbie was said to have a medical condition that a friend described to Robinson as possibly terminal. The first time Robinson phoned her, he talked to a small child, one of Debbie's children. The second time, someone answered at her home, and Debbie came to the phone. Robinson described the nature of his investigation. Debbie became emotional and started crying.

"He killed that woman's baby, too, didn't he?" she sobbed into the phone. Robinson thought that was extraordinary, though Debbie stopped and wouldn't go any further. Debbie said she didn't want to get involved. She told him to make any further calls to her boyfriend, who happened to be a cop in the adjoining county. Before ringing off, Debbie blurted out that she could tell him some incredible stories.

One of them was that on the night Brandi died, Garrett had told her, "I feel bad I haven't helped with Brandi. Why don't you take a sleeping pill tonight, and I'll take care of the baby?" Debbie said she had heard the baby cry, but Garrett had gotten up to feed her, and the next thing she knew, Brandi was dead.

The sleuth whistled to himself over these revelations.

Robinson also discovered Garrett had two different insurance policies on his daughter. This intrigued him as much as Debbie's outburst.

"The dates on the policies are very suspicious, based on the date of death of Brandi Jean Wilson coupled with the amount of the policies," Robinson reported.

Missy was told to find every scrap of paper she could get her hands on that documented her seven years of marriage to Garrett. There wasn't much—a lot of the records were in Garrett's hands. So Missy called Garrett when she was sure he wouldn't be there and put a message on his machine, asking for all of her personal belongings, photos, and the videotape that had both of their voices on it talking to their son, Garrett Michael. Missy almost blew it when Garrett called back twice trying to talk to her.

"I don't want to hear your voice," she said.

Told that Missy was harassing her husband, Vicky phoned Missy's Boston friend, Karen Thompson, complaining that Garrett's former wife wouldn't leave him alone. The go-between suggested all would be well if they mailed back the personal effects Missy was requesting. They did so, but both Vicky and Garrett would later claim they were never ever really ignored by Missy. From time to time, anonymous faxes would be sent to Garrett's employer or to their neighbors, usually labeling him both an ex-con and a murderer.

Perhaps the best move Missy ever made was changing the locks on the mini-storage room. Larry Robinson had told her to keep looking, and so Missy and her cousin, Regina Marmo, went to the storage place and found two footlockers. Garrett was a pack rat. He was not only unable to willingly give up a woman, he was also reluctant to give up a piece of paper that had his name on it. Spilling out of one of the lockers was virtually every check he had written since 1977, all of the insurance policies, and other personal papers. On top of everything was a machete.

Schrein, enthused by Missy's discovery of the footlocker and her recovery of the baby video and her personal effects, wrote a memorandum to Larry Robinson on September 20, 1994, that began, "String 'im up," stressing urgency. Patty cited what she believed to be Debbie Oliver Fennell's impending death and an immediate need to save the life of Garrett's latest child. She asked for ten pieces of information from the private eye, including Brandi's autopsy report, the divorce papers filed by Debbie, any bank records, and most important, the insurance policies. Patty told Robinson to send the information to her and to bill Missy.

Vicky and Garrett had a plan they thought would make them a lot of money. Since Vicky was getting fifty dollars an hour for what Baylor Home Health Care was billing out at nearly two and a half times that rate, they would start their own organization, provide the same services, and pocket the difference. All they needed were a few contracts. Vicky was a licensed social worker and, under Texas law, able to give physicals anywhere in the state. They named their firm Focused Care Consultants.

The two got what appeared to be lucrative work immediately. One assignment was doing physicals for the New York Life Insurance Company. They were required to do weight, height, and blood pressure measurements and then help the insurance applicants fill out a long questionnaire on the state of their health. It looked to be simple. Vicky got the pacts by agreeing to service a vast territory that jutted out 120 miles in every direction from Dallas–Fort Worth. The competition cared only about servicing the more profitable close-in metropolitan areas of the two cities.

The plan turned out to be much harder to execute than first imagined. Vicky often had to make a 250-mile round-trip to visit a single patient. Focused Care had the volume, at one time employing twenty-six full- or part-time health care workers, but most jobs were financial losers. Texas was full of vast spaces, and the competition had been smart by opting not to go after the outlying home health care business.

"Our other mistake was doing too good a job," Garrett recalled. "We spent more time than we should have with some of the older people. We cared too much about them."

Garrett remembered doing stunts in order to attract attention to their business. At one point, Vicky donned a bunny costume at Easter, visiting children and adults at a Fort Worth kidney dialysis center while Garrett badgered radio stations into covering the event. He educated the radio jocks, telling them that kidney cleansing was a normal routine of some people's day.

On February 16, 1995, Meredith Dominick and Peter Picariello, a gruff, stocky detective who was Dominick's older male counterpart in the Montgomery County major crimes division, sat down with Missy for more than an hour. Picariello, who asked nearly all the questions, wanted to hear Missy's story while trying to evaluate whether or not she would make a credible witness. He began by asking her to reenact the death of her baby.

"I would like to start off with the actual event itself. Tell us what happened," he asked.

"From the day the baby died? Okay. It was in August. It was August twenty-second, and I worked for Montgomery County public schools, and I had been off from school because I had the baby. He was born March twelfth. I had been off since the end of February.

"I had been taking care of the baby and I was going back to work the next week. I think August twenty-second was a Saturday in 1987. I was going back to work on Monday and had arranged for day care. The baby was going to be in a day care center. We lived in Germantown. It was early Saturday morning, still dark. I remember it was dark and the baby cried. I had a baby monitor. You know, we had one in the baby's room and we had one that you hear. It was right next to my ear and I woke up because I always did."

Missy had rehearsed this story in her mind for years. She had all the facts memorized.

"I was the only one that ever got up and fed the baby, and Garrett Michael woke up every two and a half hours each day of his life, practically. I got up and started to go feed him, and my ex-husband, who had never offered, never volunteered to wake up, never even asked why, well, he heard the baby crying over the monitor and woke up. He said, 'I'll go feed him, I'm going to start doing this.' He was going to take him to day care. I worked at the school system, and I went to the school earlier than he went to work. He said, 'I'm going to have to start getting up and getting used to it, so I'll go feed him.' And I said, 'Well, okay.' "

"You used a formula?"

"Yes, a bottle. And so he went in, and I was awake—"

"Do you have any idea what time of the morning this was?"

"It was still dark and it was August. It feels like it was five or five-thirty, getting close to where it was kind of daylight but it was still dark when the ambulance came because they asked me to go turn the lights on."

"Okay."

"So, anyway, it was dark and I heard him in our bedroom, he had to go down the hall to get to the baby's room. It was big, it was a townhouse and I heard him go in. He picked up the baby and it sounded like he sat in the rocking chair and fed him. Then I never heard any noise—"

Picariello interjected. Her voice was passionate, believable, but he had to get the sequence right.

"Did he go to the kitchen first? He had to go to the kitchen to get formula."

"Well, we had a townhouse and I had surgery. I had had a C-section. So from the very first week when I came home from the hospital we had a system where I had a cooler upstairs and I had a little bottle warmer."

"So the formula was right in the bedroom?"

"It was right in between the bedrooms."

"You didn't heat it up before giving it to him?"

"Yeah, I had a bottle warmer."

"Okay, a bottle warmer and a cooler were in there. So, the bottle was in the cooler and then you used a bottle warmer?"

"Yeah, right."

"Okay."

"And you know what? To tell you the truth, I don't remember him—I stayed in bed—I mean he said he would go feed the baby, and I don't remember if I heard him heating the bottle up, but I—"

Again, the cop broke in to ask a question.

"Do bottle warmers make any noise when they heat up?"

"No, it was just this little tiny—"

"How long does it take?"

"A few minutes, a few minutes."

"So, really at this point, you're unsure of the time? Right?"

"Right. It was still dark, but it had to be after four, four-thirty."

"Why do you know that?" Picariello wasn't going to let Missy get away with anything.

"Because it was getting more close to morning than versus being midnight, so it was—"

"What time did you go to bed that night?"

Missy couldn't remember. It had been 1987, and she told

him she couldn't remember what happened. She tried to help him.

"We usually watched the news, so I would say eleven, eleven-thirty."

"You're just guessing because you cannot remember?"

Missy admitted she couldn't.

"So the baby was fed every two and a half hours?"

"That's right. I do remember this. He worked late, and I had been at my mother's house because my parents had out-of-town guests and we had been with them all day. I had been over there, and he worked at a mall. He didn't get off work until after nine-thirty or ten and so it had . . . I know it was late. But honestly, I don't remember."

"So he gets off work at nine-thirty or ten. You are at your mother's."

"Yes."

"Okay. Did he meet you at your mother's house?"

"No, I just went home and he was at home."

"You just went to your house? You were still up when he got there?"

"I can't remember. I don't remember that part. I remember putting the baby to bed, but not—"

"What time do you think that was?"

"To put the baby to bed? Nine-thirty or so. I mean, I would still feed him every two and a half hours, so I more than likely fed him at midnight and that's why I'm remembering the next feeding."

"You don't remember feeding him that particular night, though? Prior to your husband getting up?"

"No, I don't. He was just five and a half months old, and he was just starting to sleep longer. You know what I mean?"

Detective Picariello cleared his throat before asking the next question. He was a father himself and knew something about the habits of babies.

"He was just stretching it out?"

"Yep. He didn't stretch it out much. He was just starting to."

"All right. Go ahead. Your husband got up. . . ."

"He offered to feed—"

"You could hear your husband in the child's room?"

"I heard what I thought was someone in the rocking chair."

"A rocking chair going back and forth?"

"I didn't hear it go back and forth."

"I mean, I want to know what you heard," Picariello said. His voice was not unsympathetic, but he wasn't coddling her, either.

"What I heard was somebody, you know, moving around, and what I thought sounded like somebody sitting down in a chair. I'm imagining it was the rocking chair because that was the only chair in there."

"Okay. What you heard was somebody sitting down. You didn't hear a rocking chair."

Picariello wanted Missy to be precise.

"That's right. Then I didn't hear anything and I thought...he didn't talk to the baby or anything while he was feeding him, and then I heard, there was no crying, there was, there was nothing. The next thing I heard a person, I thought it was him, standing up, going to the bed, it sounded like a pat, like maybe he put the baby down. It sounded like someone patting him on the back. Like trying to get him to burp, is what I thought. But then I heard this sigh. This is the noise that made every hair on my body stand up. I just heard this and...I mean it has been in my mind ever since I heard it. And it was just a sigh. It was like a last breath is the only way I can describe it. I don't know..."

Missy tried to imitate the sound she had heard for the two detectives. It came out breathy, like a bad Marilyn Monroe impression.

"That's what it was like and every hair on my body stood up and instead of just running in the room I jumped up and I had these cats and they were on me because we were up. They wanted me to feed them and we were in the town-house, I went right downstairs and I fed them and it couldn't have been a few minutes..."

Picariello knew that didn't make much sense.

"Why didn't you go in the baby's room?"

"I don't know. I wish I knew to this very day."

Picariello and Dominick exchanged glances. With the cats first and the baby second, they definitely had a problem.

NINE

AND THEN HE WAS DEAD

"So you can't explain why you went and fed the cats as opposed to—"

Missy interrupted. "I was scared. I was afraid. I don't know."

"I'm trying to make sense out of that."

"I'm trying to make sense out of it, too, because I think if I had gone in there I could have revived my child. I just jumped up and went and fed the cats and by that time, when I came up I went into that room and he was on his stomach. I went to cover him up and he didn't feel right. I put my hand under his mouth and there was foam. I couldn't see, it was dark and I picked him up. . . ."

Missy's voice was emotional now and the words tumbled from her mouth quickly, nonstop. She no longer listened to Picariello's questions.

"Where was your husband?"

". . . and then he was dead. Garrett was back in our bedroom and then he was in the bathroom when I went in. My child was limp and everything, and I just picked him up like this and I went down the hall and into the room. I was screaming 'Garrett! Garrett!' We had a bathroom in our bedroom."

"How did you normally have the kid sleep? Did the kid sleep on his stomach or back?"

"On his stomach. That was the normal routine."

"So you heard this?"

Missy was suddenly irritable. The detective seemed to doubt her. "Just give it up."

Picariello wasn't about to go off track at this point. "These questions have to be asked."

"I know, and I want to be asked because it's very important."

"I have doubts in my mind about the sequence. I'll try and clear it up. The baby wakes up, you hear him on the monitor, the baby's crying, the baby's hungry."

"Right."

"And at this point your husband, for the first time... Was this the first time?"

"He absolutely offered to get up and feed him for the very first time."

"The very first time?"

The detective had to be sure.

"Yeah, I was always the one to take care of him."

He asked the question again, watching Missy's body language, alert for the telltale signs that signaled a lie.

"The very first time he offers to get up with him?"

"Yep."

"He goes into the room and you hear activity in the room. Then you hear at some point in time—do you have any idea how long it was before you heard the sigh?"

"How long was it?"

Detective Picariello was determined to show her again he knew something about being a father. "Because I know sometimes, especially at five months, there's no guarantee the kid is going back to sleep when he wakes up."

"That's right, and he didn't ever do that in the morning at this point. He didn't ever go right back to sleep and that is probably why it seems so strange to me. He was always ready to wake up. You know. He was ready, he was hard to get back to sleep."

Pete Picariello continued to riff on what he knew about infant feeding and the sleep habits of babies for the next two minutes. Then he slipped back into the cat problem. He focused on Missy's mannerisms, still trying to determine if this was a concocted story by a vengeful wife or the tragic tale of a still-grieving mother.

"Okay, after you heard the sigh is when you got up?"

"Right."

"You went downstairs to take care of the cats?"

"Yep."

"When you went downstairs or were in the process of going downstairs, where was your husband?"

"When I went down I didn't see him. He must have still been in the bedroom."

"The baby's room?"

"Yes. The baby's bedroom. And the house was like this, it was a townhouse and the baby's room was back here and the hallway was right here and we had our bedroom here and there was one bathroom and the stairs were right here, so—"

"It was two bedrooms?"

"Three bedrooms. There were two bedrooms over here and the baby was in the back one."

"Right and left. They usually split them. Okay. All right." Picariello made a mental note to get the floor plan of the house to check it out.

"When I went down to feed them, he was still in the nursery. And by the time I fed the cats, he was out of there and in our bathroom, which was on the right."

"When you came back upstairs, he was in the bathroom?"

"Yep. I guess, because he wasn't in the baby's room. I mean . . . inside, you know."

"So from the time you heard the sigh, actually from the time your husband left the bed until you came back upstairs from the cats, you never saw your husband?"

"Exactly. I never did."

"All right, and how long were you downstairs with the cats?"

"Three minutes. I opened the refrigerator, put out the food, and ran back upstairs to the baby's room immediately."

Three minutes? How did she know it was three minutes? he wondered.

"Okay. Pick it up from there."

"I guess I was never sure anybody could do anything right but me. And so I was going to cover him up and I went to cover him up and he didn't feel right. I felt him and he didn't feel right, he was . . . I touched him and felt under his mouth, right here and there was foam and I didn't look at it. I don't know what color it was. It felt different than uh, baby spit-up. It was foam and it felt strange and I just picked him up and he was totally limp and I turned around, ran down the hall and ran into our bedroom screaming, 'Garrett! Garrett!' you know, and at that point I said, the only time I ever said this to him, until May of 1994 was 'What did you do to him?' and then I screamed, you know, 'Garrett, call 911.' He came out of the bathroom at that point and his face was white as a sheet. He didn't know what I was screaming about, but at that point he just looked at me and I screamed 'Dial 911' but I think I ran to the phone. I don't remember who picked the phone up but I put the baby down on our bed. I think it was me, but I can't be positive. I think I went to the phone and dialed 911. But I know it was me giving the address because I was going . . . because I had to think where I was, you know. I said, '11437' which was the street number and I said, 'My baby's not breathing,' and so then he was on the bed and I was praying 'God, how could you do this? You just gave us this baby,' or whatever, you know, and so, anyway . . ."

Missy stopped speaking. She was breathless. There was silence. Picariello urged her to go on. "You screamed that at him?"

"What he did to the baby? I did one time."

"And he made no response?"

"No, he never did. Now I think back on the whole thing, he never made excuses for anything. He never described what happened to anybody. Nobody ever asked. I thought there was going to be a police investigation. There never was. And Garrett just sat there. He never offered anything. But anyway, the people on the telephone told me how to do it—I mean the CPR. They told me to hold his nose and to breathe in and I was doing that and after a few minutes they said, 'Are the lights on? Can you go turn the lights on?' I said okay and they said keep doing CPR. So I handed Garrett the phone and I went downstairs because I guess the only thing I could think of was to let the experts just get here and maybe they could do something. I handed him the phone and I don't know if he did CPR like they were telling him. I guess they were going to tell him how to continue to do CPR. I went downstairs and turned the lights on and opened the front door. It wasn't but a minute before the ambulance people came. I said 'upstairs' and so she ran up and then came down carrying him and she said, 'He's still warm.'

"I said, 'Shady Grove Adventist Hospital?' and she said, 'Yeah, Shady Grove.' That was it, and then I went up and put something on and we got our keys and went out in the car. We had two cars, a Saab and a Mazda RX-7 and they were parked right next to each other. The Saab was the car that I drove. There was a car seat in the backseat strapped in. It was the regular children's seat and I . . . because we had been using the infant seat."

"The baby is transported by the squad?"

"Right, the ambulance squad. They were gone."

"You drove your car?"

"Yeah, but this is what I think was strange, and I have a hard time with. We went out to get in the car and it was my inclination to get in the car and just drive to the hospital. And the first thing he did was unlock the Saab. We could have easily just gotten in the Mazda where there was no car seat or anything. He unlocks the Saab and goes in the back and takes the car seat out and throws it in the Mazda and we go off in the Saab. I don't know why that made such a strange impression on me. I just felt, why did you do all this? All we need to do is get him to the hospital or whatever. So, anyway, when we got to the hospital I called my brother and my sister-in-law and they came. The nurses and doctors came out and said they were trying to do things and they hadn't been able to get a response."

Was there a subconscious knowledge that his son would never come home and thus the infant car seat wasn't needed? Garrett's explanation for the seemingly bizarre car seat removal is that he thought Missy might want to pick up a relative or a friend on the way to the hospital. He said he wanted to make space for them and chose the Saab because it had more room.

Pete Picariello took Missy through her first meeting at the Holiday Spa. She told him that one of the first sentences out of Garrett's mouth the day they met was "I've been married before and I lost a baby to SIDS." Picariello was interested in Garrett's feelings about the loss.

"Did he ever mention the details, circumstances, what he felt, anything about that first child to you?"

"His feelings about it?"

"Yeah."

"No, he never did."

"He never talked about it?"

"We talked about it a little bit, but I thought . . . that if he wants to talk about it we would talk about it. You know, I'll let him bring it up. I just thought he seemed to have adjusted very well. He didn't have a chip on his shoulder. That he had gotten through that death and . . ."

Detective Picariello interrupted. He wanted to know more about the child who had died and when the two had made the determination to have children. He asked her when she had decided.

"Immediately. I wanted to . . . I thought I was old."

"He never . . . okay, what was your reaction? I mean, did you start quizzing him on what happened before? I mean, did you talk about it?"

"I did. I said, 'I think we should go for genetic counseling. I am going to mention it to the doctors and you know, the people I go to.' I was a Kaiser Permanente member and I said, 'I want to mention it to the people that I go to.' The only thing I ever remember him saying when we would talk is, 'They couldn't find anything so they put SIDS on the death certificate.' They could never find anything."

"Did you ever discuss the insurance? Did he ever tell you there was insurance on the first kid?"

"Before we were married and when he was telling me what happened, he said that his ex-wife couldn't get over the baby's death, the first baby. Her name was Brandi and with the insurance money . . . He said, 'I took her to Florida to get over the baby's death and we traveled a lot and then headed back, and then the money was gone and she didn't get over it.' "

"How much money did he tell you it was?"

"I never asked him. He never hinted."

"He didn't tell you and you didn't ask?" Picariello was surprised at her lack of curiosity.

"He said it was a lot of money and they spent it all. He said, 'I spent it all on her trying to get her to accept the baby's death and she couldn't do it. And when I came back she charged a lot of things on credit cards and she wrecked our cars,' and they had all these, uh, expenses, and he said, 'I got into trouble because I was working at a bank and I embezzled some money.' I felt so bad for him."

None of this was news to the cops. Missy had told most of this part before. What Picariello wanted Missy to talk about now was why Garrett had purchased the insurance policy.

"When the baby was born, it must have been a month or two, I don't remember exactly when, and he said, 'I applied for insurance for the baby,' one day just out of the blue, and I said, 'Why?' because that made me feel really weird, because I had known that he talked about insurance before and I didn't remember my parents having any insurance on us. He said, 'Well, my dad had insurance on me and I just thought it was nice to do because later I turned it in and bought a car,' or something like that."

The detective asked Missy what was the name of the insurance company his father had policies with, but Missy didn't know.

"He never told me. They did have a lot of insurance. I know that now."

"On him?"

"On all of them."

"On all of them?"

Missy didn't say anything. She remembered some of the records from the footlocker she had found.

"They did have insurance it looks like, from things I have seen recently that were old family records of his family. His family is all dead."

"So, he was telling the truth on that?"

"Yeah. It was like they planned well for their family."

The cop went over the Allstate policy on Garrett Michael for the next ten minutes. There were several signatures that said Mary F. Wilson but Missy couldn't remember signing the documents. She said she never knew how much money Garrett got from the insurance companies for the death of their son.

"He never told you how much cash?" It seemed that was something a spouse might want to know.

"No, he didn't. He just came home one night and threw ten thousand dollars on the bed."

"There had to have been a time frame. What was it?"

"It was October or November of 1987, because he had been made manager of the store in Landover and he came home late one night and he threw all this money on the bed, and I remember his face was all lit up, all happy. He got the money out and I said, 'What is this? Where has this been?' And he said, 'This is the insurance money I collected on the baby, insurance money from the baby.' And I said, 'Where did you get this money from?' He said he had kept it in a bank."

"He told you where he got it?"

"Yeah, he worked at Landover Mall, and he said he had it in a bank over there. And I said, 'Is this all of it?' Because at one point he had alluded to the point that there was a fairly large policy. I never asked him how much. He said there was more, but he used it to buy some dining room furniture."

The detective began asking questions about the family members and friends she had told of her suspicion that her husband killed their baby. After Missy recounted each person she told, he asked for their home phone numbers. She also said she had discussed the death with John Farley.

"I remember on the day of the funeral, we came back to our house and you know how you always have food. I don't remember if I told my cousin up in the bedroom at my parents' house...but it was that day. I thought Garrett did it. I thought he killed the baby. He has a friend named John Farley, who—and I don't know whether John considers himself a friend anymore, but he's someone he has known forever, somebody that he's grown up with. John was at our house in the backyard, and I called him over and tried to get him aside. I said, 'John, do you think Garrett has anything to do with these babies?' He just looked at me and he said, 'I don't think so.' But John does not know any of the circumstances, I never told anybody any of the circumstances."

Picariello requested John Farley's phone number. Then he asked her questions about her meetings with the SIDS people and how they helped mollify Missy's misgivings about her son's death. He also wanted to know if she had ever spoken to Garrett directly about her doubts. "Did you confront him with your suspicions?"

"No, I never did."

"Never right to his face?"

"No, I never did it. And then a year—"

Picariello interrupted. "Why not?"

"I don't know. I guess—I don't know. I just honestly don't know. I guess I still thought he was a good person and bad things just happened to him and I..."

"But you didn't think that. What you thought was that he was responsible, but you never confronted him."

The detective was wondering whether a jury would buy this story. It was hard to believe they would. Missy said she had tried to put it out of her mind. Picariello wasn't going to let her get away with that. "What brought it back into your mind?"

"Well, strange things happened through the rest of our marriage."

"No more children?"

"No, I told Garrett we were not having any more kids. I told him we were not having sex. I wanted to adopt kids. I figured if he would let me adopt children, then it didn't really matter where we got them, it didn't matter whether they were ours or not. He went with me to talk to a lawyer that handled adoptions. Then I went to an adoption class and he never went to one of those with me. Somehow my dad found out, and I went to the adoption classes for six weeks, one night a week. He never went to them with me. I did want to adopt. But he got us in financial trouble."

"Yeah, but I want to know, what triggered you?"

"Okay, then we got into financial trouble and we had to move out of town."

"That has nothing to do with this."

"It does, because what I'm getting ready to tell you is how it first really got suspicious."

"Okay."

Then Missy told the cops the suspicion she had formulated in her mind. It sounded crazy, unbelievable. She was convinced her former husband's occupation was killing innocents while they slept in their beds. "I know this is what he does for a living. That he is going to do this and he is going to do it again. This is why I came to you. He got involved with another woman without me knowing it, and the whole time telling me 'I love you,' the whole thing. I never had a reason to think that he wanted out of our marriage and wanted a divorce. He claimed he was depressed and asked me to go visit a friend and I ended up being away from him and he got a job. He had been fired from a few jobs and then had gotten another job and was going to move to Texas. We were going to do this and we are going to do that and we are going..."

"This is 1992, '93, or '94?"

"I tell you I need my notes at this point. Wait a minute."

"The only reason I'm asking you is because you left 1987 five years ago."

"Right, I know, I know. In 1993."

"So, six years have passed."

"And things have made me suspicious, but . . ."

"Suspicious because of the way he deals with money?"

"Right."

Picariello had it figured out. "I guess what you are telling me, but if I'm wrong, jump in—he was somewhat of a con artist?"

"Yes. Exactly. My brother would describe him as that, exactly."

"But for six years, I mean, it's 1993."

"Right. We had gone through a lot of things, I thought about adoptions. There were times when I didn't have any idea we had money. He had trouble with money during that time, but I thought we were getting straight and going to try to adopt a kid. And what happened was I guess he lost his job. I think he was fired, but he told me he quit. That's when I found out he was running around with other women and had been running around with women always but had been lying to me for a year. He was talking to me as if everything was fine except that he was a little depressed. And I get ready to move to Texas and I went to visit him and I came back and this woman calls me."

Picariello cleared his throat. He knew Missy was not going to like what he was going to say. But he had to say it. "You told me that. I'm trying to figure out why, to be perfectly honest with you, trying to figure out why this occurs in 1987 and you contact the Montgomery County Police in 1994. Now, I'm going to play the devil's advocate. Let's say you're on the stand and I'm the defense attorney playing games with you. I'm going to say that the only reason you reported this to the police is because you got jilted."

"Exactly."

"Is that the only reason?"

"Not at all."

"Then why did you wait seven years? What is your rationalization?"

"I guess the last piece of the puzzle fell into place. Which is what I said to him."

"And what is this last piece of the puzzle?"

Missy recited what she had told Garrett. "Now that I see what you are capable of to the extent of all the things you could do."

"You mean the con artist?"

"Everything, the whole act."

"You're making a jump from a con artist to murder?"

Missy wanted the cops to accept her story. She didn't know how to make them believe her except to repeat herself. "Because there was a baby involved. There was a new baby involved. I said, 'I know what you did to my son,' and he said to me, 'You'd be dead if you were here.' "

"The problem is we have no police report."

"I know."

"And I'm trying to—did you tell any non-family members? Any medical personnel? A simple thing like who was feeding the baby. Did anybody other than you know that?"

"I think I told Mary Ann Finnegan, but I'm not sure, it's been so long ago. Because I went into no details that he was the last one to see the baby alive."

Meredith Dominick spoke up for the first time. "How about anyone at the hospital?"

Picariello liked her question. "That's what I was looking for."

"I said to the nurses and doctors, I remember standing, we all stood and they said to me, 'How did this happen?' And I said, 'He went and fed the baby, and then I went in and found him dead.' "

"He never did CPR on the baby?"

"Not to my knowledge. When I handed him the phone, he should have, but I didn't see him. Then I went to run downstairs and let the paramedics in."

Meredith Dominick asked two more questions. She became a nurse. "When you brought him into your bedroom, what was his color?"

"It was almost normal, I mean, it didn't look blue to me or anything. It didn't look like he...He wasn't stiff, either. I mean, he was just limp. It was like a doll, I mean—"

"What about his temperature? Did he feel warm?"

"Not cold, not nothing. Because I remember holding the foot and that's when I said to you—I just repeated that I said, 'Oh, God. You just gave him to me. How could you do this?' Because his foot didn't feel cold or hot. I mean, it just must have felt normal. And he didn't look funny in color."

Picariello and Dominick both knew a lot of homicides went unprosecuted. You picked your spots, and this one looked like it was going nowhere fast. The death was seven years old, there had been no police investigation, and the baby had died with an autopsy that diagnosed it with having succumbed from sudden infant death syndrome. And Missy Anastasi? It was obvious any smart lawyer could make her look like a scorned woman spoiling for revenge if she took the stand.

"And at no time did you initiate a police investigation?"

"No, I didn't. I guess I was afraid to when I thought...I was afraid to..."

"Why were you afraid to?"

"I was afraid to suggest that somebody did something as serious as murder, even though I thought it."

"But you said it to several people."

"I know, I know. I guess I was afraid."

"The suspicions you had is one thing. You had some very strong suspicions. And you allowed them to stay dormant for seven years."

"Well, one thing, too, he was always buying me things, diamond bracelets, taking me out and doing all these things. I guess I thought, How could somebody be this way and be a murderer, too? How could...maybe you're wrong. If there is a chance you're wrong, then you can't suggest something like this. That is why I didn't do it."

"But there came a point in time when you did it."

The Wilson family home on Caltor Lane. (Georgiana Havill)

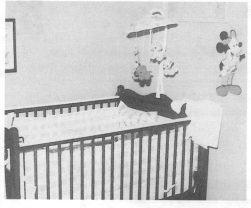

Brandi Wilson's nursery in the Caltor Lane house, where she died in 1981. (Prosecution photo)

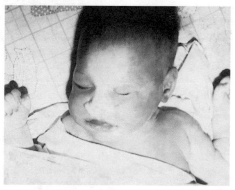

Brandi Jean Wilson, three hours after her death. The white area on her forehead and nose was where her face was pushed into a pillow, experts said. (Prosecution photo)

Garrett Wilson with Vicky on their wedding day in 1994. (Dick Vandera)

Garrett and Missy's Germantown, Maryland, town house where their infant son, Garrett Michael, died at five months of age, diagnosed as having succumbed to Sudden Infant Death Syndrome. (Georgiana Havill)

Below and below left: Garrett Wilson with daughter Marysa in 1993. (Vicky Wilson)

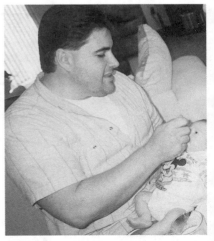

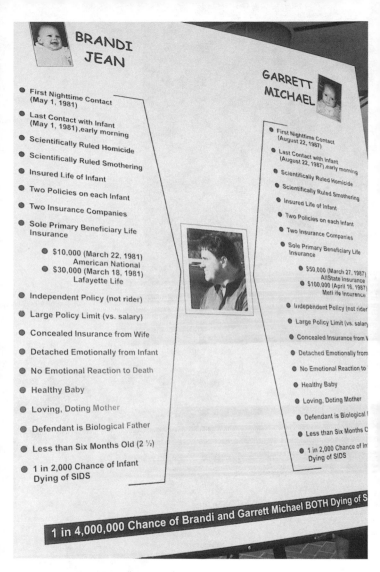

The State Attorney's Office created this "mountain of evidence" chart for its opening and closing arguments. (Georgiana Havill)

Judge Ann S. Harrington
(Georgiana Havill)

Miles James Jones, M.D.,
expert witness for the
defense. (Georgiana Havill)

Barry Helfand, Garrett Wilson's defense attorney. (Georgiana Havill)

Vicky Wilson in Barry Helfand's office, one hour before the verdict. Georgiana Havill)

The prosecution: Detective Meredith Dominick, Missy Anastasi, Jean Oliver, and co-prosecutors Douglas Gansler and David Boynton. (Georgiana Havill)

Missy Anastasi speaks to the press after the verdict is given. Jean Oliver stands behind her. (Georgiana Havill)

Jean Oliver speaks to the press. Douglas Gansler is on her right. (Georgiana Havill)

Co-prosecutors Douglas Gansler and David Boynton with Jean Oliver behind them. (Georgiana Havill)

Photos of Brandi Jean Wilson and Garrett Michael Wilson, the infant children of Garrett Wilson, were entered into evidence at his trial. The boxes in the foreground contain Garrett Michael's bed linens. (AP Photo/Leslie E. Kossoff)

The gravestone of Brandi Jean Wilson, who lived for less than four months. (Georgiana Havill)

"When I was sure I was right."

"What made you know that you were right seven years later?"

"I guess I had a feeling that he was doing it all over again when I heard there was a woman and a baby."

"Because there was another woman?"

"I found out that he had a child. So, it's like he is a liar. That's what made me realize he is a con artist, a total liar, he's a pathological liar. He has problems with money and I know this man is not normal. I was right from the beginning. I knew what he had done and I was right. And that's what made me know it. Because he's lied to me and everyone else. About everything."

Picariello had to make this point, whether or not Missy liked it. "But if he hadn't met this other woman, or had this child, we wouldn't be here now, would we?"

TEN

A ONE-WOMAN CRUSADE

Picariello and Dominick wanted to hear Garrett's version of his life with Missy. They also needed to get a better read on him without causing undue alarm. After a strategy session, it was thought he might relate better to a female than a male, so Meredith Dominick was chosen to pose most of the questions. The two cops flew into the Dallas–Fort Worth airport on the morning of May 9, 1995, some three months after their long conversation with his former wife. After lunch, they appeared on the doorstep of Garrett's house dressed in plainclothes, with a local Arlington, Texas, cop in tow, John Stanton. The trio of cops failed to rattle him, despite giving Garrett no advance warning of the visit. Garrett had just arrived home from a Technics trip to Alabama. He appeared relaxed, wearing shorts and a shirt. He was more than willing to talk about Mary Anastasi, and invited the police into his living room.

Dominick began by asking him to search his memory and tell her what happened on the night Garrett Michael died.

"All I remember is that I was in the bathroom and it was either a Friday or Saturday," Garrett told her. "I was washing my hands. I heard Missy screaming, and she came out and was carrying the baby. I called 911 and I followed their instructions by trying to give the baby CPR. It must have been close to morning, and she kept screaming until the medics arrived. I know it was almost dawn—I could tell from the drive to the hospital it was nearly light."

Who fed the baby that night? The two detectives wanted to hear his rendition.

"I think I fed the baby, but I'm not sure. I usually didn't feed the baby during the week. The baby was starting to sleep through the night every once in a while. I fed him if I got off work at Jordan Kitt's at six, but most of the time I got off at nine-thirty or ten."

How much insurance did you have on the baby?

Garrett was more than willing to tell them, and why. "I had two insurance policies on Garrett Michael. One was for $100,000 with MetLife. I had a second policy with Allstate for $50,000. My parents lost three kids, and they kept life insurance policies on each of those children and myself. I picked up this custom from them. That's why I had insurance on my child."

Dominick's heart skipped a beat. She hadn't known about the $100,000 policy. Not only was this news to her, but it provided a lot more motivation.

Garrett said he had bought the $50,000 policy because Lee Smith was such a good salesman. As someone who sold things himself, he said he appreciated a good pitch, and perhaps bought more than he should have because of Smith's hustle. He even subsequently switched his car and household insurance to Allstate because of Lee Smith, he said. He was more fuzzy about the MetLife policy, other than feeling a need for more insurance based on his own mother's experiences with dying children.

The deaths of his mother's children would have taken place in Washington, Garrett told them. He said Missy should have known about the two policies because they had a joint account, and the checks for the payment of the policies would have come out of that account.

"I don't know how she could not have known about the policies," he told the cops.

And Missy?

She was a troubled woman who just would not let go of a husband who no longer wanted her. "I feel Missy chased me for four years. I think she has a mental problem. It's all about anger and revenge. I've never accused her of anything," Garrett reminded Dominick.

"We split in November of 1992. During the Christmas holidays of 1992, I was in Maryland with Vicky. I tried to get into a storage facility I had rented to get some of my clothes, and Missy had changed the locks. I called her and she freaked out. The next day she came to South Carolina and tried to get into my apartment. I was afraid of how she would act, so I called 911. Missy told the police that she lived there, but she didn't. The sheriff's deputy had to ask her to leave while Vicky watched through the window.

"My wife is now so afraid of her that she's concerned Missy will show up in Texas and do us physical harm or try to steal our child. She wants to buy a gun to defend us," Garrett said.

Why didn't he show his sorrow when their son died?

On the contrary, it was Missy who failed to show any sadness, Garrett claimed. "I don't think Missy ever grieved. She just tried to have us adopt right away."

Garrett said he was trying to make his marriage with Vicky work. "We've been in counseling for seven months," he told the cops. "A couple of Fridays ago we were in a group counseling session, and Vicky broke down because of this. Vicky told our group about the allegations that had been made about me and the babies. Vicky had to ask the counselor if I had the character traits of a murderer. I thought we had managed to get past all this. Evidently not."

Garrett talked candidly about his divorce from Missy, saying that when the judge read the letters from her that attempted to stop the dissolution of their marriage, he had laughed. Still, Garrett recalled, the judge had delayed the final decree for ten days to see if Missy would respond to the judgment in person.

"Missy's conduct since then has been outrageous. There have been anonymous letters sent to different salesmen and customers at the firm. I know from the contents it was her. Missy called my answering machine every morning for a month after she found out I was remarried and had a child."

Garrett told them how he met Missy at the Holiday Health Spa and how, in his view, she had pursued him all throughout their courtship. "I knew what she was like. I don't understand why I ever went back with her."

Dominick asked him to tell her about how Brandi died. She watched his face for a reaction. She didn't get one.

"All I remember is getting up. I got up to do the early morning feedings about fifty percent of the time. I found the baby."

And the insurance?

"I had two small policies. One was for $30,000, the second was for $10,000."

But why, the detectives wanted to know, didn't he tell Missy he was divorcing her? Garrett said that because of his past experiences with his former wife—he told the cops the details about Missy's stalking of him and Liz Dodge at the beach—he was reluctant. Besides, he said, she was away from him so much she had to know they were separated.

"In November of 1992, we separated. I kept the apartment when she left. I told Missy it was over, but she wouldn't accept this and told me I just needed some time alone. Missy thought it was a temporary separation. I filed the divorce papers then, but I had a hard time serving her," Garrett told the lawmen.

Garrett said he was residing in Texas just to be as far away as possible from her. "This is the last place I would normally choose to live."

It was impossible, he said, that Missy hadn't known about the $100,000 insurance policy on Garrett Michael. "Missy went on a spending spree. A big chunk of the money

went for a new house in Damascus, Maryland. A lot of it
went for furniture that she selected. She was ecstatic over
the money. I don't know how she would have not known
about the two policies."

Garrett told the cops that it was Missy who made them go
bankrupt in Maryland. This was because she was unwilling
to help when they got into financial difficulties. "Her father
had a position ready for her that would have paid more
money than she was making at the time, but Missy refused
to take the job. She always took the summer off because her
job in the school system allowed it. I worked. It was the
same in Houston and in Florida, where all she ever did was
sit on the beach all day, even though she had a car to drive to
look for work."

Garrett admitted to the cops that he was easy come, easy
go when it came to his finances. "I like to make money. And
I like to spend money," he told his three guests without any
apologies.

Meredith Dominick then got down to the nitty gritty.
Would he be willing to submit to a polygraph test immediately and settle the matter once and for all? That would clear
everything up.

Garrett went back and forth on the question. "After all
this time I can't tell you how sickening this is. You're aware
of my past experiences. I don't think I'm opposed to a polygraph test, but I'm a little cynical about the law."

"Is that a yes or a no?" Picariello wanted an answer.

"A no."

But as the trio was leaving, Garrett changed his mind. He
would take the polygraph, he told them. Bill Stanton, the local cop, quickly said he would supervise the examination.
Stanton promised he would set it up and give Garrett a call
in the morning with the time and place for the test, just as
soon as he could schedule it with the Arlington, Texas, police department's polygraph machine operator.

An hour after the three left, Vicky and Garrett visited Carl
Mallory, a prominent Arlington criminal defense attorney
whom Garrett remembers as wearing a shiny polyester suit

with frayed pockets. After first extracting a thousand dollars in cash from the two for his advice, the lawyer advised Garrett not to take the test, not to answer any more questions, and if the detectives called on him again, he was to tell them to "go to hell."

Garrett telephoned Bill Stanton and advised the local cop there would be no polygraph test. Just leave us alone, he said. A few weeks later Mallory called Vicky. He mysteriously told her they wouldn't be hearing from the Maryland cops anymore. Vicky was reassured, but Garrett didn't believe him.

Ervin and Thelma Wampler, their daughter, Kathy, and Kathy's toddler daughter, Kelsey, visited Vicky and Garrett a few months after the Montgomery County Police Department's fishing expedition. They drove to Pittsburgh and flew nonstop into the Dallas–Fort Worth airport. It was the first flight for all four family members. Thelma was so nervous she refused to leave her seat, even though she felt a need to visit the plane's bathroom. While overall a positive experience for the Wampler clan, it at first seemed to be headed for disaster.

"Nan Nan fell off a bed and banged her head," Garrett recalled of Thelma. "Kathy threw out her back and then both Marysa and Kelsey got locked up at the top of the stairs and tumbled down them. But nobody got hurt badly, and in the end everyone had a great time."

A month later, Kathy's son, Jimmy, flew to Dallas to attend a cooking academy in the area. He lived with Vicky and Garrett while taking the course. Garrett, generous to a fault as always, bought him a pickup truck when he arrived, to get back and forth from the school, though he remembers Vicky's nephew's driving as too fast, saying Jimmy did "the best he could to wreck it." After graduation, Jimmy found a chef's position in a luxury hotel near Deep Creek Lake.

Garrett continued to worry about Meredith Dominick's visit. He told Vicky that despite what Carl Mallory had told her, he was afraid of the Montgomery County police investigation. It would be only a matter of time before they would try to arrest him, he said.

Missy's one-woman crusade, with assistance from Patty Schrein, was still churning along, mostly through a weekly letter-writing campaign. Missy had mailed documents on the case to Lt. F. Michael McQuillan, Chief of Homicide for the Prince George's County Police Department in January of 1995, after a successful face-to-face December meeting. Schrein followed this up by telephoning the cop and, after a long conversation, thought he sounded interested. Missy's letters began familiarly ("Dear Mike"), reminding him of her contacts by dropping in the name of her cousin Joe, the Montgomery County police sergeant, usually into the last paragraph. McQuillan was also an acquaintance of Missy's cousin, Regina Marmo. In April of 1995, when Waneta Hoyt was convicted of killing her five children, all of whom had first been diagnosed with sudden infant death syndrome, Missy wrote again. Inside the envelope this time were the Hoyt conviction stories from *The Washington Post* and the Baltimore *Sun.* Missy began to tell friends she might have better luck getting Prince George's to act than her own county police department.

Schrein continued to bombard Meredith Dominick with memos. She also wrote a nine-page single-spaced letter to Montgomery County Police Chief Carol Mehrling, outlining the case. She sent a similar missive to the liberal Democrat, Andrew Sonner, then the longtime state's attorney for Montgomery County and therefore its chief prosecutor. She argued and she threatened, writing that she would call the press if they didn't act.

In her letter to Sonner, copied to McQuillan and Dominick, Schrein cited the case of *United States* v. *Woods*, a case of infanticide originally believed to be SIDS. The woman was charged and convicted of one murder, but evidence from five other deaths believed to be caused by the defendant had been allowed into the case. Schrein ended her communication by saying, "I hope this has piqued your interest."

When little or no response was received from the authorities, Schrein and Missy began touting true crime paperbacks to their correspondence list of decision makers. One book mailed was Ann Rule's *A Rose for Her Grave*, the tale of a Seattle man who murdered two of his wives for their insurance policies. Another was Joyce Egginton's *From Cradle to Grave*, the account of Mary Beth Tinning, an upstate New York woman who had smothered all nine of her children. Schrein argued that both of these cases paralleled the case of Missy's and Debbie's babies. When these letters were met with silence, Schrein began talking about filing a civil suit against Garrett. She expressed doubt about whether or not the police were sincere by bluntly asking them if she and Missy were simply spinning their wheels.

Schrein had already spoken twice by phone to Linda Norton, M.D., the forensic pathologist who, she told friends, had "cracked the Waneta Hoyt case." Norton told her that even though Marysa was by now a toddler, she could as yet be suffocated to death by Garrett. The little girl could still be diagnosed with SIDS, Norton claimed, because some of Waneta Hoyt's children had been the same age as Marysa when they died. Schrein redoubled her efforts and implored the cops to quickly take some meaningful action. Her pleas were ignored.

A year after Missy had first notified the Montgomery County Police about her suspicions, the investigation appeared to be in limbo. Patty Schrein wrote a long letter to Andy Sonner on the day before the first anniversary date of Missy's investigation, June 13, 1995. The lawyer claimed she and Missy had no real indication the county was at all serious about their allegations, or even considered it to be a homicide at this point. Sonner had a reputation as being soft on crime, particularly in the prosecution of drug dealers, and Schrein knew it.

Schrein implied to Sonner that much of the investigating had already been done privately by Missy with her help and the cops had done little. She wanted to know if an arrest was imminent. Getting no response, she wrote to the new deputy state's attorney, Robert L. Dean, stuffing into an envelope the fat, ever-increasing stack of investigative documents. With Dean, she seemed to have hit pay dirt. He wrote her a return letter that at least gave the attorney some hope. "I have been aware of the investigation in question for quite some time, and I have asked David Boynton to work with the investigating detectives on this matter. We are treating this with the utmost seriousness," the letter read in part.

Patty fired off a package to Boynton immediately, enclosing the usual thick stack of documents. By now she had another case to cite, the *State of Washington* v. *Lough*, a trial about a paramedic who had allegedly raped five women. Patty believed the crime was a good example of what she called a "common scheme or plan," something she was convinced Garrett had carried out in the deaths of Brandi Jean and Garrett Michael. She also told Boynton that Missy was getting increasingly upset with the county's rate of progress. Could Missy meet with you personally, she wanted to know? Instead, Boynton arranged for Missy to spend another hour together with Meredith Dominick, Pete Picariello, Patty Schrein, and Missy's cousin, Joe Anastasi, on October 30, 1995.

Missy brought some of her and Garrett's joint checkbooks to the conference. In November of 1987, their joint account showed a balance of $88,000. Missy had never looked at the balances, so this was a revelation to her. Picariello and Meredith kept saying how hard a case this would be to prosecute, but Patty batted down their excuses by saying "I know you can do this" over and over again. It was a battle of wills by the end of the hour.

"We'll only have one shot at him," Picariello counseled at the meeting. He said he believed Garrett's family was nervous. They were hoping it would all go away. Picariello asked Schrein not to file the proposed civil suit against Garrett and she told them she would hold it back until a few days before the statute of limitations ran out.

Missy left, believing the investigation was still going slowly, but at least was moving forward. Patty Schrein wrote a memo the next day to the two detectives asking them to look for more potential wrongdoing by Garrett. Patty believed their suspect may have committed a crime against every company that had ever employed him. She asked the cops to call Casio, where she suggested Garrett may have fenced his Casio demonstration equipment in New Orleans and then reported it as stolen. She urged them to phone Holcombe Music, where she said Garrett was given money to come back to work for the firm, but instead he had gone to work for Westbrook Music and pocketed Holcombe's cash. She wanted them to contact Jordan Kitt's. Surely Garrett must have stolen something from them. Finally, she wanted the cops to get in touch with an insurance investigator friend of hers whom she believed might be able to uncover even more policies Garrett had taken out on the two babies.

Christmas of 1995 came and went with no action taken by the police. Missy veered back and forth from being at times disconsolate to overflowing with seething anger. For the 1996 New Year, she had stationery made up for her letter-writing campaign with her name at the top. She began signing some of her more important letters:

Mary F. Anastasi
Mother, Garrett Michael Wilson
March 12, 1987–August 22, 1987

Missy began the year by writing to David Boynton on January 3, plugging both *A Rose for Her Grave* and a new crime paperback, *Goodbye, My Little Ones*, an account of the Waneta Hoyt case written by three newspaper reporters. She also asked him to read a section on antisocial personality disorder that was in a medical textbook. She believed it described Garrett's personality perfectly. Missy ended the letter by warning Boynton that "he will do it again." When Boynton ignored her, she told friends that he should be fired.

Missy's subsidizing of the true crime publishing industry, not to mention the U.S. postal system by writing letter after letter to law enforcement authorities, had made little real progress. She was frustrated that almost two years had passed since she first contacted the police and nothing had happened. Despite her own expenditures on private investigators and a lawyer, her former husband seemed no closer to an arrest than when she first began the journey.

The investigation had become expensive. She saved money by living with her mother and taking a receptionist's job at a local company, Allied Technology. At night she took courses at nearby Hood College, trying to get enough credits for a master's degree in special education.

Nothing would make her give up the quest. She began expanding the mailing list and revisiting the names she thought could help. A local congresswoman, Republican moderate Constance Morella, got a long letter in June of 1996. Missy enclosed her thick packet of material on the case. By now, she had become more strident. Missy railed to the politician about how stunned she was by the lack of concern shown by Montgomery County officials when it came to crimes that had been committed against innocent children. Grasping for any bond, no matter how fragile, Missy mentioned to Morella that her mother worked as a librarian at a church with a woman whose daughter was married to the congresswoman's son. While that was quite a stretch, Missy was unashamed of the affinity link, ready to do anything that might get her a degree of attention. Gaining vengeance had become an obsession.

She contemplated calling Garrett and trying to get him to say something incriminating on the phone while she taped him. She discussed how this would be handled with Patty Schrein, reminding her lawyer that, "After all, he said I would be dead if I was in Texas."

A month later, Missy went above the congresswoman and wrote long letters to the Democratic governor of Maryland, Parris N. Glendening, and the very liberal U.S. Senator from her state, Barbara Mikulski. She also sent packages to the Maryland attorney general, Joseph Curran; the U.S. attorney general, Janet Reno; and finally mailed a plaintive plea to President Clinton at the White House. Despondent that little or nothing was happening in the case, Missy feared the two-year vision of putting her former spouse behind bars was over.

In her letter to Governor Glendening she said she was out of patience with the state and that he should know a baby killer was on the loose who was capable of not only producing more infants but murdering them. Missy implied that other states in the country were far more vigilant in prosecuting crimes against women and children than Maryland. She got a polite letter back from him saying he had forwarded her letter to state's attorney Andy Sonner and Montgomery County Police Chief Carol Merhling, who had already been mailed the same materials months before. Since they already had those documents, it turned out to be just another runaround.

Missy wrote a second letter to the deputy state's attorney, Robert L. Dean, in August of 1995. She reminded him that just a year before he had told her he was treating her case "with the utmost seriousness" but nothing had happened. He had ignored her since then, she said, and because of that, she was going to be seeking help from others. Dean got back to her immediately, denying the charges.

"Some investigations require considerable time and patience," he told her, reminding Missy that cases charged too early "often fail to accomplish that which is our duty to pursue—justice."

Missy got polite letters back from all the other politicians except for Janet Reno. She feared that the chief law enforcement official of the land had snubbed her until an envelope arrived in the mail. It was from the U.S. Department of Justice.

"Child abuse is Janet Reno's chosen cause," a police source said. "When the Attorney General got the letter, she forwarded it to the Justice Department, asking them to look into the case. They sent it down to their Office for Victims of Crime division. The OVC then wrote Missy a letter which said that though it was a state matter, Maryland received federal funds from the OVC to support local victim assistance programs. She was told that someone from the OVC would soon phone her attorney to let her know what avenues were open to her."

Missy got a second letter, dated August 23, 1996. An official thanked her for the letter which the OVC described as "the tragic murder of your son," and referring to "the agony you must suffer believing that your former husband caused his death." They suggested she might like to work with a Victim's Crime Advocate by the name of Ingrid Horton. The advocate, whom the OVC said had worked with Montgomery County on similar cases, might know how to help you, Missy was told. They gave her Horton's phone numbers and address.

Missy made the telephone call. Ingrid Horton would prove to be Missy's savior, helping her to get the dormant case revived.

ELEVEN

AN AUTOPSY IS CHANGED

Ingrid Horton's credentials as a victim's crime advocate had been earned though tragic circumstances. She had been sexually abused as a child, and at the age of thirty was gang-raped in Los Angeles while her daughter slept in an adjoining room. Born in England of an Austrian mother and a British father, she grew up near London. A love interest had brought her to America, where, at the University of Maryland, she graduated with a major in psychology and a minor in criminology. The slender blonde activist had taken additional courses in anatomy at Montgomery College in Rockville. This education, along with her practical experience in a number of child abuse cases, made her an ideal helpmate for Missy. She plunged into the case with zeal, working with her on a daily basis. Missy seemed grateful for the free attention. Ingrid wasn't even billing her expenses. She was optimistic, behaving as if it were only a matter of time before an arrest was made.

"I am genuinely excited to have found you," Missy gushed after they met. Missy had been despondent. She had just talked with Meredith Dominick. The detective did not have encouraging words.

"I think he's responsible for their deaths, but I don't think it is ever going to trial," was Dominick's candid assessment in November of 1996. The detective said she had received some new information, but wouldn't tell Missy what it was since the fresh intelligence was still under investigation. The cop wanted closure for Missy. To remind herself not to give up, she pinned baby pictures of Garrett Michael and Brandi on the wall next to her desk. They were given a place of honor, just below her NASCAR calendar.

Missy by now was on the edge. After the JonBenét Ramsey story broke during the Christmas holidays, she told Ingrid the case was a perfect example of how one family's money and power could thwart a criminal investigation. She believed if she had the kind of clout the Ramsey couple possessed, her former husband would already be behind bars awaiting trial. She told Ingrid she wanted Vicky investigated, too. If Garrett was Clyde, she reasoned, then surely Vicky had to be his Bonnie.

Ingrid gave Missy a series of projects designed to stop her from dwelling on every child murder case in the country and get her focused on the mission at hand. She told Missy to search her memory. She wanted a complete chronology of every week Missy had ever spent with Garrett and what happened during each of those seven-day periods. Ingrid tried to assemble a slate of potential expert witnesses to sell to the Montgomery County prosecutors. Her first choice was Linda Norton, the Dallas forensic pathologist and SIDS expert. Norton told Ingrid her fee began with a retainer of $3,000 up front. Against that she billed $300 an hour to review the case, and $2,400 a day for testimony in court plus her flight, food, and lodging costs. At first, Missy wasn't sure if the prosecutors were supposed to pay the doctor or if she would have to front the costs. If so, the outlay for Norton seemed daunting. She was relieved when she found out the state of Maryland would bear all the prosecution expenses.

Missy and Ingrid had another expert they wanted to testify. He was William Fitzpatrick, the Onondaga County district attorney in New York state who had put Waneta Hoyt in prison. He had worked in tandem with Norton in the past. In fact, it was Norton who had studied Hoyt's background and then told the prosecutor, "You know, you have a serial killer right here in Syracuse."

They wanted Fitzpatrick to be a consultant to David Boynton. Bill Fitzpatrick and Linda Norton, they believed, would make a lethal one-two punch that would surely lead to Garrett Wilson's conviction.

With Ingrid Horton doing most of Missy's bidding, Patty Schrein was no longer needed. The two parted ways amicably, with Missy prepared to lean on Ingrid the rest of the way.

David Boynton had gone far in the legal profession despite not having an elite family background. The son of a corporate actuary, Boynton had attended a public high school in Montgomery County, where he had lettered in three sports—baseball, basketball, and golf. His proficiency at hitting the little white ball might have earned him a scholarship at a large university, but he had opted instead to go to Gettysburg College, a Lutheran school in Pennsylvania. Little Gettysburg had 2,500 undergraduates and, because of its size, was not allowed to give out NCAA scholarships. Still, he had been one of the big fishes in the athletic pond there. Gettysburg had been conference champion with Boynton on its golf team.

After Gettysburg, Boynton chose the University of Baltimore for his law degree. He began as a Montgomery County prosecutor in 1983. Except for a two-year hiatus where he tested himself in private practice, he had been in the state's attorney's office ever since.

Boynton was a devout Catholic, a family man who would often sound out opinions over the dinner table when working on an important criminal case. His son and wife could sometimes be seen in the courtroom when he delivered the closing argument.

Two dead infants who might have been murdered wasn't the most horrendous case he had ever seen. Once, a young boy had been brought to him who couldn't sit down because he had been brutally sodomized by his own father. Boynton had to talk to the boy about his injury. A case of two little babies could seem easy after that.

Boynton knew he couldn't prosecute Garrett for murder with the victims' autopsies diagnosed as death from natural causes, specifically SIDS. He believed somehow both Brandi's and Garrett Michael's death certificates had to be revised. A judge would then have to allow the details surrounding Brandi's death to be allowed as evidence in any trial of Garrett Wilson. Failure to do either might kill any chance of the prosecution winning the case. Fulfilling these tasks, and knowing that others were needed to get an indictment, was a tall order.

In Prince George's County, Homicide Chief Mike McQuillan had assigned the investigation into Brandi's death to Detective Richard Fulginiti or "Fulgee" as his office peers called the chunky, five-foot-seven cop. He began by interviewing members of the Oliver family. They didn't have anything nice to say about their former son-in-law.

"Garrett showed interest in our eldest daughter first," Jean Oliver told Fulginiti, remembering the relationship. "She didn't particularly care for him, and I asked her why. She said, 'There was just something about him I didn't like.' Then he turned his attention to our youngest daughter, Debbie. I didn't like that, either. He told me, 'We're just good friends.' I told Garrett he was too old for her. I refused to allow him to drive Debbie to school. Then I found out he was coming by the school bus stop and picking her up."

Mrs. Oliver remembered that Garrett soon had Debbie feeding his horse. Her future son-in-law, she said, maintained the fiction that the relationship was only a friendship until Debbie became pregnant.

"Debbie came to me and told me. Garrett had asked her to have an abortion. She told me no, she wouldn't. Garrett came to our house a couple of days later to talk about marriage. I thought his attitude was pretty flippant."

The next part of the interview caused Fulginiti to draw a circle around her statement in the transcript he got a week later. "I told him if I had the strength, I would cut his heart out for messing up her life. I was recovering from surgery or else I would have attacked him. I certainly didn't want Debbie to marry him. But she wanted to take responsibility because it was the right thing to do."

Jean Oliver told Fulginiti what she remembered about the day before Brandi's death. She was at Garrett's home much of that afternoon.

"I went to their house to take care of Brandi and Debbie because Debbie was sick with the flu. I gave Brandi a bath, and she was very happy. She was smiling so much she couldn't drink her bottle, so I played with her for a while. She finished eating and took a nap. When Garrett came home from work, I suggested that I could take Debbie and Brandi home with me because my daughter was still very sick and not able to take care of her. But Garrett said he would bring them to our house on his way to work the next morning. He said he would care for them."

Jean Oliver said she got the call saying, "Brandi is dead," from Garrett at six the next morning. When she rushed to the Caltor Lane house he greeted her at the door.

"He was wearing blue jeans and a pull-over T-shirt. He wasn't crying and he didn't even appear upset. We went into Brandi's room and she was laying on her back. The side of her face was blue. She was so alive earlier."

At the funeral Jean Oliver remembered Garrett asking to recite a poem. She didn't think that was proper, either. "I thought it was strange he would want to read a poem. It was something about God lending us a child for a while. Garrett read it without any problems."

Jean Oliver said she was well aware of Debbie and Garrett's marital problems after returning from their Florida sojourn. She told Fulginiti that when Debbie would come home to stay with her, Garrett would call and threaten to kill himself if she didn't return. One time, she said, he fired a gun while speaking on the phone to her and then didn't say anything for a few minutes.

"We didn't know if he had shot himself or not," Mrs. Oliver said.

She also knew about her daughter's altercation with Garrett and Debra Wood. Though Debbie had charged in her divorce suit that Garrett was responsible for her breaking a finger when she ran into a camper returning home, Mrs. Oliver upped the ante. She said that Garrett had beaten up on her daughter and besides the finger, he had also broken her collarbone. Debbie's mom said a restraining order was sworn out against Garrett by the family.

And Brandi?

"I had a very strong feeling, call it a gut feeling, something wasn't right about her death. I've never accepted SIDS as the cause of death, though the coroner did rule that it was SIDS," she said.

Fulginiti got much the same story from Kyle Oliver. Debbie's dad said they had been naive. They took Garrett at his word when he said Debbie was like a sister to him, but learned too late what was really going on.

Kyle said he was friends with Eldred Wilson during his last years and Jean had sometimes driven him to the doctor. He claimed Eldred was always concerned about Garrett's spending habits. He had allowed Garrett to start handling the checkbook and saw all the money going out. He was upset about it, Kyle said. He also had a memory, a partly faulty one, of Garrett's Capitol Hill crime.

"One evening he told us he had been robbed. He said he had been held up and that the police suggested he not go home. He asked to stay at our house. We thought this was strange, but Garrett said the robbers might be after him. The next morning I got the paper and read that Garrett had been accused of embezzling money from a bank. I asked him about it. He said he hadn't and that the police were wrong.

"Garrett was tried in court and found guilty. A number of us went to the trial to be his character witnesses but the judge only allowed Reverend Edmunds to testify. The judge said how he was getting tired of white collar crimes and he was going to send a message. However, he said since this was Garrett's first offense and because he had to take care of his sick father [Note: Eldred had died the year before], he would put him on probation for five years."

His former father-in-law said that he, too, didn't like the style Garrett used in breaking the news of Debbie's pregnancy. Kyle claimed he and Jean were willing to take their daughter's baby and raise it themselves.

"Garrett said how proud he was to have a child follow in his footsteps. He had this smirky smile on his face and a cocky attitude. Jean got very upset. She told him this was a serious matter."

In spite of this, and their intimate knowledge of Garrett's crime, the Olivers admitted to the detective they had agreed to the marriage. Because of her age, parental approval was legally needed for the union to take place.

Kyle Oliver let slip to the detective that he, too, had taken the same leap of thinking as had Missy Anastasi. In his eyes his former son-in-law wasn't just a free spender and a con artist—he was a murderer. When he gave his account of Brandi's death, he began by saying, "The day before Brandi died or was killed..."

He also backed up his wife's tale of Garrett's staged suicide attempt by gun. Kyle added that when he rushed over to the Caltor Lane house, he learned Garrett had been in the basement and shot a bullet into the ceiling.

Fulginiti still needed a statement from Debbie. But his key witness wouldn't talk. She wanted nothing to do with the county's murder investigation, she said.

Ingrid Horton's anatomy classes were paying off. In March of 1997 she visited Meredith Dominick and began studying Garrett Michael's autopsy. One sentence jumped out at her.

"Diffuse edema [swelling] of the cerebral hemisphere is noted," the autopsy read on page four. She read the statement to the detective.

"Meredith, this is edema and subdural hemorrhage here," Ingrid said. "This means there was evidence of trauma to the body before the autopsy was performed."

Dominick disagreed. She thought it was more likely evidence of bleeding that had occurred when they had removed the baby's brain for examination.

"But Meredith," the victim's advocate said, "dead bodies don't bleed."

Ingrid Horton called John McCarthy, the chief of homicide investigations for the state's attorney's office. She told him of her discovery.

By now David Boynton had immersed himself in the case. He believed his suspect had a great thirst for money. He began to be convinced that Garrett may have murdered both his mother and father in addition to his son and daughter. After all, he reasoned, Garrett was the only one with them when they died. But first things first. Before any arrest could be made, the autopsies had to be revised.

On June 17, 1997, David Boynton, Meredith Dominick, Missy Anastasi, Ingrid Horton, and Pete Picariello met with the chief medical examiner for the State of Maryland in a Baltimore conference room. John E. Smialek, M.D., sat at the head of the table as the prosecutorial team began to make its case for changing Garrett Michael and Brandi Jean's autopsies. In order to soften him up, the group had yellow-highlighted the medical examiner's published works in professional journals. Smialek had either authored the articles or was quoted in them. They put the papers close enough to him so he could see they had noted his name. It was a touchy business to get a ten-year-old autopsy changed, and they wanted to use every weapon available in order to get the slim, silver-haired doctor to change his mind.

"We know you didn't perform the autopsy and probably weren't even aware of it," someone began sympathetically. The detectives showed him the insurance policies they claimed were the motivation. They gave him Garrett's credit records which showed his need for money. Garrett's two crimes were detailed. Then they laid out both Brandi Jean and Garrett Michael's autopsies, reminding him that new medical findings had found SIDS was not genetic. Finally, they gave him a transcript of the tape of Missy's interview with Pete Picariello.

After hearing them out, Smialek said he would consider their request. Both autopsies would be reviewed. David Boynton was enthused by the events and took his group to the Little Italy section of Baltimore for a bang-up Italian dinner.

Ingrid Horton was also pleased. She went to Chief Prosecutor Robert Dean, suggesting she be hired as a consultant for the state. Dean put his hands in his pockets, jingled some change, and told her he had no money for her in his budget. Afterward, a cop confided that Dean had a $300-a-day slush fund for such purposes. Ingrid was incensed.

Boynton mailed Brandi's autopsy and the same documents he had given to Smialek to Charles Kokes, the doctor who had been responsible for Brandi's autopsy determination back in 1981. Kokes was now an associate medical examiner in the Arkansas State Crime Laboratory. Kokes, a burly, bearded bear of a man, quickly changed his opinion. He sent Boynton this finding on November 12, 1997.

> I have reviewed the documents you provided to me regarding the death of Garrett Michael Wilson. In light of this additional information, I have changed my opinion regarding the cause and manner of his death. The provided investigation findings clearly indicate the manner of death was homicide. When the autopsy findings are reviewed in this context, the most likely cause of death is external airway obstruction (smothering).

A day later Smialek sent this opinion from Baltimore on Garrett Michael and Brandi Jean. For David Boynton, it seemed more cause for celebration. The case was finally falling into place.

> I have completed my review of the records of the Office of the Chief Medical Examiner concerned with the investiga-

tion of the death of Garrett Michael Wilson. In addition to these records I have studied the transcript of the tape of an interview with Mary Anastasi, the mother of Garrett Michael Wilson, and the former wife of Garrett Eldred Wilson. I have also examined the summary of an examination prepared by Detective Dominick of the Montgomery County Police Department. Here are my conclusions based on my review:

First of all, the autopsy findings in both infants, which were originally considered to be consistent with Sudden Infant Death Syndrome (SIDS), are also consistent with suffocation by smothering. Obstruction of the airway of an infant, two months or five months of age, by a soft object such as a pillow could leave no visible evidence of smothering. The appearance of their bodies in these circumstances would be exactly the same as described in these two autopsy reports. However, the fact that in the case of Garrett Michael, his brain exhibited "diffuse edema" or generalized swelling is uncharacteristic for SIDS and more indicative of an interruption in the oxygen supply to the brain such as could occur in asphyxia due to airway obstruction.

The report of the death of Garrett Michael Wilson on August 22, 1987, was significantly deficient in not having a record of a scene investigation. Since the law enforcement agency which would have had jurisdiction in this case (the Montgomery County Police Department) was not notified of the death, no investigation of the scene where [Garrett] Michael was found unresponsive was conducted. Nor was a complete medical history obtained which would have identified a previous death of the father's other child, Brandi, in May, 1981.

For your information, in 1989 a definition of SIDS was developed which set new criteria for this diagnosis, specifically requiring a scene investigation and a complete medical history.

The information provided by your investigators together with the autopsy findings leads me to conclude to a reasonable degree of certainty that Garrett Michael Wilson, died of asphyxia due to airway obstruction probably by smothering. Furthermore, it is my opinion that the manner of death of Garrett Michael Wilson is Homicide. The official records of the OCME will be changed to reflect these conclusions.

My review of the investigation of the death of Brandi Jean Wilson is continuing.

Upon further analysis, Smialek's office could not say with absolute certainty that Brandi Jean's autopsy was a homicide. After all, they reasoned, there *had* been a police investigation and there *had* been no edema of the brain. But the state would opine that the cause of death was probable suffocation, as would Ann Dixon, one of the pathologists who had examined Brandi some sixteen years before, and who still worked in the autopsy lab. Boynton thought he could now prevail in court. He could swear Charles Kokes in as an expert witness and have him give his opinion that Brandi's death was a homicide. There was enough to get an indictment.

The state could show motivation through the insurance policies. The deaths of the two children were now considered foul play. The one loose cannon could be Missy. A sharp defense attorney might be able to rattle her. They could destroy her credibility if the beach chase of Liz Dodge or the attempted break-in at the apartment in South Carolina were revisited in detail.

Boynton began making plans to go to Texas to arrest their suspect. Meredith Dominick applied for an arrest warrant with a five-page document concluding that Missy's former husband "did feloniously, willfully, and with deliberately premeditated ` malice, kill and murder GARRETT MICHAEL WILSON against the Peace, Government, and Dignity of the State." But by the time the document was approved, Garrett had disappeared. The arrest warrant had to list his address and whereabouts as "unknown." The Arlington, Texas, deputy whose job it was to drive past his house every few days had called to say the house was now empty and there was a FOR RENT sign in front. The forwarding address Garrett left was a post office box number in Tulsa, Oklahoma.

"He's on the move," the Texan told the state's attorney's office.

Boynton wasn't worried. The prosecutor was pretty sure he knew where he could find his suspect. As far as he was concerned, Garrett had only saved the state several expensive round-trip air fares.

PART THREE

There is one way in this country in which all men are created equal. There is one human institution that makes a pauper the equal of a Rockefeller, the stupid man the equal of an Einstein. . . . That institution, gentlemen, is a court. . . . Our courts have their faults, but in this country our courts are the great levelers.

—HARPER LEE,
TO KILL A MOCKINGBIRD

TWELVE

MURDER ONE IN
MONTGOMERY

Vicky asked a pal in the Frostburg Police Department for the name of the best criminal defense lawyer in Montgomery County. He told her to get Barry Helfand. Helfand had a reputation for offering potent, albeit quirky, legal arguments. Most important, he was able to avoid serious jail time for many of his clients when all odds seemed against them.

His most recent case had made him look like a miracle worker. A former Republican U.S. Senate candidate, Ruthann Aron, had tried to poison her urologist husband by spiking his chili with prescription drugs. Instead of dying, the doctor slept for fourteen hours and woke up with what he thought was a bad hangover. After that, the female politician hired what she thought was a hit man to dispatch her spouse. The potential killer went to the police. The cops taped her negotiating the amount of the payment with him.

At her trial, Aron faced thirty-six years of hard time, but after five days of deliberation, the jury was hung, eleven to one. The lone juror for acquittal turned out to have worked with some of the doctors Helfand had hired to testify on her sanity or lack of it. A mistrial was announced. The attorney then had the aspiring widow plead no-contest to a single count on what had once been multicount charges. She got three years and was allowed to serve her sentence working in the prison library at the Montgomery County Detention Center.

Helfand, who was about to turn sixty-one when Vicky first came to his Rockville offices, was the son of a Wilmington, Delaware, handyman and bar owner. He had done better than his father. Helfand was a product of the University of Maryland law school.

Because of his age, critics had begun to whisper that he was slowing down and no longer had the stamina for a long, combative day in court. Helfand would probably have yelled at anyone daring to make that statement to his face.

The defense advocate had been a prosecutor in the early 1960s. He soon discovered that litigation and criminal defense work could not only be more lucrative, but offer more rewards to the ego. Beating the big guys with their nearly unlimited budgets was what it was all about. He liked to illustrate this finding by telling the story of how he got the five-thousand-dollar gold Rolex watch circling his wrist.

"In 1984, I won a 1.6 million–dollar judgment against General Electric. I called my kids' school and told a teacher to tell them that their dad got one-point-six. I knew they'd figure out what I meant, and all lawyers' kids know how to divide by three. Then I went home and bought my wife two fur coats and she bought me this watch and we all went on a long expensive vacation."

"But weren't there a lot of tax consequences?" he would be asked. And then would come the punch line.

"There were, and this liberal Jewish Democrat nearly became a conservative Republican when it was time to fill out those tax forms!"

Helfand was not above using his religion (or anything else for that matter) if it came to winning a case. He gained notoriety when he once asked that the date of a case be moved because of the Yom Kippur holiday.

"I have to be out of here by sundown," Helfand told the judge, looking toward the heavens. "And if I'm not, lightning bolts will come down upon us. This courthouse will not be safe."

He had gotten one client, who was accused of torturing a two-year-old child by holding him down in a bathtub filled with scalding water, acquitted. Three doctors took the stand to testify that the blisters and burns were consistent with someone keeping a toddler under water. Helfand then cross-examined the medics while lying on his back on the floor of the courtroom. He had them demonstrate on him as to how the child was held down. When the physicians were inconsistent in showing the jury which way it was supposedly done, the suspect was freed.

John McCarthy, the homicide specialist for the state's attorney's office in Rockville, complained to a local newspaper that he wasn't impressed with Helfand's tricks.

"Barry Helfand doesn't know what a law library is," he griped. "He gets by with putting his thumbs behind his suspenders and getting the job done. He's a classic Clarence Darrow type of lawyer. He'll tell a joke to the prosecutor, insult his client, and then the client is found not guilty."

Helfand was able to sometimes get away with insulting judges, too. He once began an argument with this line, which got him a smile in return: "Your Honor, nobody has ever called you a fool. That is, except behind your back."

Of course, not every court approved of Helfand's comedic antics. He had been upbraided by a magistrate after causing a jury to howl with laughter. The judge had to remind him that, after all, it was a murder trial that was in progress, and a man's life was at stake.

Helfand's secretary, Brenda Goletz, liked to refer to her boss as "the Jewish Columbo" for his habit of wandering around the courtroom during a cross-examination and then asking an unexpected question. But he didn't have Peter Falk's full mane of hair. In fact, the top of his head was as smooth as a baby's bottom. In spite of that, after Vicky came to him, he began musing on who would portray him in the movie that he figured would inevitably be made from the case.

"I'll probably be played by Joe Pesci or Danny DeVito. But I gotta tell you, Pierce Brosnan could add a lot," he said.

Helfand's fee for representing Garrett was anything but a small matter. After hearing of Garrett's plight, he told Vicky he would defend her husband for a total of $100,000, which included $25,000 for a second trial if Garrett were charged with Brandi's death separately. The lawyer told Vicky if she could come up with $40,000, he would spread the costs over seven years. She would then have to pay him $250 a month with a balloon payment due at the end of the time period. Vicky's father, Ervin, he told her, would have to pledge ten acres of his land as collateral. And that didn't necessarily include the costs of expert witnesses, either, he warned.

Vicky didn't hesitate. Ervin was willing to do his part and put up the land. She borrowed $20,000 from her grandmother, and the other half from a friend. Her family believed in her husband and his innocence.

Helfand met his new client. The first thing he did was set some ground rules. "I understand you're a pretty good piano salesman," he told Garrett. "Well, I would never tell you how to sell pianos, so don't ever tell me how to be a lawyer."

Helfand went home and told his wife, Suzanne, about Garrett Wilson. She had no hesitation when she gave him her opinion about the client he was representing. "He's guilty. Hang him."

One had to wonder where the money from Helfand's fees went. His ground floor offices, two blocks from the courthouse where he practiced, were decidedly modest. Except for his son, David, who had followed him into the business, and a young assistant, Alex Yufik, Barry Helfand was pretty much a one-man show. It was Yufik, a young Ukrainian Jew whose family had left Odessa in the Soviet Union before perestroika, who would usually sit in the courtroom with him during a long trial. The associate would pass him notes containing advice and points he thought he should be making. Yufik would often try to get Helfand to operate more on the evidence and less by the seat of his pants, a plea that often went unheeded.

* * *

Bill Saltysiak, the Deep Creek Lake–based lawyer Vicky hired the day of Garrett's arrest, had tried to get bail set two days after he arrived at the Montgomery County jail, but David Boynton pulled out all the stops to keep his suspect locked up. The prosecutor said Garrett's record spoke for itself.

"This man will do whatever it takes to get his way. His entire life has been one of deceit and fraud," Boynton thundered at the arraignment. He said Garrett had three different credit cards under three different names when arrested, and that he specialized in giving out phony addresses to creditors. He would flee in a second if let loose, Boynton cautioned a judge.

Bill Saltysiak fingered Missy as the sinister force behind the arrest. He argued his client's theme that it was only after she was divorced and Garrett remarried that she came forward.

"It's curious the death of Garrett Michael was not important enough to report for eight years," Saltysiak said. He then asked for a low bond, saying, "This is not a wealthy family." But no bond was allowed at the hearing and, in fact, Garrett wasn't even in the courtroom, participating via a video-conferencing link from the Montgomery County Detention Center.

On June 30, 1998, Garrett was freed, thanks to his new lawyer. At the second hearing Helfand squashed Boynton's now familiar refrain of deceit and fraud topped by murder, in spite of his renewed protests.

"We see no good reason he's entitled to any bond," Boynton said. "The case may be ten years old, but it's a case of first degree murder where a man has killed his child for money."

Helfand answered that the state had no evidence. It was relying totally on the circumstantial motive of insurance proceeds as grounds for a conviction, he claimed. As far as the changing of the autopsy document to read *homicide*— well, that was conjured up from whole cloth.

"Two people did the autopsy and they said it was a natural death. Then they changed the autopsy report without any additional evidence."

Garrett's bond was set at $100,000. He was warned not to leave the area, especially not the state. Vicky raised the $20,000 that a bail bondsman demanded by giving him most of the jewelry her rich second husband Paul had bestowed upon her, along with some of her husband's. The adornments would not be returned.

Garrett was free for the moment, but kept looking over his shoulder. He feared a second murder charge in Prince George's was on the way. He had planned to reopen the shuttered Wampler-owned Green Lantern restaurant after settling in western Maryland, envisioning a piano bar where he could perform. He was enthused to learn that the place had once served 1,500 cups of coffee a week until someone told him the coffee had been twenty-five cents a cup with free refills. Still, he was willing to take a shot. The new career as restaurateur was postponed.

Instead, safe in Vicky's mountain valley home, he took a minimum-wage job as a daytime desk clerk at a Hampton Inn, just off I-68. He was soon let go after an employee, a girlfriend of one of the members of the far-flung Wampler clan, discovered his identity and complained to a manager that he wasn't doing his job. Garrett told Vicky she was jealous of his marketing abilities. Ervin then used his contacts to help get his son-in-law a job selling musical instruments. Garrett was too good at that to be terminated.

John Farley called and asked him if he'd done it, and Garrett said no, he had not. "I've done a lot of terrible, stupid, mean things in my life, but I could never ever stoop that low," Garrett told his friend emphatically.

John believed him. When Helfand asked if he would accept a plea of murder two or manslaughter, Garrett shook his head.

"I'm not going to plead guilty to something I didn't do," he said.

* * *

The prosecution was winning the battle of public opinion through the press. It was also reaping a bounty of former Garrett girlfriends from the news stories. Many of them were stepping forward to tell of their romantic, and, even more damaging, monetary experiences with him. There were almost too many to choose from. Julie Stinger called to give her story, as did Elizabeth Dodge, now married, with the last name of Bahlman. Liz sounded almost sorry for her former fiancé.

"We broke up because I found out he was married to Missy," she told Meredith Dominick. "During the time he was repaying his debt to me, Garrett would tell me how miserable he was in the marriage and how horrible she treated him. He said they had violent arguments where she would throw things at him. She followed him wherever he went, almost stalking him. He told me he made a mistake."

Julie Stinger was an avenging angel. She called Dominick the day after Garrett's arrest hit the newspapers, telling of her many meetings with a con man who she said "could sell air conditioners in Alaska." She claimed Garrett had been fired from Jordan Kitt's for stealing both money and property. She said she had always suspected Garrett of killing his son.

"Garrett Michael's death and my suspicions have been eating at me for the last ten years," she told the cops.

The state's attorney's office apparently believed that media coverage listing Garrett's many sins, with little or no mention of any virtues, could only help to win the day for it at his trial. A potential juror who was familiar with the case through news stories might be eliminated if he admitted it during a voir dire process. But they also knew that jurors who took the oath sometimes failed to tell the truth about their knowledge of a case. At each scheduled pretrial hearing, the prosecution took time to reemphasize Garrett's criminal record, the purchase of the insurance policies, and the ages of the two infant children. At one such court session, in July of 1998, David Boynton revealed he had visited a mystery forensic expert in Dallas.

"She is renowned in her field. She is an essential witness and an expert in child death and sudden infant death syndrome," Boynton said, speaking of Linda Norton, but not mentioning her by name.

Another pretrial hearing, held ostensibly to allow Garrett permission to sell pianos in the states adjoining Maryland, evolved into a rancorous debate. The argument was on the key question of whether the details of Brandi's death should be allowed as evidence into Garrett's murder trial for his son. David Boynton and his co-prosecutor, Debra Grimes, seemed to think they could get a conviction without the Brandi intelligence, but Boynton hedged.

"The case we have can stand on its own merits, but knowing about the Prince George's case would be important to a jury in deciding," he said.

Helfand strongly disagreed. "The state is desperately trying to get him charged in Prince George's so that evidence in that case can be used to show other crimes or bad acts."

The judge at the hearing, Ann S. Harrington, was about to learn her name had been drawn to hear the trial. She granted Helfand's travel request for Garrett. She did not rule on the more important issue.

Helfand managed another small victory. Garrett's loquacious ramblings on the day of his arrest were ruled out as evidence. Helfand said Garrett's interview should have ended when he said that he wasn't going to "sit here and talk to you without a lawyer," even though he had kept on chatting with the cops after he said it. Harrington agreed.

Boynton then leaked the story that his secret medical expert would be forensic pathologist Linda Norton. One newspaper described her as the doctor who "headed the team that exhumed the body of presidential assassin Lee Harvey Oswald in 1981." Another said she had "helped convict Green Beret doctor, Jeffrey McDonald, of killing his family."

Helfand described Norton as a hired gun.

There was still the question of whether or not Harrington would allow the evidence surrounding Brandi's death into the trial. By the end of 1998, Garrett had yet to be charged in that case. Another hearing was held to permit Boynton and Helfand to argue the matter again as 1999 began.

"There is a unique pattern in both cases," Boynton began. "If we could show that in 1981 a death occurred in the same manner as the one in 1987, then it helps the state's case."

Helfand said any jury would be prejudiced by hearing what he again called "letting other bad acts" into the trial. He also reiterated that the revised autopsy reports were a sham, saying there had been insufficient findings to support any homicide ruling.

On January 20, Harrington ruled that information on Brandi could be allowed in as evidence. Her opinion read in part:

> The court is persuaded that the state has demonstrated substantial relevancy of the circumstances surrounding the 1981 death of Brandi Wilson as to issues of identity, motive, lack of mistake or accident, intent, and common scheme or plan.

It was Helfand's worst defeat in the pretrial hearings. He felt the ruling would prejudice any jury, making his battle against the prosecution an uphill one that would be difficult to surmount.

"They can now say two kids are dead, so he must have killed them both. This case will now be tried on the odds that he did it, not beyond a reasonable doubt," he complained.

The person heading the state's attorney's office in Montgomery County must be elected. In November of 1996, after twenty-six years of holding the title, liberal Democrat Andy Sonner was made a judge. Upon his retirement, his assistant, Robert Dean, replaced him. Dean was considered the frontrunner to win the 1998 election until it was revealed he'd had an extramarital affair with one of his female prosecutors. The love letters and poems he wrote to her were leaked to *The Washington Post*. A sample stanza:

Your lips as they turn to a smile / When they touch mine, / They speak their own language.

This made for juicy reading and sealed his fate at the polls. In the Democratic primary of 1998 he lost to a young upstart by the name of Douglas F. Gansler. Gansler, a thirty-six-year-old wunderkind and scion of a powerful political family, jogged door-to-door campaigning against Dean, beating him by 8 percent. He had already won a measure of fame as a U.S. government attorney by prosecuting broadcaster Ted Koppel's son Andrew for assault, and a diplomat for a drunken hit-and-run. Both cases were successes. The diplomat, from the former Soviet Union state of Georgia, had killed a sixteen-year-old Montgomery County girl in a Washington traffic accident. Despite technically having immunity from prosecution, he received the most severe sentence ever given a foreign envoy for a crime and served his time in a North Carolina federal prison.

After much mudslinging, Gansler also won the November general election, becoming the youngest state's attorney ever, while Dean burned his bridges by supporting his Republican opponent. Eager to show his mettle, the newly elected state's attorney chose the Garrett Wilson case as the first one that he would personally prosecute. He kept David Boynton as his co-prosecutor.

Gansler immediately called a press conference. He expressed regret that his office was unable to ask for the death penalty in Garrett's upcoming trial, as well as for Hadden Clark, an already convicted murderer and confessed cannibal, who was facing another trial for killing a six-year-old girl.

"If I could ask the jury for the death sentence in either of these cases, I would. However, neither is a death penalty case because they don't contain the aggravators required by law."

(Maryland law has ten statutes for the death penalty. Among these are murdering a law enforcement officer, killing someone during the course of a kidnapping, hiring a contract killer, and dispatching two or more people at the same time.)

"Both of the defendants are alleged to have murdered multiple people and to have preyed upon utterly helpless children who had no ability to defend themselves," Gansler said.

Helfand, already appalled by the one-sided media coverage, was incensed at Gansler's attack. He attempted to counter the young upstart.

"These news releases are being issued for only one reason, to poison the potential jury pool before a trial. While the state has an absolute right to protect the public, I think they should limit their press releases to what they intend to seek and not talk about the rationale for it," he said.

The aggressive Gansler threw a curve ball at the court the next time there was a hearing. He asked that the jury be allowed to question all witnesses, an unusual practice that was rarely allowed anywhere.

"It's a way of involving jurors," Gansler claimed. "It's a way of getting to the truth."

Harrington said she could see hundreds of questions coming from the jury. She also thought the length of the trial could double.

"I see this as being bad for everybody," she said.

Helfand shrugged. He would go along with it, he said, as long as he had the privilege of stopping the procedure at any time. Furthermore, the jury was not to be told who stopped it or why.

Gansler agreed to Helfand's request.

The press corps by now hungered for the courtroom clash. Gansler and Boynton in one corner and Barry Helfand with young Alex Yufik trying to keep him in check in the other would be welcome news on any day. Stir in an accused baby killer, two altered autopsies, and a pair of murders going back nearly twenty years. This was right out of a Patricia Cornwell novel.

Hold the front page, momma!

Gansler had warmed up for the trial by putting boxer Mike Tyson behind bars in February. The convicted rapist lived in a Bethesda mansion in one of Montgomery County's best neighborhoods, with his new wife, Monica Turner. She was a doctor who also happened to be the former mistress of a cocaine dealer. In November, they had been involved in a fender-bender near their home. Incensed at the dent in his car, he'd lashed out by kicking one of the motorists, a sixty-three-year-old man, in the groin and punching the other passenger. Though both declined to prosecute after being paid off by Tyson, one of Gansler's lieutenants, Carol Crawford, prepared a fat presentencing report totaling 151 pages. The package not only listed the fighting thug's trespasses, but contained negative articles from newspapers and sports magazines. The compendium of material was enough to send Tyson off to the Montgomery County Detention Center with a year's sentence. Gansler, not one to hide from publicity, got his name splashed on every network news show and most newspapers in the country the next day, described as the man who put Iron Mike away.

The new state's attorney clearly appeared to be a young man in a hurry. Unlike David Boynton's public school and small college credentials, Gansler was a Thoroughbred groomed for the Kentucky Derby. His blue-blood background made Boynton's look blue collar in comparison. He had gone to the posh Sidwell Friends prep school in Washington, whose most recent celebrity student was Chelsea Clinton. He had not been quiet about his ethnicity and was proud he had once worked on a kibbutz in Israel. His undergraduate school was Yale, where he had been an All-American lacrosse player. After that there was law school at the college of Thomas Jefferson, the University of Virginia. His father, Jacques "Jack" Gansler, was Undersecretary of Defense in the Clinton administration. His wife was a prominent lawyer with Nasdaq. You could find no takers in the state's attorney's office willing to bet Gansler would stay around for twenty-six years like Andy Sonner.

On February 12, 1999, Detective Richard Fulginiti presented a four-page arrest warrant to a court in Prince George's County. It charged Garrett with the death of his daughter, Brandi. The last paragraph read:

This investigator believes that a pattern of deception for monetary gain is apparent and also believes that probable cause exists to charge Garrett E. Wilson with the murder of Brandi Jean Wilson.

Three days later, five cars—one from Prince George's County with Fulginiti in it and four state trooper black-and-whites—showed up to arrest Garrett a second time. Fulginiti, who had been David Boynton's guest at the first arrest, felt his suspect would offer no resistance, based on observing Garrett at Ervin's house nearly a year before. This time, though, there would be no bond. The cop who handcuffed Garrett had not yet gotten the message.

"Don't worry," the lawman told a tearful Marysa as he led the five-year-old's father away. "Your daddy will be out tomorrow."

THIRTEEN

THE FACE OF AMERICA

Ann S. Harrington was unlike any other judge in Maryland, if not the country. The distinction was that she was beautiful, not merely attractive. She was too smart, one would think, to have ever been a beauty queen, but in fact, she was just that. She had been a runner-up as Miss College Park in the Miss Maryland pageant when she was a university student. The memory had become so fogged among some courthouse clerks that she was often gossiped about as having been the titleholder herself.

She was a queen in her courtroom, too, ruling it with lace gloves rather than an iron fist. Nobody could ever remember her using a gavel. A look or a few quiet words were all Ann Harrington needed to establish order.

In court she wore skillfully applied makeup and false eyelashes. There would never be a Judge Judy white doily collar around *her* neck. Instead, she made sure a gold chain or a pearl necklace peeked above her black robe, and on the days she abstained from wearing jewelry, there would usually be a saucy silk scarf visible.

Others might have thought she could have been an actress and, if so, they would have been right. There were courthouse lawyers whose saliva glands would overproduce at the mere remembrance of her singing and dancing her way through *Kiss Me Kate*, in the role of Bianca. She had performed in the musical version of William Shakespeare's *The Taming of the Shrew* and *Fiorello*, too, in Rockville Little Theater productions during the 1970s.

That was when she was a young prosecutor. Now nearly fifty and married to a local criminal attorney, she was still willowy, blessed with what she claimed was a high metabolism rate. But as a Circuit Court judge, well, one could not rule over life and death matters by day, and tread the boards by night, could one?

Like Helfand, she was a University of Maryland law school product. It wasn't Yale, but not anything from which to hide either. She thought her career had always been interesting, if not always so pleasant. As a judge, she, like David Boynton, had seen far more gruesome cases than a parent charged with smothering infants.

One of her more famous trials was that of triple murderer Lawrence Horn. The former Motown record technician had hired a hit man to kill three people in 1993. The first two victims were his former wife and a daycare nurse, both shot between the eyes. The other was his seven-year-old quadriplegic son, Trevor, who died when the contract killer simply unplugged the child's respirator. The hit man committed the acts after consulting a published how-to manual on how to perform murders for hire. Horn's reason for ordering the killings was so he could corner nearly two million dollars that his child was about to receive from a medical malpractice suit. Harrington gave the hit man, James Perry, the death penalty. Horn got life without parole.

Ruling on these kinds of cases was light-years away from musically interpreting the works of Shakespeare. She looked forward to the start of the Garrett Wilson case, now set to begin on the morning of July 19, 1999.

After his second arrest Garrett Wilson was kept in a special protective custody cellblock at the Prince George's Correctional Center. There was no choice. Baby killers or child molesters, accused or convicted, were prime targets for inmates—such is the code of convicts. Harming a child in any way is a major taboo among prisoners. Those who are convicted of doing so usually suffer extreme violence, often being silently dispatched in state penitentiaries during their first years inside the walls.

Vicky often became angry with Helfand before the trial to the point where she considered firing him. Once, when the colorful lawyer had come to western Maryland and the two had lunch, he upset Vicky by playing keno at the bar instead of discussing the case. Vicky and Helfand were on the outs when Fulginiti had shown up to arrest Garrett. It was left to Steve Friend, an Allegany County attorney pal of Vicky's, to attempt to get Garrett released on bond. It was futile. The Prince George's courts weren't about to consider letting a person accused of murdering two babies walk for any amount of money. When Friend failed, he gallantly refused to bill Vicky for his services.

Unlike the ten-cell PC unit in Montgomery County, the H-cellblock for protective custody prisoners in Prince George's called for twenty-three hours a day in solitary confinement without a radio or television. Garrett's one-hour outside his cell allowed time for him to make over-priced collect phone calls or take a shower. He tried to do both, but it was impossible. His only diversion came when a plastic trash bag full of books would be dragged by his cell once a day. He was allowed to select two. By the end of the month, he had exhausted the limited supply. There was one newspaper allowed per day, and it was *The Washington Times*, the conservative local paper with a great sports section but hardly any comics, perhaps reflecting the political beliefs of his captors.

"I'm a voracious reader," he told a visitor. "I always have been."

And his tastes?

"Tom Clancy, Jack Higgins, Robert Ludlum, Stephen Coonts. I just read my first Sue Grafton book."

"*N Is for Noose?*"

"No, *L Is for Lawless.*"

Montgomery County had a much better system, he thought. There, the prison librarian was the infamous Ruthann Aron, and you could order on a computer from the county library system. You could lift weights, too, and even if you were in the isolation cellblock, you could come out to see video movies twice a week. Garrett thought Montgomery County's facility was a resort compared to Prince George's. Montgomery allowed you to have a Walkman radio in your cell. He got into the habit of listening to the Rush Limbaugh broadcasts on the AM powerhouse, WMAL, when they were repeated at midnight. During the day he listened to the FM classical music radio station, WGMS, especially when the velvety voice of Renee Chaney could be heard. He remembered listening to her during his Friendly High School days.

The only advantages Prince George's had over Montgomery County were its canteen and the visiting system. There was a wider selection of food. It was cheaper, too. In Montgomery, a small jar of peanut butter was five dollars. He had bought it anyway with money sent by Vicky. Anything was better than the moldy baloney sandwiches and powdered eggs that were slid through a slot in his cell. He wouldn't drink the juice. There were rumors about the contents. Saltpeter and sedatives were mixed in it, he was told. Garrett began to long for the simple feel of ice in his mouth when he drank warm water from the prison's faucets. In Montgomery, ice had been readily available. Here, even that was denied.

Yet, anyone could visit a prisoner in Prince George's. There was no approved visitors' paperwork necessary for a half-hour chat.

The trip to his new home added 100 miles to Vicky's already 270-mile round-trip. She would come down from the mountains for night visits with her sister Kathy, Ervin, Marysa, her Aunt Inez, or her friend Belinda Lavin, but more often alone, trying to make the round-trip and not fall asleep at the wheel by consuming Snickers bars, drinking coffee, and listening to loud country music. She would get back to Allegany County after midnight, arriving at her $36,000-a-year county social worker job the next day tired, trying not to let it show. When Kathy accompanied her, a redneck guard had picked up her Appalachian accent and flirted, calling her his "hillbilly" and making the term sound somehow lewd. Vicky and whoever was keeping her company would be sent to an enclosed cubicle, where they would take turns shouting at Garrett through the perforations at the bottom of the thick windows—the kind you yell into at movie theater ticket booths—until the talk sometimes turned to tears.

Garrett Wilson tried to show a sense of humor, given the macabre set of circumstances that had brought him to this point in his life. Once, when he called collect to a prospective visitor, he used this wry opener: "I'm trying to plan my evening. Are you coming to see me at the jail tonight?"

Who were his other callers? John Farley came a few times. Bill Boyer Jr., the Wampler family's pastor at the Welsh Memorial Baptist Church, made the trek to the jail on one occasion, even though he had a bad shoulder. The reverend had a weekly message put in the church bulletin which read: "*Pray for the Garrett and Vickie* [sic] *Wilson family.*" He was a poor driver and his parishioners worried that he would have an accident navigating the busy highways around Washington.

The congregation, which often brought the latest Beanie Babies to Sunday services to show them off, was backing Garrett. Its richer members slipped cash into Vicky's pockets as she played the organ on Sunday mornings.

She tried not to buckle under the pressure, but Vicky could see Garrett losing weight with each visit and getting the pasty white face many prisoners acquire over time. Garrett tried to keep his usual self-confidence up, but it was hard, particularly while wearing a V-neck orange jumpsuit with INMATE and SIZE 2XL stenciled on the back. He had once been a person who was fastidious in what he wore, what he ate, and how he looked. Now, there were neither food nor wardrobe choices. However, in phone calls from his cell, he seemed to believe it was just a short matter of time before he would be set free. The trial would vindicate him, he said.

"When I get out, we'll celebrate," he told a visitor.

"Sure. You can have champagne."

"No. You'll have the champagne. I'll have a pitcher of Diet Coke with lots of lime. And I'll buy."

The Prince George's facility was in the middle of nowhere—two miles from the courthouse in the village of Upper Marlboro—surrounded by fierce razor wire. Despite the location, the P.G. system found ways to gouge its mostly indigent visitors. It had installed seven-day-a-week meters in front of each parking slot in the giant lot. Most of the poor would leave their cars down the road and gingerly walk along the rough shoulders rather than pay.

The Wilsons began writing love letters to one another. One piece of his correspondence read: "When I get out I'll kiss you on the lips and go from there!" Vicky's would always include the lyrics from a Shania Twain CD, the song that rhymed "bless" with "happiness." Garrett wrote to Ervin and Thelma and Marysa. He would beg friends to take Marysa a box of doughnut holes. The yeasty dough balls were a treat they had once shared and that he knew she loved. He asked that Marysa be told they were from her daddy.

On Memorial Day weekend of 1999 he wrote to Ervin. "Dear Pappy," the note said. "Hi! it's Memorial Day. It's time to remember what you gave to all of us. I still love our country and I do love you." And to Thelma he began: "Dear Nan Nan, The last five years have been the happiest of my life..." Garrett told his mother-in-law he was cleaning so many bathrooms that when he got out he was thinking of getting a Mighty Maids franchise.

Garrett couldn't wait for the trial to begin. He had no doubt that with Barry Helfand as his defender he would soon be walking out of Ann Harrington's courtroom a free man. On May 24, 1999, he was switched back to the Montgomery

County Detention Center so Helfand could have closer access to prepare him for trial. His new cell in the protective custody wing had just been vacated by Mike Tyson, paroled early some six hours before.

A protracted murder trial is like a long play with four acts. The opening consists of the jury selection, followed by dramatic opening arguments. In the second act there is a parade of evidence from witnesses favoring the prosecution. During part three, the defense responds in kind. And in the final quarter, both the prosecution and the defense sum up the case and make their final arguments. The prosecution always gets two bites from the apple by making both the first summation and then taking the opportunity to respond to the defense. Courts allow this because the prosecution has the greater burden of proof and must prove its case beyond a reasonable doubt.

A good defense lawyer knows that reasonable doubt is not always what juries base their judgments upon. Rather, cases are usually decided on emotion. Certainly, a trial with pictures of two dead babies and accounts of how they died was sure to produce tears and sobs on all sides. Making the emotion work in one's favor is what both the prosecution and the defense wanted to accomplish. Facts were one thing, but pathos would rule.

Ann Harrington had the opening day of the trial moved to Courtroom One of the Judicial Center, the largest such venue in the county. It seated several hundred people on hard brown wooden benches. The seats were identical to the pews one finds in country chapels on Sunday, but without the comfort of a church's fabric-and-foam cushions. Toward the end of a long day in Courtroom One, there was much squirming among the hardy souls still in attendance.

The courtroom was on the third floor of the nine-story stone-pebbled concrete building. It placed the jury to the public's left. The witnesses sat in a box between the judge and jurors. The prosecution and the defense sat side-by-side across from the jury at long tables, with the defense closest to the judge. Ann Harrington, of course, was elevated above everyone in the center, her back to the wall and the obligatory furled flags. In front of her was the legal combat zone, called the well. It was here that exhibits were placed on easels and attorneys ranted as they attempted to sway the jurors with a combination of facts and hyperbole.

On the trial's first day Barry Helfand was in the courtroom before anyone. He wore a navy power suit and a red tie, a costume that usually impressed jurors. Alex Yufik followed with books of discovery documents. Vicky was already in the front row on the right, poised to take notes. Doug Gansler was next to arrive, speedwalking down the center aisle with David Boynton in pursuit, while a young assistant wheeled in exhibits on a cart behind them.

Helfand had walked the two blocks to the courthouse from his office. On the way over, he expounded on an angle he planned to explore during the trial.

"Ever hear my cat theory?" he asked.

His astonished listener had not. Helfand explained how the old wives' tale of cats smothering babies might, in fact, be true, and that he was considering calling in a veterinarian as a witness to back him up.

The courtroom was filling up. Ingrid Horton sat near the front on the left, the press side. Missy Anastasi, dressed in black, had her supporters grouped together. She had prepped for the trial by going through cosmetic surgery (eyes, chin, liposuction). Her brother, Frank, sat with his wife, Susie. All three were on the witness list and would have to leave when actual testimony began. Today, attendance was open to all, a time for choosing jurors. The task was expected to be difficult. Near the rear of the courtroom was a mystery couple. Both appeared to be in their mid-sixties. The woman was in a wheelchair. They turned out to be Garrett's cousin, Paul, and his wife, Jacqueline Sandoe, who knew of Garrett's four years of breastfeeding and Ethel's pregnancy difficulties. They had not heard from him for years, but had read about the charges and were determined to attend.

The accused arrived in the courtroom handcuffed. No prospective jurors were in the courtroom who could be prejudiced by seeing the manacles. A sheriff's deputy removed them. Garrett Wilson wore a lawyerly suit of muted stripes. Unlike Helfand's, it looked to be a bit tight. His choice of ties was a novelty style, a merry road of black-and-white piano keys cascading down the silk. He would wear the costume each day of the trial. When Vicky had asked Alex if she should bring him a change of dress, she was vetoed.

"It's okay. We don't want him to look too prosperous," Alex said.

There were a few housekeeping questions before 150 potential jurors filed in. Doug Gansler had both a curve ball and a change-up to throw this time. First, he wanted the four alternate jurors not to be told of their status so they would pay more attention during the trial.

"Intriguing, but not within the rules of this court," said Judge Harrington. "Mr. Helfand, do you want people not identified as alternates?"

Helfand didn't seem to think it mattered.

"Then the last four chosen will be the alternates," she said, adding that their status would be revealed.

Gansler threw another pitch.

"In terms of motions, can our chief investigator Meredith Dominick sit next to us? We're not going to be calling her."

The specter of a Detective Meredith Dominick, brass badge flashing at the jury in order to underscore the prosecution's arguments, was not lost on her honor.

"Investigators do not sit at the prosecution counsel's table," she gently chided.

"We also have a chart that we want to use during the opening statement," Gansler said.

Helfand appeared bored.

"If you want to use a chart, go ahead."

Helfand was more worried about the two cops from the sheriff's office standing just behind Garrett and the prejudicial appearance it gave.

"The defendant has an absolute right to be present during

the jury selection. But if he has to move, they will move with him. I'm asking that they not move," Helfand said.

Harrington said that was beyond her control.

"I don't direct the sheriff's office, but I'll see what I can do," she said.

Gansler then complained that he had never been given access to Helfand's expert witnesses as required. He wanted to know what they would testify about. Helfand was not about to assist him.

"In general? They will not help the state's case." He said one of them might be a veterinarian. This remark, alluding to his pet cat theory, seemed to shake the prosecution and drew raised eyebrows from Ann Harrington.

The posturing ended and 150 potential jurors filed in. They were the face of America: Half of them were white while the rest were either black, Asian, Hispanic, or Arabic. Jamaican and Haitian patois and whispered Central American Spanish blended with English filled the courtroom as they sat down. Unlike the rest of those already in the courtroom, casual comfort appeared to be the jurors' only concern. Only two of the men wore suits, while the rest were either in knit collared shirts or tieless tailored cotton blends without jackets. Some of the black women were cornrowed on top. They were attentive, curious. The jury pool appeared to be one of honest citizens all, caught in the great maw of the law and pulled away from their jobs for the opportunity to serve justice for fifteen dollars a day. Harrington told them how they might get out of serving in a trial she admitted could take up to a month.

"Do you know something about this case? Do you know the attorneys? Have you received information about this case? Or is there another reason why you should not hear this case?"

Jurors began standing in an attempt to disqualify themselves—nineteen in all. They wanted to be the first out the door before the woman wearing the black robe changed her mind.

"Mr. Wilson, please stand. Are there any of you who knows this defendant?"

Ann S. Harrington got no takers on the question. She asked if anyone knew Barry Helfand, David Boynton, Douglas Gansler, or Alex Yufik. Then she wanted to know if anyone had religious convictions that might disqualify them. Now several more stood. She further weaned the jury pool by asking these questions.

"Are you more or less likely to believe a witness, simply because of the person's occupation? Example: A doctor or a policeman. Are there any prospective jurors biased in favor of the defendant or the prosecution on what you have heard or learned so far? Do any of you have medical training—are any of you doctors, nurses, or scientists?"

A total of eighteen stood up on the last question. It didn't mean they were automatically disqualified, but enabled the prosecution and defense to note who they were, in case they wanted to issue a challenge and dismiss them later on the basis of their occupation. Judge Harrington began asking the jury pool even more pertinent queries.

"Is there any prospective juror that has familiarity with the term 'sudden infant death syndrome' or 'SIDS'? Is there anyone here connected with the SIDS Foundation?"

A dozen more stood up.

"Have any of you ever sold life insurance? Is there anyone who has had experience with the death of an infant?"

Two. The questions got even more specific.

"Is there any prospective juror who doesn't believe that a parent is capable of killing a child? Is there any person here who believes that a person is likely to be more guilty or less guilty, simply because he has been arrested by the state?"

With that, one of the two suits, a man who had said he was from the Washington law firm of Hogan and Hartson, stood up. He was dismissed.

"The defendant is presumed to be innocent unless the state is able to prove its charges. Is there any prospective juror who would lower the state's burden of proof strictly because the death of children is involved? Are there any members of the juror pool who feel they cannot be a fair juror because of the subject matter of this case?"

Another twenty-five people stood up.

"Have any of you ever been charged with a misdemeanor or a felony?"

Another twenty.

By now more than half of the jury pool had been eliminated. The 150 number was down to just over 70.

At noon, the press corps began drafting story leads. The slant for the evening newscasts would be that a jury pool of 150 might have so many of its numbers eliminated on the first day that a second group of jurors would have to be shipped in. There would be no opening statements. In the building's cafeteria at lunch, Jim Neustadt, a bearded producer wearing a navy blazer from WRC-4, a Washington television station, and Chris Gordon, his reporter, discussed whether they had a package. The term was television jargon for all the visual elements needed to put several different news reports together. Channel 4, an NBC-owned station, did three straight hours of local news in the afternoon that didn't end until seven and led into Tom Brokaw, who added another half-hour. Gordon, who had just returned to Washington after a stint at *Court TV*, went through what they had on tape.

"We've got Missy, we've got the wife. Helfand's done. Gansler came in under the building, but he's not ducking us and nobody's trying to go in a side door."

Neustadt took a bite of his tuna fish sandwich before commenting, "This is like shooting fish in a barrel."

Gordon agreed.

Gansler quickly gave the two their wish. After Harrington dismissed everyone at three, he immediately came down from Courtroom One to a velvet-roped press corral on the ground level of the courthouse. He gave the media a feeding that was in time for the afternoon deadlines. Gansler tried to begin with a canned speech.

"I think it's important for a case like this to be tried..."

"Who are you trying to weed out?" a reporter interrupted.

"People who have a proclivity to either side."

Gansler then made a surprising statement, considering the drama expected in the days ahead. He said the trial might not be able to hold all of the jurors' attention over a four-week trial, particularly the alternates, who would know of their status.

Outside on the sidewalk, with a camera catching some of the words on the building spelling out MONTGOMERY COUNTY JUDICIAL CENTER over his left shoulder, Chris Gordon touched up his makeup in the hot summer sun. He straightened his tie and then kept practicing his opening lines over and over as he stared up at the clear blue sky, waiting to go live for his first news report of the day.

"They've been at it all day here at the Montgomery County Courthouse, trying to select a jury in the murder case of Garrett Wilson, a man charged with killing two of his children..."

Gordon frowned. That didn't sound quite right. He began the lines again.

FOURTEEN

HE DID THE UNTHINKABLE

The prosecution and defense had conducted a partial voir dire in private the day before, bringing in the remainder of the jury pool by tens into the chambers behind the courtroom. Both had goals. Helfand wanted as many men as possible on the jury in the belief that males would be less emotional and more analytical. Gansler and Boynton wanted adults who had families—spouses and children. Many of the prospective jurors at the voir dire simply begged to be sent home. They would be glad to serve in a jury they said, but not in this instance, where the suffocation deaths of two babies were about to be explored in every detail.

On the second day of the trial, a final, more public selection took place. Called "striking from the box," a total of sixteen men and women were chosen from the decimated jury pool. A dozen would become jurors and four would be alternates. Helfand and Gansler took turns excusing some of them based on notes they had from the day before.

"Strike her, please," Helfand said of an Asian woman. He did the same to a stern-looking elderly woman.

"Strike him, please." Gansler pointed to a black man after consulting with David Boynton.

Both knew what they wanted. After more winnowing,

with their numbers replaced from the disappearing jury pool, they were ready to begin Case 82490, *The State of Maryland versus Garrett E. Wilson*. Both believed their wishes had been fulfilled. There were eight men and four women. Of the primary twelve, all but one were married with children. Six were white, five were black, and there was a single Hispanic male. Kristina Vaquera, Harrington's ice-blonde, microskirted young law clerk, passed out paper and pencils for the jurors to make notes. After each day, it was her duty to collect the legal pads for safekeeping.

Courtroom One was cleared of all witnesses who might possibly testify for either the prosecution or the defense. That meant Vicky and Missy. The two women would spend their days outside the courtroom seated as far away from one another as possible. Most of the time Vicky was alone while Missy was surrounded by a horde of female supporters, all dressed in dark clothing. The bailiff read the single charge in archaic language passed down from English law.

"Count number one: Murder. If guilty you will say so. If not guilty you will say so. And say no more."

Harrington instructed the jurors. She warned them they could be hearing the case for as long as four weeks. The news was not greeted with any applause.

"As a body, you possess the knowledge that these counsel want. We have gone through a meticulous trial to choose you. You cannot discuss this case with your family and friends or even each other. Listen to all the evidence on both sides. Do not do any independent investigation on your own."

She told them how the trial would unfold. The opening statements, then the state's case, followed by the defense.

"The burden of proof is that the state has the obligation to prove their case beyond a reasonable doubt. Decide this case on evidence and not on the opening statements or the last ones. I expect there will be objections and you should not hold it against either counsel when they do object. That's their job."

Harrington warned them not to read newspapers or listen

to broadcast accounts of the trial. She also said there would be no reading back of questions as the county had no court reporter, but rather the proceedings were audiotaped only. She was covering all her bases. If there were a mistrial or an appeal it would not be due to any misruling she made, Harrington hoped.

She was ready to begin. Gansler bounded to his feet. His voice still had a teenager's ring, and his speech patterns sometimes sounded like a high school valedictorian's at commencement exercises. But his energy and the fearlessness he displayed as he looked straight into the jurors' eyes made up for any vocal deficits.

"On April 30, 1981, Debbie Fennel placed her beautiful, healthy daughter, Brandi Jean, down for her night's sleep. Early the next morning, between three-thirty and five-thirty A.M., the defendant snuck into Brandi Jean's nursery and did the unthinkable."

Gansler had the jury's attention with those two sentences.

"The defendant smothered his own daughter until he killed her. Six years later, here in Montgomery County, in Germantown, Missy Anastasi took her beautiful, healthy, energetic five-and-a-half-month-old son, the brother that Brandi Jean would never know; she took him and placed him in his crib for his night's sleep. Early next morning, the defendant crept into Garrett Michael's nursery. And again, he did the unthinkable.

"He, the defendant, took Garrett Michael and smothered him until he died."

Gansler had moved toward Garrett now and was wagging his finger within inches of his nose. Helfand was having none of that. He immediately established a ground rule.

"I object. Please, remove your finger from my client's face," he said calmly. Harrington didn't need to say anything. Gansler walked away, back toward the jury. He had made his point.

"That man, the father of Brandi Jean and Garrett Michael, killed his own babies, and his motive was greed.

He snatched their futures away from them before they took their first steps. He did it for money, because what he did before he killed those two babies, was he bought life insurance on both of them. He placed a value, a monetary value, on those innocent, adorable infants. He placed a $40,000 value on the life of Brandi Jean and he placed a $150,000 value on the life of Garrett Michael.

"Now, I just briefly described two murders. But I want to make it perfectly clear from the outset that the defendant stands trial here for the one murder, the 1987 murder of Garrett Michael, the murder that occurred here in Montgomery County. The 1981 murder occurred in Prince George's County. So you will not be asked to return a verdict on that murder. However, during the course of this trial you will hear a great deal of evidence about the 1981 murder so you will be able to see the striking similarities between the two cases.

"Let us begin back in 1977 when Debbie Fennel, then named Debbie Oliver, was herself a young, vulnerable child. She was twelve years old. This is where the story begins about a man, that the evidence will show, manipulated women to his advantage, floated from state to state and job to job, spent money without restraint, and finally, and ultimately, was willing to kill to support his spending habits.

"Debbie Oliver was twelve years old when the defendant, a twenty-year-old divorcé, induced her and seduced her into having sexual relations with him. In fact, for the next three years, from the time Debbie was twelve until she was fifteen, the defendant repeatedly had sexual relations with her. Indeed, he got Debbie Oliver pregnant five times from the age that she was twelve until the age that she was fifteen."

That was a new accusation. A couple of the older women jurors looked toward Garrett. Five times? Can I strangle him myself?

"He had so much control over her that she got an abortion for each of those first four times. He had her go and abort those potential children. And then she got pregnant with Brandi Jean. The problem with Brandi Jean for the defendant was by the time Debbie got to the doctor to have the abortion the defendant wanted her to get—she was a child, she listened—she was five months pregnant. The doctor would not perform the abortion. So now she had to accept the consequences of his act."

Four abortions before the age of fifteen? The women jurors appeared ready to rule on his guilt before the trial was under way.

"She told her parents and she will tell you what her relationship is with her parents and she knew how difficult that was to tell her parents that she was pregnant—she felt she had to marry the defendant. In fact, she had to leave school. When she was five months pregnant, in October of 1980, the defendant and Debbie did get married. Two months later, when she was pregnant seven months and Brandi Jean had not yet been born, the defendant asked her: 'Are you going to be okay if something happens to the baby?'

"On February 26, 1982, Debbie gave birth to a healthy baby, named Brandi Jean. She named her Jean after her mother, and she named her Brandi because she liked the name. Brandi Jean, for the short period of her life—over two months—was a completely healthy child. She went for her well checks, her well visits—she never had any health problems at all. During those two months of Brandi Jean's short life, the defendant was emotionally and physically detached from his child. The defendant didn't change Brandi Jean, ever. The defendant didn't feed Brandi Jean. The defendant never got up at night with Brandi Jean. He never was a father."

With Garrett Wilson painted as a cold, uncaring father, Gansler told what he believed happened on the night of Brandi's death.

"We move to the evening of April thirtieth. That night, Debbie had a severe cold. Debbie's parents, Jean and Kyle Oliver—who you'll meet—were at the defendant's house that day. Debbie's parents said, 'Look, you've got a severe cold. Stay here tonight. Let us help you take care of Brandi

Jean—you don't want to be getting up during the night.' But the defendant said, 'No—I'll take her home—I'll take care of her.' "

And then Gansler described how he believed Garrett took care of her.

"He gave her pills, which he told her were vitamins. Brandi Jean went to sleep and he gave Debbie pills that he called vitamins. Debbie, who throughout her life was a moderate-to-light sleeper, had never missed hearing her child's tears or her cries in the middle of the night. She slept through her cries this night. In fact, the very next morning on May 1, 1981, Debbie had to be physically awakened by her parents. She missed Brandi Jean's cries, she missed medics showing up at the house or the police showing up at the house, and when she got up and saw her mother there, she said, 'What's wrong? Where is Brandi Jean?' Now, the reason why her mother and her father were even at the house was because after the defendant killed Brandi Jean he called—not 911—he called Debbie's parents. He told them and they came over and what did he tell her parents? He said he walked in to check on Brandi Jean when he heard her crying and then he found her dead. When the parents showed up at the house that day, and they'll tell you this, the defendant, to them, looked like he had been up all night."

Gansler shot a hard look at Garrett, who looked straight ahead and avoided a staring match.

"You'll hear from Mark Cashman, the fire department guy from Prince George's County that showed up. You'll hear how he found the baby. You'll learn he found Brandi Jean lying in her crib with her fists clenched, as if there had been a struggle. And you'll see the pictures of Brandi Jean as he found her. You may be disturbed by them, but it's important that you see these photos. You'll also hear from people who will tell you she was blue and mostly red throughout her body, and you'll hear medical experts tell you why that is, but what you'll see, and Mark Cashman will tell you what he observed, was that the front of her face was completely white right here."

Gansler pointed to the bridge of his nose to indicate.

"There was no blood. That will become significant as this case goes further. You'll also hear from Terry Montague. He's a Prince George's police officer. And you'll hear about the different reactions of Brandi Jean's father and Debbie.

"Debbie was hysterical. She had to be restrained by the police; they wouldn't let her see Brandi Jean dead. The defendant was nowhere to be found. But the defendant was in the house, roaming around. Mark Cashman saw him very briefly. Terry Montague was there forty-five minutes and never saw him. That was because the defendant was downstairs in the basement, shooting pool. And that was before he later went out flying with a friend.

"But what he did before he went out flying—he had time to make a phone call. And he called George Smith. Who is George Smith? Well, George Smith was the agent that sold the defendant his insurance policy. George Smith was not a friend of the defendant—he'll tell you he was a mere acquaintance and met him a couple of times. The defendant solicited him for the opportunity to buy some life insurance. So, now he calls George Smith and says, 'I didn't know who else to call.' He told George Smith he had found Brandi Jean in the crib that very morning of her death and he said he had no one else to call."

Gansler continued to pound on Garrett by describing him as cold and unfeeling.

"The defendant never comforted Debbie at any time. He was completely unemotional, and you'll hear how unemotional he was at Brandi Jean's funeral. There was no police investigation into the death of Brandi Jean, and you will learn during the course of this trial the significance of the fact that this death took place in 1981 and that the death of Garrett Michael took place in 1987 and where we are today in 1999.

"The knowledge about SIDS has advanced tremendously. Back then they didn't do investigations. There were, however, photos, because the police showed up that time—it's a Prince George's County policy—if the police show up at any unattended death—and what they mean by unattended is not at the hospital. So they showed up and took some pictures and that's why we have the photographs that we do.

"But there was no suspicion, there was no investigation of the defendant. And the death was ruled SIDS. Only later, closer to now, was it learned that the defendant was the sole beneficiary of two life insurance policies on Brandi. He bought the first one on March 18, 1981, for $30,000 from Lafayette Life and he bought the second one on March 22, 1981, for $10,000 from American National. Of course, you'll note, Debbie knew nothing about these policies. She was not the beneficiary of these policies and she never benefited from the policies.

"In fact, while Debbie was spending her time grieving from the loss of her baby girl, the defendant went out and bought himself a brand-new Pontiac TransAm. She told her mother and father and her friend Diana McGoldrick about her suspicions of the defendant's involvement, but she didn't go to the police. Shortly thereafter, Debbie left the defendant, they got divorced, and she wanted to forget about this case forever. We made her remember.

"She didn't want to talk to law enforcement when we came to her. She wanted nothing to do with this. She didn't want to relive it.

"Our story moves to 1985. Missy Anastasi meets the defendant at the health club where the defendant was working. And in their very first conversation he feels the need to tell her that his first baby died of SIDS. Missy and the defendant get married in March of 1986. Unknown to Missy, the defendant was also scheduled to marry Elizabeth Dodge Bahlman, in June of 1986. She found out in May that the defendant was already married to somebody else. The defendant also meets a woman named Julie Stinger in 1986. They started getting serious and discussed marriage during Christmas of 1987. Early in 1987 the defendant tells Julie Stinger that he wants to leave Missy and marry her. He wants to leave Missy, so they can be together."

The women jurors weren't looking pleased whenever

they gazed toward the defense table. Patty Schrein's cry of "String 'im up" seemed too good for Garrett at the moment.

"On March twelfth of the same year, Garrett Michael was born—a healthy, energetic, bountiful boy. You will see for yourself—you'll see home videotapes of Garrett Michael, and you can decide if he was healthy or not. Again, the defendant had almost no contact with his baby. He doesn't change him, doesn't feed him, doesn't get up at night to support his wife while she's feeding him.

"Instead he borrows money from a variety of people and gets himself in economic straits, including borrowing $5,000 from Julie Stinger. The defendant and Missy have a trip planned to go to the beach in August of that year. Before they go, the defendant tells Julie Stinger, 'I'll have the money for you when I get back.' Missy and the defendant went to the beach on August twelfth, and while they're there Missy says to the defendant, because of the previous SIDS death—she had been reading up on it a little—'Today's the five-month anniversary of our baby. We're out of it, we're out of the woods and he's not going to get SIDS, he's not going to die.' They come back from the beach and the defendant tells Julie Stinger, 'Don't worry, the money's coming real soon.' And five days later, Garrett Michael's dead."

Garrett kept his eyes on his writing pad as Gansler spoke, taking so many notes, a new arrival in Courtroom One might have mistaken him for Ann Harrington's stenographer. Alex Yufik wrote his observations as well. From time to time, he would slide notes toward Helfand.

"At six-fifteen on the morning of August twenty-second, through the monitor, Missy hears Garrett Michael crying. She goes to get up, like she had done every night for five months. She thought the defendant was going to lie in bed, as he had done every night for the first five months. But he says, 'No. Let me do it tonight. You're going back to work soon. Let me do it, let me take care of it.' So, she does. And she, Missy, hears, through the monitor what's going on. She hears the defendant with the baby. The baby's alive, he's being fed. About six-forty-five in the morning, Missy hears

Garrett Michael being put back into the crib, but she doesn't hear Garrett Michael. She hears him being put back in the crib and hears a strange sigh. That sigh worried her. That sigh was—she didn't think it was the unthinkable—the defendant killing her kid, her infant, but the sigh bothered her so she got out of bed and because her cats had been troubling her, she went quickly to feed them, get them out of her hair, and then ran upstairs to find out what was wrong.

"She gets into Garrett Michael's nursery and the defendant's no longer there. He had left and gone into the bedroom. She walks in to put a blanket over Garrett Michael and realizes something's wrong. He's stiff. She picks him up.... She screams! She runs into the master bedroom where the defendant is in the bathroom and she says, '*What did you do to my boy?*' He doesn't answer. He walks out of the bathroom as white as a sheet and just keeps walking. There's roughly one or two minutes since Missy hears the sigh and the time she comes back upstairs. And what you'll learn from the doctors is that, in infants, if you suffocate them, once they stop breathing—which takes about twenty seconds—they don't reopen their mouths once you release them to start breathing again. And it takes about four minutes for them to die.

"So, Missy calls 911. The paramedics arrive, and you'll see—this is important—there's a strip that's called an EKG strip—which shows that the baby is dead and that it happened very recently because it shows heart murmurs which means it's dead but still has these murmurs. The paramedics take Garrett Michael off to the hospital. The defendant and Missy get in the car to follow them. And the defendant decides that he needs to take the baby seat out of the car before driving to the hospital... and a neighbor will testify to seeing that. Missy told her mother, friends, and relatives about her suspicions, but again they said, 'You're a grieving mother, this is SIDS.' There was no police investigation, no photographs, and the police were never notified because it was an 'attended death,' and in this case he was pronounced dead in the hospital. Again, there was no reaction, no emotion showed by the defendant at the funeral, while Missy was incredibly distraught as a mother who had just lost her child.

"Later, it was learned that the defendant had bought two life insurance policies on the life of Garrett Michael. A $50,000 policy, which he purchased from Allstate, on March 27, 1987, and a $100,000 policy, which he purchased from MetLife, on April 16, 1987. Like the two policies before, and like these two policies, it was the defendant who solicited the agent to buy the insurance. Like the previous policies, the defendant was the sole beneficiary of that $150,000.

"The defendant bounces around for a few years and winds up divorcing Missy in Florida, in 1993, without even telling her about it. And eventually Missy finds out that the defendant had married a fourth wife, Vicky Frihse. She questions whether or not she should go to the police at that point to tell the police what her suspicions are, but she doesn't do it then. She does it, and reports to the police what had happened to her, when she finds out that the defendant has a child with Vicky, his fourth wife. That's when she goes to the police.

"Eventually, the Chief Medical Examiner for the state of Maryland is given the two cases, reopens them, looks at the cases, and, given the new knowledge we have about SIDS and how it manifests itself, in November of 1997, Dr. Smialek, who you'll meet, ruled Garrett Michael's death was a homicide.

"Now you know more details about what occurred, you will see many similarities in the two murders."

Gansler had the chart up now, the chart he would always refer to as his "mountain of evidence." It showed the similarities in the two deaths. He went through it step-by-step.

"Both cases, two insurance policies . . . both cases, was the sole beneficiary . . . both cases, fed the baby for the first time."

It was time to speak of SIDS.

"SIDS is a term that some people know a lot about and some people don't know much about. Sudden . . . Infant . . . Death . . . Syndrome."

Gansler spoke the words slowly, drawing them out. He wanted the jurors to feel that these were important words.

"Think about that. An infant died suddenly. We all agree that these two infants died suddenly. The question is how? You will learn that SIDS is not a disease, SIDS is not something you die of—you die because you're murdered or in an accident or have some sort of medical condition. If these children had been sick from the time they were born, and there were an autopsy done and they had meningitis, that would be detected. But when they did an autopsy, particularly back in the early eighties, if they weren't able to determine a medical reason why an infant died, they would rule it SIDS. It's a catch-all, it's a basket category. It's not a disease."

Gansler told the jurors how difficult it was to perform an autopsy on an infant. He said because "infants can't fight back and they're small," there would be no struggle marks if they were murdered by suffocation. He explained that four doctors would testify for the prosecution, including Dr. Linda Norton, whom Gansler described as "one of the chief experts in the United States on SIDS and infant death." He said all four doctors would say there was no SIDS in the deaths of both Garrett Michael and Brandi Jean. And three of the four would say that in the case of Garrett Michael, it was a homicide.

"SIDS was only discovered in 1969. It's a relatively new phenomenon. You're going to hear what a negative autopsy is . . . which means that during the autopsy the doctors discounted any possible cause of death. They did a thorough autopsy, but they weren't looking for homicide.

"The defendant smothered, killed Brandi Jean by placing her face down on her stomach, and the blood collected there, except for the part where her nose was touching the crib.

"And Garrett Michael . . . you're going to hear about brain swelling. You would not have brain swelling in a crib death. You're going to hear about Garrett Michael's expanded lungs. That's important, because Garrett Michael took a breath in, and was smothered. If a baby died of SIDS, he would breathe out and expire."

Gansler began talking about the credentials of Linda Norton. There was one statistic he wanted to get out.

"She will tell you that there's a one in two thousand chance of an infant dying of SIDS. She will also tell you that SIDS is not genetic. She will tell you that the only way SIDS is genetic, is if there is a murderer in the family!"

Gansler paused and then spoke more loudly to let a last statistic sink in.

"The final thing she'll tell you is that there's a one in four million chance that Brandi Jean and Garrett Michael both died of SIDS. That's simple math."

He demonstrated by multiplying two thousand times two thousand with a black magic marker on a white paper chart. The jury made notes.

"And she'll flip it for you. She'll tell you that of four million births, three million, nine hundred and ninety-nine thousand, nine hundred and ninety-nine killed their kids. And we suggest that the defendant is not the one who didn't."

With that, Gansler went to the defense table and sat down. Ann Harrington declared a lunch recess. And Barry Helfand began earning his six-figure fee. He spoke to a press corps eager to see his reputed magic powers.

"We're going to come back from lunch and the jury is going to hate my client and me," he told them as several television cameras jockeyed for position. "The prosecution's case has a lot of holes in it. Their numbers are flawed, and I don't know if the judge will even allow them in. This doctor Linda Norton goes all around the country making a living out of witnessing at SIDS cases. We'll see how she makes out in a Montgomery County court."

FIFTEEN

JUST A BUNCH OF STUFF

Like any good orator, Barry Helfand started slow and tried to build. He walked toward the jury and faced them, speaking in a meek, quiet voice.

"My name is Barry Helfand, and as strange as you will find this, it is my privilege to represent Garrett Wilson in this trial. He is accused of murdering his two children.

"In fairness, Her Honor told you that an opening statement is not evidence. I want to repeat that, one more time. It is not evidence. It means that what I'm about to tell you or when I read certain things to you means that it is not evidence until someone admits it and says these things as a fact or a document comes into evidence or someone comes into this box, looks you in the eye, swears to certain facts, and after you judge their credibility, their motives, the reasons they are saying things, and you accept it—then it becomes evidence—for or against my client.

"You went through a long, exhausting voir dire. We know something about each of you. It would be foolhardy of me to believe that each of you, each of you—no exclusions—have not formulated an opinion that my client is worse than the devil, that he is the man who has murdered two children, and that in fact, as you just heard this, you believe that. You just heard the prosecutor give you a powerful opening statement. You heard the prosecutor tell you what he intended to prove. He listed all of these things, and he said, 'I'm going to prove each of these, each one of these, so you will have no doubt, no reasonable doubt that man'—how did he do it? 'That this man murdered two children.'

"All of you have promised to be fair. You have said, 'I will be fair.' You'll listen to this evidence. And the prosecutor is going to tell you so you'll have no reasonable doubt. So you have become our gods. This is the big leagues. I am here to tell you that you cannot convict this man. All you have heard is motions and emotion."

Helfand opened a Bible and began reading from the second book of Samuel.

" 'Oh my son, Absalom. My son, my son Absalom, would God I had died for thee. Oh Absalom, my son, my son.' "

It was a daring move. Helfand seized on the moment. He became excited, talking fast. He spoke loudly and began gesturing with his hands.

"You have heard the prosecutor. He told you that my client had no emotional attachment to the baby. Guess what? He's wrong. He didn't tell you all the facts. He has evidence that directly contradicts this. But he didn't tell you that. He was selective. He was selective and now it's my job to tell you all the facts."

Helfand began pacing in front of the jury.

"I'm not dancing now. The state has told lies. You have heard the phrase, 'scientifically called a smothering,' and that's wrong. That's not correct. You will recall that he said, 'Brandi had no illnesses.' Perfect health. Wrong! She was discharged at birth severely jaundiced. She held her breath when she was being bottle-fed by the defendant. That's not right? They told you he never held the baby. She had nasal stuffiness at night. And that's according to her mother.

"The second mother believes he killed his child. She attracts the attention of the police because—and oh, this is a sexy case! He had insurance, so, oh, let's change our opinion. So they changed the autopsy because he had insurance.

It's the one thing that gave him a motive. Someone examines a body. Sixteen years later they change their opinion. Her death is attributed to probable suffocation. Suffocation means you don't get enough air. But they say that's a homicide in one case and undetermined in the other.

"Mr. Gansler was correct when he told you about SIDS. What is the cause of SIDS? They don't know. Babies die. They don't know the cause. Until you know the cause, you can't do anything."

Helfand appeared to be furious with Gansler.

"In regards to the other child—I hesitate because of my anger. My client is accused of killing a son—a son he has named after himself. They changed the autopsy because of brain swelling. A scientist wouldn't change an autopsy because of insurance, would he? We say he did."

Helfand continued to pace back and forth in front of the jury. He began talking of their expert, Linda Norton. It was clear he despised her.

"She's a self-styled expert who goes on the talk shows with no more scientific evidence than the man in the moon. They went down to her office in Texas and this is what happened. He told her there were two babies dead from SIDS and he had insurance, and she goes—*BING*—'Murder!'

"So what they have is a whole bunch of stuff. Stuff! Does a brain swelling make it smothering? No. I talked to her on the phone—in my own stupid style—and she's going to curve it when she gets in here. But I have the tape.

"And I want you to judge Missy Anastasi. Does she have a motive? Does she have an ax to grind?"

Helfand had gone back to the defense table. When he said the word *murder*, he put his right hand on Garrett's left shoulder comfortingly, as if they were brothers facing down the judges of the Spanish Inquisition. Then his voice rose in anger again.

"She said from the get-go, remember, '*What did you do to my child?*' I'm just asking you people to apply a little common sense to this trial. When you do, and you say, 'What did you do to my child?' whether you're a woman or a man—what do you think? Do you think the evidence will show you the natural course? Do you think the evidence will show that she hated him? She loved her baby, she's a doting mother, he's murdered him, she finds out there's insurance, you'd think she would want to get rid of him. Your answer as you sit here is, 'I'd either take a knife and do it myself or else I'd leave him just as fast I could leave him.' But the evidence will show she didn't do that—ever.

"Although the state will tell you this woman immediately suspected her husband of murdering her baby. *Her baby!* Then he went off with another woman—and I'm not trying to justify the womanizing—you can find that to be as bad as you want, but that doesn't make him a murderer. But you will learn that's not what she does at all. In fact . . ."

Helfand paused, rifling though some papers, looking for the exact phrase he wanted to hammer home. He stalled with some patter as he looked for the document.

"In fact, and this is what you're going to find out from the evidence. Ladies and gentlemen . . ."

Finding it, he leaned in to the jurors. He was as close as he dared. Less than a foot from one man's face.

"At some point my client wanted to get a divorce. He was getting a divorce in Florida. In 1993. And this woman will be coming in here and telling you all the things he did and how emotionally detached he was, and how he never changed a diaper in 1987. But she did this—she wrote a letter—on October 12, 1993.

> " '*Please be advised that neither Mr. Wilson or myself have lived in Florida since October of 1992. It is my best understanding that Mr. Wilson was in extreme distress at the time he initiated this action. Neither he nor I desire this course of action at this time. We have worked out our difficulties. Should any further court be involved it will be in the state where we reside.*' "

Helfand stopped to let Missy's letter sink in. Garrett later said he saw two of the male jurors nodding their heads affirmatively.

"She signed it. Trying to stop a divorce from the murderer of her baby. The murderer of her baby! Then on November 18, 1993, this very woman writes:

> " *'I object to the action being taken in this order. I did take written action at the time. I have not had legal advice or time to respond. I am not able to afford to travel to Florida at this time. My husband and I were reunited in Texas in August of 1993 and had decided to try to work out our marriage. We had sexual relations at this time. He was under the impression he did not have to do anything further and that this case would be dismissed.'* "

Helfand read the last sentence slowly, pausing after each word much the way Gansler had stretched out "sudden infant death syndrome."

> " *'I...absolutely...do...not...intend...to...be...dissolved...of...this...marriage....Dismiss...this... case!'* "

He paused again.

"Remember, I've asked you to consider this type of evidence when you hear the testimony of Missy Anastasi. When you hear such facts as 'He's the one, he never took care of the baby, he never got up, and it was only this one particular night that he did.' If you believe her, so be it. If you believe her...just understand and ask of her...Does she have a motive?

"But it doesn't end there. Because, there are certain things that should make sense. Particularly when you go to convict somebody of murder, something should make sense. And ladies and gentlemen, the state sort of glossed over what I'm about to tell you, but I'm not going to let them gloss over it.

"They told you that the facts in this case will reveal that, with regards to the very night Garrett [Michael] died, they say my client, for the first time got up and took care of the baby. They did not consider that up to that time he was working and she was not. She was going to start going back to work and so he was helping with the baby. And he had helped with the baby. But she says now, to make the case of murder, he was the last person with this baby and so he killed this baby . . . but we'll leave it to you to judge all that.

"But here's what the evidence is clearly going to show: 'I went. I heard a sigh. I was in bed and I heard a sigh. I had a monitor near my bed and he had already told me he had had a baby die from SIDS.' He told her that and so she had a monitor in her bedroom. She heard him go in, she heard the rocker, she heard him put him down. Then she heard a sigh that was unmistakable, it was sort of bloodcurdling, and she knew it was her child's last breath. She was so alarmed, so alarmed, by that fact that she leapt out of bed . . ."

Whether by design or accident, Helfand went into a soliloquy on the correctness of his English. It allowed the "leapt out of bed" phrase to sink in.

"She *leaped* out of bed? If I don't correct it, my wife's going to give me pain if I don't use the right word. She got out of bed quickly, okay . . . ? Fast.

"But where did she go? Where did she go? You know what the answer is, don't you? I know you do. She ran immediately, immediately, to the aid of her child who was in such distress. Wrong! Wrong! Wrong! Somebody write her a note and ask her to explain this next part. . . .

"She didn't go to her baby on his last gasp. Instead, her answer will be, when she's asked, 'Where did you go when your baby, when you heard the last gasp of your baby?' her answer will be, 'I went to feed my cats!' "

Helfand repeated the last phrase to make his point.

"If that's wrong, you can punish us. But if that's right and that's where she went, somebody better start doubting the testimony of Missy Anastasi."

He stopped speaking again, pausing next to the jury and

leafing through some documents. He was doing it on the wing, but the jury was listening raptly.

"The evidence will be, unless it becomes denied, that she gave a statement they gave us. She said to Detective Peter Picariello, and he talks to her and he says, 'Okay, that's what you heard, someone is sitting down and you didn't hear a rocking chair.' And she said, 'That's right. And then I didn't hear anything, and I thought, he didn't talk to the baby or anything while he was feeding him, and then I heard, there was no crying. There was nothing. The next thing I heard was that I thought a person was standing up, I thought it was him going to the crib. It sounded like a pat, like maybe he put the baby down. It sounded like somebody patting him on the back. Like trying to get him to burp, is what I thought. But then I heard this sigh, and this is the noise that made every hair on my body stood [*sic*] up. I just heard this and it's been in my mind ever since I heard it and it's just a sigh, it's like a last breath, is the only way I can describe it.... and instead of just running in the room I jumped up,. I had two cats and they were on me because we were up, they wanted me to feed them and we were in a townhouse and I went right downstairs, and it couldn't have been a few minutes ...' "

The way Helfand was telling it, nothing seemed to make sense.

"Okay? Magical question—why didn't you go to the baby's room? Answer: 'I don't know. I wish I knew to this very day....' 'I don't know?' Last gasp, but now she's sure as heck that every fiber of her body is telling her that my client murdered this baby. This is the woman that you're going to hear all about my client from—this is the woman that you are going to glean facts from, and you are expected to say, 'Oh, I don't have a doubt, she's telling the truth, she makes a lot of sense.'

"Insurance? Oh! Oh! Oh!... The bright shining light of guilt. It's not scientific, but it's the insurance that's the motive. 'Oh yes,' they will say, 'concealed insurance from wife.' A fact—the same conversation with Detective Picariello: 'I never talked to an insurance agent. If I had been asked, I probably wouldn't have wanted insurance.' Detective: 'You never signed any forms?' Missy: 'I never signed any forms. I never was talked to or told that he wanted insurance.' Detective: 'Did you know that there was an insurance policy taken out?' Missy: 'When the baby was born, it must have been a month or two, I don't know exactly when, he said'—and she will tell you he concealed the insurance—but she said he came home and said, 'I applied for insurance for the baby.' That's really great concealment!"

Helfand appeared triumphant, as if he were revealing secrets that would surely clear Garrett's name.

"He told her, 'I applied for insurance for the baby.' And she adds, 'one day, just out of the blue, and I said, "Why?" because that really made me feel weird, because I had known he talked about insurance before and I didn't remember my parents having insurance on us,' and he said, 'Well, my dad had insurance on me. I just thought it was the right thing to do . . .' "

Judge Harrington interrupted. She asked Helfand, Yufik, Boynton, and Gansler to approach her. They did, and she pressed a button which sent a loud static sound—the kind a television set makes just after a late-night channel sign-off—through the courtroom. If all the lawyers had shouted loudly simultaneously, observers could not have heard the off-the-record conversation. Whatever was said, it didn't seem to be to censor Helfand. He went on.

" 'I didn't like the sound of it,' says Missy. 'Then shortly before the baby died—I think it was in the summer—he came with a policy of insurance—and it was a big notebook' . . . and he gives it to her. He gives her the insurance policy and she throws it in the bottom of the closet and never looks at it again. Does she know what the amount was? No! No! She finds out later.

"Then the officer starts to talk to her about signing forms. Did you ever file a claim with the insurance company after the death? Answer: 'Never, I never talked to anybody, I never filed a claim. I know his name, because I have my car insurance with him, I have it with him now.' Then the detective says, 'I should have had this ready instead of wasting time'... and she says, 'With my name on it,' and he says, 'Well yeah, there are several things on it.' He says, 'See, you're listed here as the beneficiary.' She says, 'It wasn't me, because I would have never put Mary F. Wilson.' He says, 'All right, here's a claims statement notifying the insurance company of the death, the amount signed September 1, 1987.' Missy Anastasi: 'That does look like my signature. I never saw this piece of paper,' and he says, 'Is that your signature?' and she says, 'That is my signature,' and he says, 'Then explain to me how your signature got on that paper if you didn't see it.' Her answer is, 'I have no idea.'"

Helfand seemed to be making points by relating this he-said–she-said conversation. The jurors were making notes. They looked attentive. He paused again to let his argument sink in before switching the subject.

"SIDS is the sudden death of a child. No cause. That was the old-fashioned way of defining it. That's basically what it was—then they changed the definition. SIDS is a sudden death with unexplained causes, and that after a careful examination it is a natural death. It is my intention to show you that medical science has no clue what really causes a baby to die. There are babies who die—not homicides—babies who die and they have not been able to find out the cause. Well, obviously they die of something. Medical science does not yet know the cause, and we don't believe any expert will come in here and tell you they know the real cause of the death of these babies. You will learn that Dr. Smialek himself wrote an article that talks about how he was defending people accused of killing more than one baby. Dr. Smialek wrote an article that says, in general, that there can be multiple deaths of SIDS twins. These kind of cases do exist. One can only wonder why and how these cases do happen.

"I don't know where it's going to come from. Maybe, there's some study yesterday, or as I speak, that says there is no genetic effect and that they have ruled out any genetic component to SIDS. Anybody with a medical degree can get up here and express an opinion, but we'd like to see them prove it with medical documents...because you'd have to rule that out, too, before you say that this man murdered his two children."

Helfand sensed it was time to stop.

"The only disadvantage to talking after lunch is, when you talk too long, it's too hard to stay awake. I know you're trying and I appreciate it, but I'll save the rest of it for this trial.

"When we started this case, let's all remember—every one of you has been told this is emotional. We wouldn't even want you on this panel if you thought it wasn't. Both sides. You just have to have some common sense.

"Please understand the difference between motive and proof. A motive may cause some suspicion, but is it proof of anything? I suggest you know that there's only suspicion. We ask you to look for the scientific reason that the State has proven when he says, 'you know' and you can suddenly say, 'I know what caused this baby to die and therefore I know that he did it.'

"I'm carrying this load on behalf of this man in the face of all this emotion...in the face of all the people. Maybe some of you absolutely just hate me for defending anybody. I will carry this load until the very end of this case. I swore to do that and I'm doing it honestly and to the best of my ability. There will come a time when it is your turn. You will be Solomon. Your task is deadly serious, and for real. I ask each of you to listen to each other's arguments. At the end of this case, just be sure you can say, 'I have suspicions. There was a motive. But I'm not satisfied. There's no real proof that he did it. I've weighed the people. I've examined who they are, and what they've told me. I'm just not satisfied and prepared to convict a man based on this testimony.'

"I think if you honestly get over all these preconceived notions...I pray that some of these things I've just told you, that I've just read to you, that weren't in any newspaper article, you'll see that you have to listen carefully to this evidence. I ask each of you, if you find him guilty based on an honest assessment, then so be it, but we believe, when you hear it all, you will never truly be satisfied, and at its worst, will only have suspicions. And Her Honor's instructions will be, if that's all you have, it is your sworn duty to acquit him."

Helfand sat back down, exhausted, and Judge Harrington called a recess. He could only hope his arguments had leveled the playing field.

SIXTEEN

YOU THINK HE KILLED BRANDI?

Gansler and Boynton had Helfand backed into a corner. They could put on a parade of witnesses who would destroy Garrett Wilson's character while they testified to what they knew about the deaths of the two babies. Helfand's client could not refute their allegations by testifying on his own behalf. If he did, the details of his two criminal convictions could then be explored in full. As of now, that part of his history was legally excluded. Gansler dared the defendant to try to take the stand. He confided to friends what the very first question would be from his mouth.

"So, Mr. Wilson, if you didn't have the courage to shoot yourself directly in the stomach during your 1982 bank robbery, how did you find the nerve to kill two innocent babies?"

Let Garrett recover from that beginning.

Helfand didn't know who his defense witnesses were going to be. He had a list of experts, but he was unsure if Vicky was going to be able to come up with the cash to pay them. Earlier, he had made a bold motion to Ann Harrington that the state put up the money. His reasoning? Garrett hadn't been able to work because he was being held without bond and thus he was indigent. The judge knew Helfand's services were expensive, so it was hard to view the defendant as destitute. She ruled against him.

Vicky could testify, but the infidelity in the early months of their marriage would surely come up. Marysa was raised without insurance and she was healthy and alive. That could easily be twisted in favor of the prosecution. John Farley was another question mark. Certainly he could speak about observing a loving relationship between Garrett and his first two children. He had witnessed him with both Brandi and Garrett Michael. But he would also be questioned about Garrett's free spending and his many adulterous relationships. Helfand thought he would have to play it by ear until he saw how the trial was unfolding.

Ann Harrington was telling the jury members of their right to ask questions of the witnesses. They seemed a bit surprised.

"In this case we will allow you to ask questions. You will write down your questions and I will ask them to the witness. If I do not pose the question, the juror should not gasp or speculate. You are not to be advocates for one side or the other."

Harrington was ready for the first prosecution witness. It was Debbie Oliver Fennel, obviously recovered from her near terminal illness as reported by Chesapeake Investigations.

The years had not been kind. She was still blonde, her hair back in a single pigtail, but the once-slim teen had become a dumpling. Her pale round face was fleshy, without makeup or earrings. A gold chain worn around the neck was her only adornment. She was here reluctantly. She had been pushed to the courthouse by her parents and the threat of a subpoena appearance before the grand jury.

"I didn't want any involvement," she admitted at the start.

Yes, she was twelve when they met, she said. The implication was that she had begun dating Garrett at twelve, rather than thirteen, the age he claimed they had became romantically and sexually involved. Twelve sounded so much worse than thirteen, and who was going to refute her?

"He would show me attention. He sent me roses, took me bowling and bought me things."

And your relationship?

"It was pretty stormy."

Why did you have the four abortions?

"Garrett just decided."

She talked about getting pregnant in the tenth grade and quitting school after Brandi died in the eleventh. Then she dropped the first bombshell.

"When I was about seven months pregnant, he asked me if I would be okay if something happened to the baby. I don't know what I answered, but I told my mom."

Was he in the delivery room with you?

"No."

Garrett whispered to Helfand that he had been there. Alex Yufik made a note to find the obstetrician who had delivered Brandi and subpocna him. Garrett said he was in Springfield, Virginia, and would back up his claim that he had been present. Despite having the physician's phone number, Yufik would fail in his attempt to serve the doctor and get him into court.

What was the defendant's reaction to the birth of his child, Brandi Jean?

"He didn't have a reaction."

Did he ever feed her?

"No."

Did he ever change her?

"No."

The prosecution was ready to bring in its heavy guns. Up came two blown-up photos of Brandi Jean's empty crib. Debbie began weeping audibly the second she saw them.

What are these photos?

"It's . . . it's Brandi's room," she sobbed.

Tell us about her health problems?

"She didn't have any."

The prosecution took her through the night of Brandi's death, the "vitamins," her father, Kyle, breaking the news that her daughter was dead, and Garrett calling a friend and going flying. It was all damning.

"The police officers wouldn't let me in Brandi's room. My daddy held me by the door and hugged me."

Debbie Oliver wasn't giving Garrett an inch. She couldn't remember him taking any part in making funeral arrangements, or reading his poem at the funeral. Garrett was, and always had been according to her, a block of ice when it came to his daughter.

"He didn't ever appear distraught," she said, between sniffles.

The first time she had ever heard of SIDS, Debbie recalled, was when the police appeared at her door two years ago. They told her about Missy Anastasi and her suspicions.

"I didn't want anything to do with it. They went to my mother. And they told her, 'With or without a subpoena, she's going to have to talk to us.' So I talked to Meredith Dominick and Mr. Boynton."

The prosecution showed her a picture of a healthy one-month-old Brandi to identify, which provoked more tears, and then it was Helfand's turn. Garrett's former wife was a problem. Hit her too hard and he came off as Rasputin. He had Debbie start by telling him of their early dating days.

"We went out for pizza, went roller-skating. He wooed me, he swept me off my feet. I guess he liked me."

Helfand, always good for a chuckle from the jury, got one when he asked about Garrett's involvement at the Fort Foote Baptist Church.

"In case you haven't noticed, I'm Jewish. What do choir directors do?"

Helfand was wanting to get to the abortions. Debbie claimed she had been pregnant five times over a two-and-a-half-year period. That couldn't be, could it? But when he asked her on what dates she had become pregnant, she couldn't remember.

Where did the abortions take place?

"I don't know."

He tried to pin down the area, but all she could remember was the state.

"Yes, they were in Maryland," she confirmed.

How did you get there?

"Garrett drove me."

How far along were you?

"I don't know."

"How quickly did you resume having sexual intercourse?"

"I don't know."

Helfand gave up. He asked her about the pills Garrett had given her. She had perfect recall there. She had taken three or four, and they were little, hard ones, she remembered.

She also knew exactly what had been in Brandi's crib when she died, from the stuffed animals to the type of fiber in the blanket.

"It was a white puffy one that's made out of cotton."

"Do you recall telling a detective that you had numerous problems during your pregnancy."

"No."

Helfand dropped that subject, too.

"Do you have any pictures of Brandi with Garrett?"

"No."

Debbie finally admitted that she did have thirty pictures of Brandi that Garrett had taken. Helfand went into how the insurance money had been spent. Debbie said he didn't spend any of it on her. No jewelry, trips, or flowers—nothing. Free-spending Garrett had become a piker.

Helfand let her go and the jury asked its questions, as voiced by Ann Harrington.

"What were his working habits?"

"He wouldn't get home from work until eleven-thirty."

"Who told you to pick out the casket?"

"My daddy."

Before she left, ducking out a side door, Debbie let slide to Helfand that she was separated from Steve Fennel. The former Mrs. Wilson seemed relieved her turn as a star witness was over.

* * *

Day three, July 21, 1999, began with a silver-haired Jean Oliver taking up where Debbie had left off. Dressed in a sharp, two-piece black suit with gold buttons and matching black hose, she appeared ready for a funeral. There was little doubt she hoped that it might be her onetime son-in-law's. Her lips were pursed, threatening to erupt into rage at any moment. She first remembered meeting Garrett in 1976.

"I kept seeing things in him I didn't like," she said.

How did you hear of Debbie's pregnancy with Brandi?

"She came to my bedroom early that morning. She said, 'Mama, I have something to tell you.' Then she told me, and we both cried. We talked about how people would react. We talked about how she needed to finish school. Kyle and I didn't want this. She was too young. But we tried to make the best of the situation. Who doesn't love a baby?"

Jean Oliver had a tissue out and was dabbing at her eyes.

Did you ever see the defendant feed or hold the baby?

"No."

Jean Oliver repeated most of the story she had told Detective Fulginiti. She added details.

"Garrett didn't say anything. He was matter-of-fact. He didn't look like he had slept all night."

And how could she make that judgment?

"When someone has slept, they have puffy eyes and tousled hair. He didn't have the wrinkled face where you've laid on a pillow. He looked wide awake."

She demonstrated to Doug Gansler how she had tried to awaken her daughter that morning. She used her hands to demonstrate using Gansler's shoulder. She had, she said, almost violently shaken her daughter awake.

"She was a light sleeper, even as an infant. She looked at us and she said, 'What's wrong? Where's Brandi?' Then she bolted down the hall. The police had to restrain her. She struggled with them."

Jean Oliver painted the contrast for Gansler in bright colors.

"Debbie was devastated. She was very emotional. He was just . . . there."

A gallery of nine blown-up photos of a dead, facially distorted Brandi, was placed on an easel. Her little face was a loose patchwork of red and blue blotches, reflecting where the blood had settled. Jean Oliver blinked back more tears. But Garrett, who had been portrayed as being unemotional by the prosecution and both witnesses, broke down and wept.

Doug Gansler wasn't about to let him get away with it.

"Have you ever seen the defendant cry?" he immediately asked his witness.

Jean Oliver gave Gansler the right answer.

"No, never."

Garrett continued to weep. Helfand asked for a five-minute recess and got it. The press corps was also unimpressed by the drama.

"How hard do you think he had to bite down on the inside of his cheek to get that reaction?" Candus Thomson of the Baltimore *Sun* asked rhetorically.

Gansler wanted everyone to know Garrett was faking as well. He let the press know his opinion during the recess.

"It's ironic he didn't cry after Brandi's death or at her funeral," he told the reporters. "But eighteen years later, he breaks down after hearing testimony about what he did."

Helfand defended his client.

"He was in distress. I could hear him sobbing."

After the recess Helfand had his turn, asking Jean Oliver if she had always felt Garrett had killed Brandi.

"Call it a gut feeling. Call it intuition . . ."

"So you don't like him for that."

"You're judging me, sir," Jean Oliver retorted. She wasn't about to let a lawyer put words in her mouth.

"But, you think he killed Brandi?"

Jean Oliver was more than willing to answer that one.

"Yes, yes," she agreed, nodding her head.

The questions between Helfand and Jean Oliver got more

rancorous. She described Debbie's illness and how she dealt with it.

"If you're a mother, you can't just cave in to a headache. It hit her hard. You have an ache all over, you're weak, you're coughing. It all goes with the flu—fever and headaches."

"So, did you offer some motherly advice?"

To Jean Oliver, Helfand was the enemy. "No, I don't practice medicine, sir," Debbie's mom said.

Helfand took her through the funeral arrangements and Jean Oliver did more damage. She turned toward the jury and addressed them before Helfand could stop her by objecting.

"Garrett never paid for the funeral—just a few hundred dollars of it."

Notes were made.

And when Helfand asked her what the prosecution had told her to say, she was more than ready.

"They said to tell the truth. What I remember."

The jury looked forward to asking their questions, but Gansler's legal experiment was over. Helfand said later it was Ann Harrington's idea to stop.

Kyle Oliver followed his wife with more accusations. He said Garrett hadn't even touched the baby at the hospital.

"The nurse handed her to me. She hadn't been cleaned up yet, but I didn't mind loving that little girl."

Mr. Oliver said he had never seen Garrett so much as hold Brandi. He echoed his wife's description of the death scene.

"She was all blue. Blue around her mouth and her face. When you see them like that, they're dead."

The paramedic, Mark Cashman, took his turn in the box. There was no doubting where he stood either.

"I saw the baby laying face down. I turned her over. I signaled to my partner she had passed."

"Please describe her appearance."

"There were purple splotches on her face. The mouth was open, the arms were straight out, her fists were clenched. The way the baby looked, it just wasn't right."

"Objection!" Helfand rose to his feet.

"Sustained. The jury should disregard the last remark."

But Cashman's opinion was already memorized by each juror.

"I had to stay in the room until the police arrived. I told them there was a little more here than meets the eye."

"Objection!"

"Mr. Cashman is not a medical expert and cannot give an opinion," Judge Harrington told the jurors, striking the remark.

The former Prince George's cop, Terry Montague, followed Cashman with more of the same.

"There was a young teenage girl and two parents. I never saw the father. She was very emotional. We had to restrain her. Her father had to help us."

Montague said he had chalked it up as a SIDS death from the start, but put quotes around SIDS in his report.

"Why did you put quotes around it?"

"It's, uh, like a title."

Debbie's childhood best friend, a still youthfully pretty Diana Coon McGoldrick was next. She admitted for the first time that Garrett had read a poem at the funeral, albeit not with much emotion.

"He read it quietly and slowly. It was a long poem. I remember saying I couldn't believe he got through it."

Helfand didn't let her get away with the remark.

"Is the point of your comment because you couldn't have read it and since he did, then he's a killer?"

Now it was Gansler's turn to jump up.

"Objection!"

"Sustained."

Diana McGoldrick told the tale of Garrett taking Debbie out near the end of her pregnancy. She described her as being so drunk that she had fallen down.

Helfand was angry now. He asked if she was trying to indicate that Garrett wanted Debbie to fall down so she would miscarry.

"Let's stop dancing. Just answer the question."

"Objection!" Gansler was on his feet suggesting that Helfand was badgering his witness.

Harrington sustained the objection.

Helfand was mad at the portrait being drawn of a cold and unemotional Garrett Wilson. He asked McGoldrick if she had seen Garrett at the funeral.

"I'm sure I did."

"And did he put his arms around you and embrace you or did you stand there like a stone?"

"No, I'm sure he did."

George Smith, the Lafayette Life insurance salesman, took the stand. He said Garrett had given him a check for $68.64 for the $30,000 policy. The settlement check was for $30,279.55 he said, which included interest. He admitted Garrett also bought a policy for $25,000 on Debbie's life, but said he had let it lapse. He remembered the call from Garrett, the day Brandi died.

"He said, 'They found her in the crib,'" Smith told the jurors.

When Helfand did his cross, the defense lawyer appeared disturbed. Is this the entire policy? Well, no, it wasn't. It seemed that a woman from the state's attorney's office, sitting in the audience, had it. Sheepishly, she brought it forward.

There was a rider attached to the policy, it turned out. Garrett had paid extra for it. The addendum guaranteed Brandi future insurability, regardless of her health. Helfand scored it as a small victory. Did the jurors think the prosecution had tried to hide it? Helfand hoped they did.

Eddie Aragona, Garrett's former weight-lifting and drinking buddy, as the former Debbie Oliver Wilson described him, was the day's final witness. He wore a gray double-breasted suit that advertised his bodybuilder's physique. Aragona was no longer an insurance agent, he testified, but a D.C. cop. Whether or not he was being genuine, he failed to recognize Garrett. The prosecution had to point him out. Aragona was quick to let the jurors know that he and Garrett were acquaintances and not friends.

"I met him through Diana Coon McGoldrick. He let it be known he wanted insurance. It was the first policy I ever sold."

Aragona said he had asked Garrett if he had other insurance on Brandi, and Garrett said he hadn't. He said the defendant would have been rejected by his company if he had another policy.

The insurance-agent-turned-cop left the stand with a slight smirk directed toward Garrett. He was the last witness of the day.

In the daily press conference, Barry Helfand was still ticked at Diana McGoldrick. Her insinuation that Garrett had wanted a drunk Debbie to fall on her face and miscarry gnawed at him.

"I wanted her to answer. I was trying to be a lawyer," he told reporters.

Mary Floyd Anastasi was scheduled to take the stand early the next morning. Helfand went back to his office to prepare for her.

SEVENTEEN

HE REALLY DID IT!

David Boynton questioned Missy first. He took her through a condensed version of her first meeting with Garrett, their early life together, the birth of Garrett Michael, the night of the baby's death, her suspicions, their bankruptcy, and her years with him in Florida and Texas. He ended by having her relate the "You'd be dead if you were here" conversation and her telephone chat with Vicky, though Missy referred to her throughout as "Victoria." A blown-up photo of her healthy infant son was shown, and tears were shed. Missy had worn a black suit with a black shell underneath it. Her pale face and nearly white hair gave her a ghostly glow. She was calm and measured, determined not to lose her composure no matter what sort of legal tricks Helfand had in store for her.

The highlight of the testimony was a darkened courtroom and the home video of a healthy, gurgling Garrett Michael shown to the jury. The jurors got the message. How could such a normal-appearing infant die so suddenly?

There were law students and courthouse attorneys in the courtroom waiting for Helfand's shot at the prosecution's other star witness. At first Helfand appeared to be more interested in how often Missy fed her cats than in Garrett Michael. He wanted to know their weight (thirteen pounds), even the brand of cat food she used (Tender Vittles). But then he dropped the subject, failing to even insert the inference that the cats did it. Instead, he attacked her on the subject of Garrett's detachment.

"I never said Garrett was a stranger," Missy answered coldly. "I would have left him if he had not been somewhat normal. He was away a lot at work."

Helfand made some points by playing the parts of the baby video that the jury hadn't seen. On this portion, Garrett appeared to be taking a more active part and directing the video. His voice could be heard affectionately saying to Garrett Michael, "All you need are some shades and a telephone and you'll be just like your mother."

He took her through the incident in South Carolina. Helfand managed to get her to talk about picking up the log to break in the window and then being stopped by the police. Missy stayed icy cool. She did not come off as loony.

"Did you see another woman?"

"I saw a cat. It wasn't my cat."

Helfand tried to bring up the stalking story of Garrett, Liz Dodge, and Missy at the Delaware beaches.

"Oh, here it comes. Look out, Missy," Ingrid Horton would later remember telling herself. But the prosecution objected as soon as Helfand used the word "stalked." It wasn't within the scope of the inquiry. Since Boynton had not brought it up, Helfand was blocked. He tried another tack.

"Ma'am, do you remember Detective Picariello saying, 'Why is it in 1997 that you had all this information in 1993 . . . I'm trying to figure out—' "

"Objection!"

Harrington motioned the combatants forward.

Jean and Kyle Oliver had stayed for the rest of the trial. They held hands during Missy's testimony.

"She's starting to make me nervous," Jean whispered to Kyle as the judge called the lawyers forward.

The attorneys approached Harrington. After several minutes, Helfand came back and tried again.

"Ma'am, isn't the real reason you've come forward is that you loved him, he cheated on you, deceived you, married another woman, and jilted you?"

"No."

It was Helfand's final question. Boynton couldn't get to his feet fast enough for the redirect. He had one question.

"Why did you?"

"Because there was another child involved, and I didn't want it on my conscience."

It was time for the cameos. Susan Anastasi, a sad-faced munchkin, wore a navy blue outfit topped by a fitted, scallop-edged jacket. She had devastating emotional testimony.

"Missy grabbed my hand real tight," Susie said of the day Garrett Michael died.

" 'Susie, he did it. He really did it! He did it! He did it! He did it!' " she said her sister-in-law told her.

Missy's sister-in-law had a second remembrance. The ride home from the hospital was very dramatic. She was in the backseat, justifying Garrett's removal of the rear baby seat.

" 'My baby. My baby, my baby, my baby. I can't leave without my baby,' " she remembered Missy wailing.

Susie said Garrett gave this response: " 'Be quiet. I'm going to hit you if you're not quiet. You've got to settle down.' "

Helfand was unable to shake her.

"Just in general, is it fair to say you dislike the defendant?"

"Now? Yes."

"Did he ever reach out to comfort her?"

Susie took the opportunity to score again.

"No. He said to calm down or he was going to hit her."

Missy's mother, Amanda, said much the same.

"She just blurted out that Garrett did it. I tried not to react. I tried not to make an accusation about it."

Mary Ann Finnegan, Missy's co-worker from the county school system, had a similar story. Megan Churchill, Garrett and Missy's former neighbor, told her tale of witnessing

Garrett toss the baby seat into the other car. The witnesses' stories differed slightly, with some saying Missy had told them Garrett was in bed after she discovered the baby, instead of being in the bathroom. These were small twists and not enough to turn the case around.

It was time for some of Garrett's other women. Elizabeth Dodge Bahlman, in a red-and-black Mondrian-pattern dress, and Julie Stinger, wearing a loud flowered frock, were studies in contrast. Liz seemed almost sorrowful to have to give her recitation, while Julie appeared to relish her chance to expose him. Helfand tried to work in the beach incident when he cross-examined Liz, but since it had never been mentioned by the prosecution, he was stopped again.

"Did you ever tell the police Missy had stalked you?"

"Objection!"

The prosecution wasn't about to let Missy be portrayed as an unbalanced stalker. They had erected a wall that even Helfand couldn't climb over.

David Boynton focused on Garrett's finances with Julie. It was damaging testimony.

"Money was always on his mind," she said, repeating verbatim what she had told Meredith Dominick.

Garrett's uncle, Donald Ward, followed Garrett's former girlfriends. In case Helfand had a witness who could confirm Garrett's claim of his mother having three children die before he was born, and thus begin building a genetic argument, Boynton wanted to issue a preemptive strike. Ethel had had only one miscarriage prior to Garrett, Ward said.

"I would have been aware if there was more than one. She had the miscarriage at home."

Uncle Don, at times glaring in the direction of his nephew, said he had never been paid back the thousand dollars he had lent him back in 1980.

Helfand, who had Garrett's cousin, Paul Sandoe, ready to testify that there had been three dead children before Ethel gave birth to Garrett, tried to pin him down.

"It is only one miscarriage that you heard about?"

"Yes."

Boynton and Gansler had been thorough. The two had twenty-nine witnesses prepared to testify. They eliminated some as they went along. Others, like the former Montgomery paramedic, Anthony Lombardi, were on and off the stand in less than five minutes. Gansler had claimed the case had a "mountain of evidence." The pair appeared to be halfway to the summit as the first week of the trial ended. David Boynton was pleased to note that three members of the jury scowled whenever they looked in the direction of the defense table.

On the morning of Monday, July 26, Helfand asked for an early morning hearing. It was a last-ditch attempt to block the testimony of the state's insurance expert, Alan Meltzer. Helfand contended Meltzer wasn't an expert, but a salesman. He might have sold two billion dollars' worth of policies, but he would be expressing his opinions, rather than quoting scientific studies, Helfand claimed.

"It would be prejudicial for him to come in here and say, 'I've never sold a policy on a child,'" Helfand told Harrington.

"Apparently people only buy insurance on babies for burial expenses," Gansler said.

"But that's not all. He doesn't have knowledge of that," Harrington answered.

"The insurance part of this case is as emotional as any part of this case," said Helfand, adding this one-liner: "Even my weight can't even up the scales of justice on this one."

The judge said Gansler could proceed, but with caution.

Helfand was in a joking mood while waiting for the jury to come in. He was wearing a yellow tie he had purchased in 1975 from a defunct Rockville haberdashery called Larry Alan.

"I'm looking around the courtroom and I think that you and I are the only ones old enough to remember Larry Alan," he said to Ann Harrington. His faux pas drew a weak smile.

Gansler passed a book to a reporter. It was *The Death of Innocents*, a 640-page, near-encyclopedic 1997 tome by a husband–wife team on the Waneta Hoyt case. Missy had given Gansler the paperback edition. On the inside front cover she had written a personal message.

Lee Smith of Allstate Insurance, and the Metropolitan Life salesman, Dan Sullivan, preceded the prosecution's insurance expert. Most damaging was Sullivan's testimony that Garrett had claimed there was no policy on his son that was already in effect or pending. Records showed he had bought the $50,000 insurance before getting the $100,000 policy from Sullivan.

The MetLife agent said Garrett had put his six-figure pay-off in a special controlled checking account on October 3, 1987. By January 20, 1988, the account had $6.56 left in it.

Helfand tried to chip away. He got Sullivan to say it was standard operating procedure for proceeds to be put in such an account. And he had Sullivan admit the policy Garrett purchased was Universal Life, a policy Sullivan admitted was "more of an investment."

Meltzer, who followed the two, was totally checked. Helfand objected to every question posed by Gansler. He got the first six of seven sustained. The handsome Massachusetts Life agent, whose steel-gray hair and slim physique made him appear more like a male model than a rumpled insurance salesman, didn't spend much time on the stand. The only question he was allowed to answer was one favoring the defense.

"Can insurance be used as an investment vehicle?"

"Yes."

As Meltzer was leaving the stand, Garrett, feeling his side had finally won a big victory, scribbled Helfand a note on his yellow legal pad.

"The insurance expert bombed," he wrote.

Never one to miss a chance to speak with the media, Gansler held a prelunch press conference to protest the defeat. He said parents without life insurance just did not buy policies on infants.

"It never happens. He's never sold a policy like that. I think our expert witness should have been allowed to testify. Instead, he added no value to our case."

* * *

Helfand was confiding to those closest to him that he was winning the case. At worst there would be a hung jury and a mistrial. The state may have aroused suspicions that his client was a killer, but had they proved it beyond a reasonable doubt? No way. All he had to do was neutralize the four expert witnesses the prosecution was going to throw at him. Then he would counter with his own expert. That is, if Vicky came up with the cash.

Was it bravado or a genuine belief? Listening to Helfand, one came away with the feeling that Garrett was going to walk out of the courtroom a free man.

Ann Dixon, the pathologist who did the original autopsy on Brandi, was the first expert for the state. The doctor had been with the Maryland Medical Examiner's office for two decades. She was there to play the role of teacher for the jury. Dixon's cropped hair hugged her small head as she talked softly in a Scottish lilt that had never disappeared despite decades of living in America.

"Forensic pathology is a subspecialty of anatomical pathology. It encompasses the effects of injuries on the body. We do the investigative aspects of death," she said.

She went through the examination she had done on Brandi.

"We opened the body cavities. We made sure there were no abnormalities. We removed all the organs and examined them organ by organ. There was no evidence of disease. Death was attributed to sudden infant death syndrome or 'crib death'—the death of an otherwise healthy infant. It was natural."

But she had changed her opinion, she said, based on new information.

"The death is caused by probable suffocation. Her air was cut off by external means. The manner of death is undetermined. It could be anything. I'm not saying it's a homicide. I just don't know."

Helfand asked why she had changed her opinion, if even slightly.

"Did they tell you about insurance?"

"Yes."

"Oh, yes!" Helfand exclaimed. "What is there about life insurance policy—it's legal—that causes you to change your opinion?"

Dr. Dixon wasn't sure.

"We're not dealing with an isolated fact here," she reminded Helfand. "I believe Brandi was suffocated. It was not a natural event."

The bearded teddy bear, Dr. Charles Kokes, followed. He was prepared to go much further than Ann Dixon.

His special interest was pediatric forensic pathology, he said. Kokes told David Boynton that the chance of a second baby dying of SIDS when one child had a cerebral edema, or swelling of the brain, was one in a hundred million. He based his arithmetic, which Helfand would label "mathematical sorcery," on studies which showed one or two babies out of a thousand died of SIDS and brain swelling occurred in less than one percent of SIDS deaths. When that was added to the statistics on a second SIDS death happening in the same family, he said, you got one out of 100 million.

"The likelihood of Garrett Michael dying from SIDS is so low as to make it impossible," he said.

Helfand objected. He was now so angry at the numbers being thrown around by Kokes that he got up and made a standing objection to the doctor's entire testimony. Harrington said she would note it for the record, while at the same time overruling him on every one of his demurrals.

Kokes graphically demonstrated how he believed Garrett Michael had been murdered. He pinched his nostrils with one hand and put his own hand over his mouth.

"Garrett Michael had an obstruction—either a hand or something akin to a towel or a pillow—placed over his airways long enough for him to cease breathing."

He faced the jurors as if they were his students. (Following his testimony, Nikola Nixon, the girlfriend of Alex Yufik, would describe the jurors as "particularly attentive." She was about to get her doctorate in psychology and had been in the courtroom trying to "read" the jurors for Helfand's team.)

"This is the second infant death associated with the father. So this is cause for alarm. You would be reluctant to view it as SIDS on that basis. Swelling of the brain is very uncommon."

In his cross-examination, Helfand tried to tear Kokes to shreds. His questions were laced with derision, as if he couldn't believe the doctor quite knew what he was talking about.

"You say it's one or two per thousand based on death certificates. Where did the death certificates come from?"

"I don't know. The number is generally accepted as evidence by forensic pathologists."

"Can you name the study?"

"I can't give you the name of the study."

Kokes couldn't name the author of the study, either. Then the doctor said the study was done in 1979. It was not just twenty years old, but, he admitted, it had excluded African Americans from the sample base. And it was a survey of only 971 cases. Kokes had said earlier that one needed at least a thousand respondents to be statistically accurate. Helfand kept peppering him with questions, hoping for larger gaffes.

"Do you believe there can be two children in the same family with SIDS?"

"Yes, it's possible."

Helfand read from a National Institutes of Health manual. "Siblings of SIDS victims are likely to be subject to increased risk. The literature on the risk of subsequent siblings does not provide for clear answers. Some studies say there are increased risks, and some say there is not."

He put down the textbook. Would the doctor dare differ with the esteemed National Institutes of Health?

"I can't agree or disagree with that," Kokes said.

After dismissing Kokes, Helfand made a motion for a mistrial. All testimony from medical experts should be excluded, he said, adding that they had infected the jury.

"Odds are a dangerous thing to employ. Their testimony

was speculation based on facts. The opinions are based on probabilities. It's flimsy stuff that is not verified," Helfand pleaded with the judge.

Harrington paused before speaking.

"I'll deny the motion to strike, I'll deny the motion for a mistrial."

"Yesssss!"

The long hissing cheer came from the Anastasi section of the divided courtroom.

John Smialek, the chief medical examiner for the state of Maryland was a gray-appearing man in a gray suit. Perhaps he was someone who saw death too much. David Boynton wanted to establish that Smialek wouldn't simply change a determination of the cause of death strictly on rereading an autopsy.

"What information do you consider?"

"Information provided by family members, investigators, and then a reevaluation of the autopsy," Smialek said.

Boynton zeroed in on the swelling in Garrett Michael's brain.

"His brain was swollen. That abnormality suggested to me that some event had blocked his air supply. I looked for any injury to the head, scalp, or brain cells. There was no evidence of that."

"What was there evidence of?"

"The death of brain cells is caused by the lack of air. The fact that Garrett Michael's brain was swollen indicated his oxygen had been deprived for several minutes. On reviewing the information, there was nothing in his crib that could have blocked his airways. I looked at various information provided by the state's attorney's office. This led me to conclude the manner of death was a homicide."

Boynton cleverly asked another question which made Smialek repeat himself and say Garrett Michael's death was caused by another person.

"The manner of death is a homicide. It is the active work of another individual," Smialek said.

It was Helfand's turn. He got out of his chair looking a little weary. He started to draw a chart.

"What's the cause of SIDS?"

"It is an abnormality in the central nervous system that interrupts the heart and the breathing system."

Helfand brought out an article Smialek had written in 1986. In the paper, Smialek had studied nine sets of twins who had each died of SIDS.

"You did a personal study of twins because you wanted to dispel the notion that when twins die of SIDS, the parents shouldn't be looked upon with suspicion, right?"

Smialek said it was an unexplained phenomenon. They fenced verbally on the twins study and the brain swelling for ten minutes. Helfand read a question that Garrett passed to him.

"Could the emergency medical technicians have ever done anything to Garrett Michael that would cause this edema or brain swelling?"

"None of what they did would explain the swelling."

"Are you basing your indication of homicide on scientific fact?"

Smialek slam-dunked the question.

"I consider the investigation and the autopsy both to be scientific. The examination of the brain got me to a point where I determined there was an obstruction. The rest of the statements and the insurance information are scientific when evaluated."

"Did you consider in reaching your homicide conclusion that my client was considered cold and unresponsive?"

"I read that, but I didn't consider it."

"Did you read where she heard the last gasp of her child and then fed her cat? Is that normal?"

Smialek seemed to shrug. "People do strange things."

"So different people react different ways to certain events. True?"

"That's certainly correct."

Helfand stopped. He hoped the jurors got his point about reacting different ways to different events. He had been reading the newspapers and was planning to compare Garrett with the Kennedys in his summation. John F. Kennedy, Jr., had just been killed in a plane crash, and some of the family had responded to the news of his dying by going sailing. People really did react differently to death, he thought.

EIGHTEEN

BATTLE OF THE EXPERTS

It was hard to believe Linda Norton, M.D., could add much to the testimony of the three doctors who had preceded her. But one could never be too sure when it came to figuring out what information juries would seize upon and what they would reject. David Boynton believed it was his team, not Helfand's, that was sitting on the safe lead. He was anxious to pile up points with this final witness for the prosecution. Norton came to court on July twenty-seventh ready to testify. She appeared to be very much the professional witness in a black turtlenecked suit, her brunette hair efficiently cut in a severe military style.

Boynton first gave her a chance to extol her credentials. Norton proved to be self-effacing. The doctor said she had been doing SIDS research for twenty-five years, but had only written one paper on the subject.

"I'm a lazy writer. The rest has been lectures and workshops...I work in civil and criminal cases—it's now about fifty-fifty—with all sorts of murder and mayhem."

Norton was practiced. She also had a sense of humor. Each time she answered a Boynton question, she swiveled to face the jury. While Kokes had done the same, Dr. Norton seemed more adept at the art.

"I've testified in ten states as an expert witness, if you include Maryland. After today, I can always say Maryland."

Boynton asked Norton what evidence she had looked at to reach her conclusions. She seemed to have read everything. The doctor raised her hand above a railing to show just how much. In case the message was not getting through, the prosecution measured the imaginary evidence with a yardstick to show she had read documents that were more than a foot and a half high. While it was far from a mountain, it appeared to impress the jurors.

"You can't get too much information. That's why I requested you send me everything. A forensic pathologist who works in a vacuum is likely to reach an erroneous conclusion," Norton said.

Was that a deliberate slam at the earlier autopsies? One could only wonder. Boynton got to the meat of her testimony right away.

"Were you able to reach a conclusion as to Brandi Jean's death?"

"Yes. She was suffocated. It was a homicide," Norton said flatly. "There was compelling evidence to make you suspicious. Then, with the little boy's death in 1987, you are basing your decision on a developing pattern."

Norton looked right at the jurors. It was clear she was referring to "you" as meaning each one of them. The photos of the mottled, distorted face of Brandi Jean Wilson materialized on an easel near her. She pointed at the red and white areas of the face with a laser pen.

"Normally, smothering deaths of babies are difficult to analyze. But what is striking about this picture is the pattern of lividity, the settling of the blood. Where you don't see lividity there is no blood. That's suspicious right off the bat. There is pressure against the surface of the face. The pressure was on the nose. No infant sleeps with their head face down. The notion that a baby would sleep smack-dab on its face is like flipping a coin and having it land on its side. We're dealing with a child whose face was pushed into a mattress until she stopped breathing, and then left in that position."

Norton graphically demonstrated with her hand how one could grasp the back of a baby's head. Then she slowly moved the hand down, pantomiming pushing the head into a mattress. Ann Harrington's courtroom grew very quiet.

"And Garrett Michael?"

"This child was also suffocated. It was also a homicide. I based my opinion on the fact it was the only time he cared for it. I based my opinion on the statements of the mother. I based my opinion on the totality of the circumstances. And, I couldn't ignore the insurance money. I was in the enviable position—if you can call it that—of being able to go back in time and being able to look at everything."

Norton gave her definition of sudden infant death syndrome.

"SIDS is a term developed in the late 1960s or early 1970s. It was an undetermined cause of death that had medical authorities stymied. So, we invented a term, SIDS. And now we had something to tell the parents. SIDS became a diagnosis—it's really a nondiagnosis.

"The SIDS term became abused. In Texas, where I live, there are 254 counties and sometimes a justice of the peace simply writes SIDS to avoid an autopsy that's unpleasant for everyone. In the future, we're going to see the end of SIDS diagnoses. They are going to go away. In the next decade SIDS will be inappropriate to be put on death certificates.

"They began to write SIDS as a convenience beginning in the late 1970s. It's not genetic. If it crops up over and over again in the same family—if you discover what's really going on, and I think the Hoyt case brought that out—the parent is killing the children."

Boynton then got to the numbers. "What is the incidence for SIDS in live births occurring in the United States?"

"The figure I use when I lecture are the numbers that come out of good medical examiners' offices. Not fifteen-month-old babies who are reported as dying from SIDS—it's one in two thousand live births."

"And what is the likelihood of two SIDS deaths occurring in the same family?"

"One in four million."

Norton reiterated that SIDS couldn't be genetic, but could be familial. Her example of a familial case involved parents who repeated a dangerous practice such as putting successive children down on a soft mattress on their stomachs.

Boynton was through. Helfand was ready to attack. He needed to knock down her measured foot-and-a-half-thick "mountain of evidence."

"Did you talk to Missy Anastasi?"

"No."

"Did you talk to Debbie Oliver?"

"No."

"Did you talk to any paramedics?"

"No."

"Did you talk to Detective Dominick?"

"Only after I formed my opinion. She picked me up at the airport and we chatted as we drove in."

"How long did you talk with Mr. Boynton?"

"Several hours."

"And Mr. Boynton told you his theory of the case?"

Norton appeared to have heard the question before. She gave a nonanswer.

"I have never taken an attorney's word for anything."

"Why?"

"They might leave out facts. I like to form my own opinion. Sometimes they're fairly accurate. Sometimes they're so bad my mind is boggled. My opinion is based on the totality of the records. You assess whether a statement makes sense. Is it supported by medical records?"

Helfand said he wanted to go through every page of the foot-and-a-half-tall stack of documents Norton had read.

"It's eight hundred and fifty pages. So let's begin."

Helfand did. But he wasn't going to rattle a pro who had testified in ten states, exhumed Lee Harvey Oswald, and helped nail a Green Beret who tried to cover up killing his entire family. Still, he had to try.

He pointed out the discrepancies in the stories of Missy Anastasi and her neighbor, Megan Churchill. In their separate statements, the times they remembered events happening on the day of Garrett Michael's death were as much as an hour apart.

"Did you rely on this?"

"Somewhat. It doesn't matter."

"You don't know whether the facts are true and say it doesn't matter?" Helfand appeared incredulous. "Why doesn't it matter?"

"It's not unusual for a story to be added to or deleted from. This kind of disagreement makes me comfortable. Nothing bothers me about the two statements."

Helfand stopped asking questions on the differing statements and tried to pick apart her SIDS numbers. Norton answered him like a guru speaking to a follower.

"Isn't it true that the statistics regarding SIDS are unreliable?"

"What is unreliable are the conclusions that are drawn," Norton said.

"What is the cause of SIDS?"

"It depends on who you talk to and when you ask. SIDS has been in evolution and flex since 1972."

"Isn't it true that the people who report SIDS deaths are unreliable?"

"There's going to be some numbers that are unreliable. The statistics depend on where they come from."

Norton had no problem disagreeing with those who had preceded her. When Helfand tried to bait her with John Smialek's article on twins dying from SIDS as an example of a genetic component, Norton slammed Maryland's chief medical examiner.

"With all due respect to Dr. Smialek, I thought he was being extremely naive. I chuckled over it. I thought he was still under the 1972 influence of Dr. Alfred Steinschneider."

"So, we were in the dark ages in 1986?"

"I wasn't." Norton wouldn't back down an inch.

"You said you considered insurance?"

"Yes. It certainly supplies motive."

"So, you became a medical detective, right?"

"Insurance is a very reasonable motive. I don't know anyone who insures a child without insuring themselves."

"But one might take out an insurance policy to insure the future insurability of a child. Ever hear of that?"

"Honestly, I haven't."

"Have you ever done a study to see how many parents take out insurance policies on their children?"

"No. I haven't."

Helfand complained about two articles Norton had sent him on SIDS, particularly after Norton admitted she disagreed with the findings in them. He seemed upset she had given him the unreliable material.

"You were asked to produce a study that you relied on . . ."

"There is no such study. Statistics on SIDS vary from here to here and vary with ethnic groups and countries."

The study Norton had sent Helfand said that "in a family, the odds of a second child dying from SIDS varied between five per thousand and ten per thousand," but warned it was more likely a familial occurrence. Helfand could hang his hat on that, but Norton was saying she didn't believe the study she had mailed him.

He was frustrated. "Why didn't you send me something you relied on?"

"I didn't want to send you a whole bunch of journals that have numbers that range from here to here, counselor."

Norton made a sweeping motion with her hands to punctuate her answer. Helfand asked if she knew exactly how Garrett Michael was killed.

"Was he pressed down on a piece of plastic, a mattress, on his forehead? . . ."

"Any of those. The actual mechanism could be done many different ways."

Garrett's defender took desperate action. He went back to his cat theory.

"Remember, she heard the two cats? Do you know how much they weighed?"

He tried to suggest that cats could get on top of a baby. Norton dismissed the suggestion by saying "impossible."

Helfand then tried a series of ploys that met with sustained objections. He ended his assault on Linda Norton with this question: "Would you agree that your opinion as to the manner of death differs from that of the Maryland medical examiner?"

"Objection!"

"Sustained."

With that, the state rested.

It was time for the defense. Helfand believed the state had not proved its case. He became a minimalist. He dismissed Vicky Wilson, John Farley, and even the Sandoes as his witnesses. He told the Sandoes their recollection of Ethel's giving birth to three dead children would be ruled hearsay. Instead, he played it safe by putting Garrett's former pastor, Joseph Edmunds, on the stand. The minister repeated his observations that Garrett was crying, upset, and in shock the day Brandi died. Gansler wasn't about to let him off the stand without an attack.

"Everything you know about the baby comes from the defendant. Isn't that right?"

"I had met Debbie," Edmunds protested. "And I had been pastor of a church Garrett had attended."

Edmunds might have been the devil in disguise as far as Doug Gansler was concerned. He showed no deference for the man of the cloth before letting him go. Edmunds was the last witness of the day.

At his daily press conference, Gansler gave a victory statement.

"We've achieved our objectives. We proved that the defendant murdered Garrett Michael."

Derrill Holly of the Associated Press wasn't so sure. "Are the various statistics going to confuse the jury?"

Gansler expressed confidence they would not.

"Why didn't you consider lesser charges?" Holly asked.

"All of the evidence shows premeditation. Anything else would be fiction."

Helfand followed. As usual, he started with a joke. "I

must be winning. We went from one in one hundred million yesterday to one in four million today. If the trial lasts two more weeks we'll be at even money."

Then he grew somber. For the first time he expressed doubts. "I'm very frightened we're going to lose this case. It was a mistake to bring up the odds. I can only argue from the evidence. My client has lost two children."

The comment drew snickers from Gansler and Boynton. Helfand suggested that Judge Harrington had paved the way for an appeal because she had allowed the mathematical statistics to come in.

"I'd like to stop this case right now. The judge made her call. And I'm making mine. But she's wearing the black dress, and I'm not."

Vicky had found some new money, so Helfand was able to put one expert on the stand. Miles James Jones, a forensic pathologist from Missouri, was every bit the professional witness Linda Norton had been. He even charged more— $550 an hour. Jones, who looked like Gary Coleman on steroids, was expected to resonate with the African-American jurors. But in truth, he was not one of them.

The doctor was a Princeton undergraduate, a Howard University medical school alumnus, and a country club Republican. He told the driver who picked him up at the airport that a GOP ticket of Elizabeth Dole and Steve Forbes could save America.

Before Jones took the stand, Helfand made a final effort for a mistrial. He said Norton had testified, "That would be enough proof to convict beyond a reasonable doubt." Since the defendant always is entitled to the presumption of innocence, Helfand said, Dr. Norton had breached the presumption with her statement. Harrington wasn't buying the argument, despite Helfand's quoting of case law—*Robinson* vs. *the State of Maryland.*

"No one made a motion when she said that," Harrington ruled. "The jury has to believe her or not believe her. It's my opinion your case is deficient."

Gansler rubbed it in. "It was counsel's question and he has to live with that."

Boynton and Gansler seemed to be conducting a scorched earth policy with any witness the defense presented. After Helfand went through the doctor's qualifications—"I made *Sixty Minutes* once," Jones boasted—which included nineteen years as a pathologist and testimony in twenty-two states, Boynton attacked his qualifications. He asked Jones a dozen questions designed to impugn his reputation, suggesting his expertise was more in gynecology than SIDS.

Jones became prickly. "I understand some graduates of Yale have trouble understanding English," he said of Doug Gansler when his resume was questioned.

"Let's not get personal," Harrington chided, a half-smile crossing her face.

But when Boynton attacked again, Jones gave another snide answer. "We do understand the problems of some Ivy League schools' education," Jones said, looking toward Gansler. He was spoiling for a fight.

Jones began by calling both autopsies "unprofessional." And when Boynton asked if he had ever worked in the office of the medical examiner for the state of Maryland, Jones had another retort.

"Ninety-nine percent of the finest forensic pathologists in America have not set foot in the Maryland medical examiner's office," he said.

"So, in a word, no?" Boynton said, answering for him.

Still, he was an expert who gave Helfand the answers he needed.

"Was there any anatomical or pathology reason to call Garrett Michael's death a homicide?"

"No."

"Look at this autopsy—I believe it's Garrett Michael's. Do you see the part that talks about a cerebral edema. What is an edema?"

Jones talked to the jury much like Linda Norton. But his toothy smile appeared overconfident. His words seemed forced.

"An edema is a collection of fluids. You can get an edema from a bee sting. It will swell into the tissue. A cerebral edema is the body's natural defense to injury. Garrett Michael's edema occurred before death. It's most common in seizure activity. After a seizure an infant can be in a daze. This individual was suffering from a viral infection."

And there you had it. Jones had given the jury an alternate reason for Garrett Michael's death. He could only hope they were absorbing it. Helfand asked Jones to give the reason for Brandi's mottled face. The doctor did not disappoint the defense attorney.

"The baby was on her face for an hour. Lividity happens after death. After four or five hours, lividity became fixed. We use lividity in criminal scenes to show whether or not the body has been moved," Jones said. He suggested Brandi's death may have been the result of what he called a "fatty-acid oxidation problem."

Jones expounded on some of the other medical reasons that could have caused the deaths of Garrett Michael and Brandi Jean.

"There can be holes in the heart, there can be tumors in the heart, there can be other abnormalities not detected at birth—disorders of the lung, asthma, abnormalities of the brain—they can all lead to unexpected death."

"The fact that insurance—$40,000 on one, $150,000 on another child—"

"Objection."

Helfand was stopped, but Jones had his answer ready. And he got it out.

"The fact that someone has insurance on his children. I mean, there but for the grace of God—I have insurance on my children."

"Objection!"

"Sustained."

"With regards to statistics, what is the risk of a second child having SIDS?"

"Objection!"

"Overruled."

Jones set it up by first saying he used to counsel SIDS parents. "It's three-point-five to five-point-five per thousand. There is an increased risk of having a second child die from SIDS. But I always counseled them to have the second child."

Point counterpoint, Dr. Norton.

Boynton tried to tear down the testimony, but couldn't.

"So in your opinion, the case is undetermined?" Boynton asked.

"There is insufficient information. There is no determinable cause of death based on the information available."

Boynton shuffled his notes. He tried to cheapen Jones's credentials.

"Do you have an Internet site?"

"No."

"Mr. Helfand didn't contact you on the Internet?"

"No."

Boynton sat down and Helfand rested his defense. He made several more motions, particularly on the bandying about of statistics that had been a central part of the prosecution's arguments. Harrington waved off his various protests as if absentmindedly brushing off a fly attempting to settle on her black robe.

At the afternoon press conference, Helfand seemed pleased. "We ended on a high point. It's a lawyer's call and maybe I'm wrong," he said.

It was all over except for the closing arguments.

NINETEEN

A DECISION IN ROCKVILLE

After David Boynton made his final statement to the jury the next morning, Barry Helfand called it "The finest closing argument I've heard in thirty-five years of practicing law. He believed in his case, but of course, everything he said was wrong."

This is part of what David Boynton told the jurors in a crowded courtroom that included Vicky and Ervin Wampler, the Anastasi family, Meredith Dominick, Ingrid Horton, Elizabeth Dodge Bahlman, Kyle and Jean Oliver, and Boynton's own wife and son. Before he began, Alex Yufik gave Garrett a long embrace, as if expecting the worst. Ann Harrington read the jury its instructions on how to weigh the final arguments.

"It is your duty to decide the facts. You cannot decide by sympathy, by prejudice, or public opinion," she said. "You are not required to believe any of the witnesses that are expert. You may consider statistics only with the weight of the evidence."

Harrington went on for another seven minutes. Then Boynton got up.

"For the last week and a half you have heard from witnesses about the life of Garrett Wilson. It's a life that's unthinkable to most of us. It's been a life of deceit, and it's been a life of greed, and it's been a life of murder. You've heard about the deceit in every aspect of his life, with everyone he's known, with every situation he's dealt with. You've heard about the greed he's had in his life, a man of limited means who was out spending more than he could ever make. He wanted to make people believe he was a very important man and rich person and, in the end, the greed overcame him and he ended up murdering two children to collect money. You are the first people to ever hear all the facts of Garrett Wilson's life. He was able to have the ability to compartmentalize the people in his life so that they never were aware of what was going on. He was able to separate his wives from his girlfriends, from his fiancées, from his employers, from his friends. They never knew what he was truly about. Everyone who first met him would always think, what a wonderful guy. He teaches music, he plays with children, and by the time he ended up leaving their life, he had destroyed their life. That's the life of Garrett Wilson. You are the first people to ever hear this about his life, and you are the ones who have to decide what actually happened.

"The state has charged Garrett Wilson with the murder of Garrett Michael Wilson, his only son. The unthinkable act of killing his only son—but in fact, that's what happened."

Garrett stared impassively straight ahead as Boynton became his biased biographer. Boynton kept his hands clasped in front of him. He told the story calmly, methodically, without gesturing. The jurors didn't need histrionics at this point. They held his eye as he went through Liz Dodge, Missy Anastasi, Julie Stinger, and the acts Garrett had allegedly perpetuated upon them. But Boynton lost his cool demeanor when he got to the death of Garrett Michael.

"Missy was a neurotic mother, she was the perfect mother, she wanted everything to be perfect for *their* son. Early in the morning she heard a cry on the baby monitor as she had every day for five months...this morning when she heard the cry, the defendant was already awake. She was surprised. And she laid there and said, fine...the man who loved her, the man who cared for her, the father of this infant... she certainly didn't think he was going to suffocate his child. Then something evil happened."

Boynton was breaking down. The normally impassive stony face of David Boynton was choking back sobs in front of his wife, son, and everyone else in the packed courtroom of Ann S. Harrington. Did he believe in this case? You bet, and he couldn't have let the jury know in any better way.

"She said, '*What did you do to our baby?*' and what did he say? Nothing. And what did he do? Nothing."

Boynton tried to stay in control, taking deep breaths, as he retold the rush to the hospital with the paramedics.

"And... they couldn't save the baby's life."

Why didn't Missy leave Garrett then?

"She had this incredible emotional bond to the man that she loved... she's struggling with this whole event. She's besieged by people who want to help her. The autopsy comes back. It's SIDS. It couldn't be murder. No one wants to believe another human being can kill a baby. No one wants to believe that your husband can do that."

Boynton went on, describing "blood money on the bed" as he composed himself. He continued for twenty more minutes. His phrasing may not always have been elegant, but it was always compelling. He ended his statement with these paragraphs:

"Garrett Wilson is a person who always felt he could get away with just about anything. He believed he could talk people into just about anything. He always believed he could deceive people, because he was good, he was a salesman, he could convince them of anything. But he messed up.

"He never counted on the photographs of Brandi Jean Wilson being taken and preserved all these years. He never counted on leaving his wallet behind in Liz Dodge's bedroom. He never counted on Julie Stinger finding out about Missy. He never counted on the multiple insurance policies being discovered. Who would know? And he never counted on Missy finding out about Vicky in Texas.

"Imagine the audacity of pursuing your former wife and

inviting her to Texas when you're in Texas, remarried, with a ten-month-old baby. That tells you how brazen this man is—he believes he can get away with anything, and until today he has! He has gotten away with killing two of his children. I can't help but recall the words of Jean Oliver. She was the grandmother of Brandi Jean, and she said, 'I trusted him with my daughter.' He broke that trust.

"The defendant was entrusted with the most precious thing that a person can have, and that's an infant, a child, of your own flesh and blood. He broke that trust and he murdered these children for money. You are the community. He's gotten away with this for eighteen years. He has to be held accountable. He's the only one who could have killed these two children. He is the man that murdered Garrett Michael Wilson."

David Boynton sat down. Ann Harrington declared a recess. And Barry Helfand prepared for his final argument that he believed would set Garrett free.

"In the course of doing this case, it's become abundantly clear to me that what this case has been about is that I have a client who is a womanizer and he is a murderer. And he is a murderer because he is a womanizer.

"I'm not on the side of the case that can give you the emotion. Because the emotions have always been and will remain with the people who bring the accusations. They bring the charge, they investigate the charge, and they plan the way they want to try to prove it. They write the script for the play with you as the audience so you can hear it, and if you applaud, you find the defendant guilty of murder in the first degree.

"They started this investigation five years ago . . . it was five years in the planning . . ."

Now Helfand was telling his version. The vengeful Missy, the medical lobbying, and the reluctant Debbie Oliver. "It's all smoke and mirrors. The facts they have presented are incorrect, incorrect. Forgive me if I get angry. . . ."

Helfand rebutted the state's assertions point by point.

Was he reaching the jurors? They appeared relaxed, impassive. Had they made up their minds?

"Does she have a motive?" Helfand said of Missy. "What is her motive in all this? What is the family's motive?"

He answered his own question. "They hate him! They hate him! They believe he killed the baby. And the descriptions they employed of him were destroyed with one single witness, and that is Pastor Edmunds. They said he was unfeeling and went downstairs to play pool. Who saw him playing pool? No one."

Helfand was jumping all around now. He started to use the Kennedy analogy on Garrett's reaction to death, but jumped out of it so fast the jurors didn't get the message.

"The triggering event occurs. The triggering event is that there's another woman, there's a baby, 'My heavens, I know his plan, I know what he's going to do, he is going to murder this next baby for money, I know it, I'll go to the police.'

"That was five years ago. Garrett Wilson didn't know she had gone to the police five years ago. And she was wrong, wasn't she? There is a living five-year-old child she was wrong about."

The jurors had made up their minds. It showed in their eyes. It was unlikely there would be a hung jury. But for whom? One couldn't tell.

Whether Helfand thought he had won or lost, it was his duty to go on, to do the whole thing. And he did.

He attacked the numbers. "The most dangerous part of this case is that if you start to believe these numbers, and to equate them with real proof of something. Their numbers don't add up to diddly! They never have!"

He attacked Linda Norton. "She's a self-styled expert in two minds—hers and Mr. Gansler's. Who said she's the leading expert? Has someone come in and said that? But that's what you were told. They're just words, just words."

He attacked Brandi's revised autopsy. "It's not just suffocation. It's probable suffocation! And that's the basis for the first murder and therefore blah, blah, blah, blah."

Helfand went on and on. The jury seemed weary. Even

Ann Harrington appeared impatient. He stopped to address her.

"Judge, as you know, I don't have a clue as to when I'm going to stop."

"Tell me how much more time you need."

Helfand shuffled some papers.

"Uh . . . fifteen minutes. Okay?"

And he was off again on SIDS and genetics and insurance and motives and experts who were "hired whores coming to testify." And then he ended with this statement:

"If they had brought the indictment earlier, perhaps we would have had a chance to look at all of the evidence. The fact is, materials are missing. And now you sit as the ultimate judge. There is only going to be two who will ever judge him, and you're the first. The state of Maryland gives you what they want you to see and then they tell you this is a mountain of information. Look at all the exhibits. You certainly don't have it all.

"In this case, we suggest, there is more than reasonable doubt. We believe you should have plenty of doubt. The real problem is between you and your personal courage. Do you really have the moral courage to say, 'I have a reasonable doubt'? If you had given me enough, trust me, I would have killed him myself! But you didn't give me enough, and I have a doubt, you have not proven it. I have a genuine doubt. It is an honest doubt. My oath is to find him not guilty.' We have an abiding faith that when you're back alone, you will get down to exactly what I just told you. The emotion is now gone. It's cold, hard facts, and you have plenty of them."

Helfand sat down, exhausted.

It was Doug Gansler's turn. After a forty-five-minute lunch break, he went right at the tear ducts of the jury and attempted to open them. He put Garrett Michael and Brandi Jean's enlarged photos up and went for it without an ounce of subtlety in his voice.

* * *

"What is the case really about? It's not about wet or dry cat food, it's about these two babies. It's the worst crime you can do, kill your own children.

"Because he did that, this little girl and this little boy will never walk; will never have an ice-cream cone; will never go to school; will never go to a dance; will never go to college; will never get married; will never have their own children. And their mothers, their mothers have suffered the whole time."

Was that a juror, a male juror at that, biting his lip?

"I was thinking, what is going through his mind when he does the most cowardly act imaginable? Sneaking into these rooms in the waking hours of the day, looking at these children who depend on two people—the mother and the father—and looking into Garrett Michael's eyes. 'There is my daddy,' he thought and then his life is snuffed, it is snuffed out. How could he do it?"

Gansler piled it on. If this could he won on tears and torn hearts, he would win going away. He used these potent summary sentences:

"The first thing he did that day, after he killed Brandi Jean, was to call the insurance agent."

He pointed to the two infants' photos. "The only witnesses are right here . . . and they can't testify."

He looked at Garrett, who wouldn't meet his eyes.

"You don't have to hate the defendant. But you've got to hate what he did. This is a guy who said, 'Shut up or I'm going to hit you.' That's a relationship that some of you may understand. It's part of this whole domestic battered women's violence syndrome. And she stayed with him."

And he said this of Missy and Debbie: "They didn't want the money. They wanted their children."

Doug Gansler pointed to the photo of Garrett Michael. "I have just one question for you. The question is, what is this child's life worth? To him, it was worth $150,000. What is it worth to you?"

The prosecutor sat down. It was the middle of the afternoon on July 29, and the press wondered how long into the night they would have to wait before a decision was reached. Judge Harrington told the jurors they could deliberate until six, then either have dinner and continue, or go home and begin again in the morning. The jurors disappeared into chambers and the predecision press conferences began.

Gansler told the press he would not be able to accept defeat. "If the jury comes back and says not guilty, then this child died in vain."

Helfand praised his expert witness, Miles James Jones of Missouri. "He was from the Show Me State, and he said 'show me,' and they didn't."

Garrett's lawyer retired to a Rockville bar with instructions to be called on his cell phone if a decision was reached. Vicky waited on the leather sofa in his office. The prosecution team went back to its offices on the fifth floor of the courthouse.

Someone was gasping, then shouting. The doors of Courtroom One were reopening and it had been just two hours. The jury was back and Gansler was already inside, looking happy. He was joking with Boynton, pouring water for the both of them.

Helfand looked depressed. He cupped his hand and whispered into Garrett's ear. "This doesn't look good. Whatever happens, I want you to suck it up and take it like a man."

The jurors walked in. They wouldn't look at Garrett.

"How do you find the defendant? Guilty or not guilty?"

The juror closest to Harrington, the one who had been chosen to read the verdict by her, spoke softly.

"Guilty."

Garrett blinked back tears and pressed his palms into his thighs. His chest heaved back and forth as if he were hyperventilating. Helfand put his right hand on his client's shoulder to comfort him and left it there. Vicky and Ervin Wampler showed no emotion, something they had steeled themselves to do by mutual agreement outside the courtroom. Gansler and Boynton stared straight ahead, determined not to gloat.

In the Anastasi camp, Missy put her hand to her throat and smiled, while Frank, her brother, let out a soft "wow" before he began spreading the news on a cell phone. Jean Oliver, already in a celebratory red dress, wiped away tears and blew her nose.

Everyone wanted to hug Meredith Dominick. The winners left by the center aisle as if departing a wedding reception. There were kisses and handshakes all around.

Doug Gansler made a statement for the cameras, as did Missy Anastasi and even Jean Oliver.

"Justice does prevail, even though it has taken so long," said Jean Oliver. Missy thanked her supporters and her family.

Gansler stayed in pugnacious character. "There was a lot of evidence the jurors didn't hear. If they had, the verdict would have taken less time."

Just outside the press corral, separated by glass a few feet from where Doug Gansler was making his victory speech, Vicky Wilson stood with Ervin Wampler and smoked her Salem 100s furiously. They kept their backs to him and the festivities taking place inside.

A Montgomery County sheriff's deputy took Garrett down to the parking garage in an elevator and out to a waiting squad car that would take him back to Prince George's County. There, he would await trial for the death of Brandi Jean. The cop taunted the convicted murderer.

"So, how did you like the verdict, Garrett?"

His prisoner said nothing. He looked straight ahead.

The cop couldn't resist a final dig as he put his hand on Garrett's head, guiding him into the rear seat of the black-and-white. "Gotcha!" he exulted, slamming the car door shut.

"His sentence is our sentence," Vicky Wilson wrote to Ann Harrington before Garrett appeared in public a final time on September 9, 1999. On that day, Vicky gave an emotional speech to the courtroom. She said she had always believed in Garrett's innocence and still believed in his innocence.

Vicky said Missy had destroyed Marysa's life and eventually "revenge will eat her to pieces."

After Vicky's six-minute speech, Doug Gansler wouldn't let it go. He asked for permission to cross-examine her and got it. There were tough questions, objections by Barry Helfand, and spirited denials. For a few moments, it seemed as if a retrial of the case were about to take place.

Helfand, who was now talking—perhaps in jest—about building an Indian casino in partnership with Ervin Wampler on his land, stood up and made a short, halfhearted plea for leniency, and then it was Garrett's turn. He spoke for a long time. He talked about God, his life, and his love for Vicky and Marysa.

In one of my many conversations with him, he asked that this portion of his comments be included in any account I gave of his life. It was delivered in a choked, breaking voice. "I thank God every day for Vicky, for sustaining me and allowing me to sustain her through those first years that were very difficult. We were raising a child, learning how to do those things. I am very proud as I stand here today, as I have always been, to say that I have a wonderful daughter, she's intelligent, she's very sensitive, she's very caring, and she has a great sense of humor. She likes to tell a joke.

"I also have a well-spoken, intelligent wife who is loving, and loved by me. She is devoted to me. It has been so remarkable to me for six years, from the moment I met Vicky, that we have had a passion with each other that has not lasted for a few weeks or a few months or a few years. Our relationship has gotten stronger every day. I thank God for this relationship that I have enjoyed. She is the finest person ever.

"If I was given an opportunity to go back seven years, and if somebody said to me, You're going to know everything that's happened to you for the past seven years, but you're going to have to give up Vicky and you're going to have to give up Marysa. We're going to take you back seven years and you're going to be with Mary Anastasi, and, of course, if you stay with her, none of this is going to happen. There's not going to be any trial or any conviction.

"Well, I couldn't do that. I wouldn't do that. I wouldn't forfeit what I've shared with Vicky, and I would never give up the creation and the birth of my daughter, Marysa."

Garrett said he had loved Brandi Jean and Garrett Michael, denied he killed them, and asked for leniency. He said he hoped that one day he would be free to be with Vicky and Marysa again. Judge Ann Harrington though, had the last word.

Harrington detailed Garrett's prior crimes and empathized with the suffering of Vicky's family, the Anastasi family, and the Oliver family. She quoted from Vicky's letter, which said, "Garrett wrapped his arms around Marysa on a daily basis."

Then she said this: "But what this case is about is another baby. And I think, as the jury has spoken, there was another baby that Mr. Wilson, as a father, wrapped his arms around. But with that baby he didn't wrap his arms around with love. This jury has determined his father's arms were around him for the purpose of murdering him. Because he loved something more. And that was money."

Ann Harrington gave Garrett a life sentence without the possibility of ever being paroled.

EPILOGUE

At this writing, Garrett Wilson is presently serving his life sentence at the Maryland House of Corrections in Jessup, Maryland, as prisoner #287923. On Sundays he plays an electronic piano at church services, has organized a men's choir, and during the week teaches the basics of computers to other inmates. He supplements the prison meals with purchases of canned lobster meat mixed with rice. Money for these luxuries still arrives regularly from the Wampler family. Members of the Welsh Baptist Church in Frostburg have given him a new television set for his cell. Several appeals are pending and a second murder trial for the death of Brandi Jean will eventually take place.

Garrett's health has deteriorated. He has inherited his mother's osteoarthritis to such a degree that handrails have been installed on each side of his metal toilet so he can pull himself up after using it.

Missy Anastasi has told her story to *The Washingtonian* magazine, *Reader's Digest*, and *Redbook*. She has also sold her story to the *Star* tabloid and has appeared on the daytime talk show *Leeza* with her brother Frank, his wife, Susie, and David Boynton. She is attempting to start a foundation that will educate other women on infanticide.

"It's a good thing he didn't get the death penalty," she says. "Being in jail will kill him." She also wishes Garrett could have felt the terror her son felt during the last moments of his life.

Vicky Wilson still believes in Garrett's innocence, but has become more pragmatic since the conviction. She has divorced him, but continues to take Marysa to visit her father. At a recent prison picnic it seemed like old times. While her former husband played the piano, she stood next to him and gave an impromptu concert, singing "Over the Rainbow" and "Amazing Grace."

John Farley is also standing by his boyhood friend. By coincidence, Garrett's prison is less than fifteen minutes from John's home. During a recent visit, Garrett joked to him that this was the closest they had lived to one another since they were children.

The Case That Shocked the Nation

THE MOTHER, THE SON, AND THE SOCIALITE

The True Story of a Mother-Son Crime Spree

Adrian Havill

Once mistaken for a young Elizabeth Taylor, the weathered, 64-year-old Sante Kimes may have lost her movie-star good looks, but she never lost her pathological ambition to con, steal, and murder, and to use her emotionally explosive son as a pawn in her twisted schemes. Eighty-two-year-old Irene Silverman was suspicious of the surly young man she had just rented a $6000-per-month apartment to in her Manhattan mansion and was planning to throw Kenneth Kimes out. Then she suddenly disappeared without a trace—except for the bloodstains outside of her luxury townhouse. Linked to an unbelievable cross-country crime spree that may have included as many as four brutal murders, police finally caught the Kimeses. In the sensational trial, damaging evidence was presented that left no doubt in the jurors' minds as to the Kimes' guilt in the murder of Irene Silverman. Now, *The Mother, The Son, and the Socialite* takes you behind-the-scenes to reveal a story of two master criminals who thought they would get away with anything—including murder...

"Crime journalism at its best! Well-written, carefully researched, and as timely as the headlines that captured attention from coast to coast."
—Jack Olsen, bestselling author of
Hastened to the Grave and *Salt of the Earth*

Visit our website at: www.stmartins.com

**AVAILABLE WHEREVER BOOKS ARE SOLD
FROM ST. MARTIN'S PAPERBACKS**

MSS 04/02

THE DARTMOUTH MURDERS

Two kindly professors...
Two teenage suspects...
One brutal crime...

Eric Francis

On January 27, 2001, popular Dartmouth College professors Half and Susanne Zantop were found slain in their home in the wooded outskirts of Hanover, New Hampshire. Both had been stabbed repeatedly in the head and torso with twelve-inch combat knives. The crime—unprecedented in the bucolic college town—sparked a nationwide manhunt. Then, weeks later, a CB-radio call aroused the suspicion of an Indiana cop, leading him to a truck stop east of Indianapolis—and the arrest of two suspects. Their identities would be as startling as the crime itself...James Parker and Robert Tulloch were two clean-cut, straight-A, Vermont high school students with impeccable reputations. Investigators couldn't imagine any motive they might have had for the vicious killings. Could these boys have snuffed out the lives of perfect strangers with such intense, cold-blooded fury?

DAR 04/02

THE GOOD DOCTOR

The Shocking True Story of
A Prolific Serial Killer

WENSLEY CLARKSON

Fifty-five-year-old Dr. Harold "Fred" Shipman had a noble dedication to his profession, winning the trust of his patients with ingratiating charm and an old-school bedside manner. In fact, he even made house calls—but his unsuspecting patients had no idea of the evil that lurked behind the friendly façade of the kindly doctor....After thirty years of practice, Dr. Shipman's true nature was finally exposed—that of a calculating killer who delivered his own prescription for death. Authorities eventually unearthed the shocking possibility that the fatherly physician had killed as many as 297 people. The search for answers would take investigators into the life of a man who forever changed the stereotype of the sweet country doctor...